Study Guide

to accompany

George E. Rejda

Principles of
Risk Management
and Insurance

TENTH EDITION

Michael J.McNamara
Washington State University

PEARSON

Addison
Wesley

Boston San Francisco New York
London Toronto Sydney Tokyo Singapore Madrid
Mexico City Munich Paris Cape Town Hong Kong Montreal

Copyright © 2008 Pearson Education, Inc.
Publishing as Pearson Addison Wesley, 75 Arlington Street, Boston, MA 02116

ISBN-13   978-0-321-46320-3
ISBN-10   0-321-46320-X

1 2 3 4 5 6 BB 10 09 08 07

Contents

Preface

This *Study Guide* was written with you, the student, in mind. Each chapter opens with an overview of the text chapter, the list of chapter learning objectives, and a listing of the chapter's key concepts and terms. Next, short answer, multiple choice, and true/false questions are provided, as well as two thought-provoking cases. Problem sets are included for chapters in which quantitative material is covered. Answers to all of these exercises are provided, so you will receive immediate feedback on how well you have mastered the material.

Some key features of the *Study Guide* include:

- Emphasis on Terminology. A common question my students ask is, "How should I study for quizzes and exams?" I suggest a review of key terms and concepts. Not only will a command of the terminology assist with quiz and exam preparation, but it will also be of great assistance to you as an insurance consumer and if you plan to work in the insurance industry.

- Variety of Exercises. Several types of questions are used to help you review and test your mastery of the material. Working through these exercises and checking your answers will improve your test-taking skills. The multiple choice questions in the Study Guide are patterned after the multiple choice questions in the test bank that your instructor may be using. Working through the exercise and checking your answers will improve your test-taking skills.

- Problem Sets. *Principles of Risk Management and Insurance* is not a mathematics book. However, quantitative material is presented in some chapters. For each of those chapters, a problem set appears in the *Study Guide*. Topics covered in these problem sets include actual cash value settlements, coinsurance settlements, other insurance provisions, reinsurance settlements, calculating how much life insurance to purchase, determining the cost per thousand of life insurance, and how to calculate insurance premiums.

- Current with the Textbook. Textbooks are periodically revised to assure that the content included is up-to-date. It is frustrating when learning aids, such as study guides, are not revised to correspond with material presented in the text. Care was taken to match the *Study Guide* with the revised text. Questions pertaining to material not covered in this edition of the text were deleted, and questions covering material new in this edition of the book were added.

- Emphasis on Accuracy. The answers to the exercises have been thoroughly reviewed.

I would like to thank Professor George Rejda, author of the text that this *Study Guide* accompanies, for his comments and suggestions on this edition and previous editions of the *Study Guide*. I would also like to acknowledge Donna Battista, Addison Wesley's Acquisitions Editor for Finance, Allison Stendardi, Assistant Editor for Finance, Heather McNally, Supplements Editor for Economics and Finance, Marianne Groth, Digital Assets Manager, and Nancy Fenton, Managing Editor for Economics and Finance for their assistance in preparation of this edition, and past editions of the Study Guide. Bethany Tidd, Senior Media Producer, is also recognized for her assistance with the website study aids. You will find multiple choice practice quizzes and internet exercises at the website that accompanies this text: http://www.aw-bc.com/rejda. While these individuals are acknowledged for their assistance, any errors are my responsibility. If you find an error, please contact me or the Finance Editor at Addison Wesley.

It is my sincere hope that this *Study Guide* will help you to master the material in this course.

Michael J. McNamara
Mutual of Enumclaw/Field Distinguished Professor of Insurance
College of Business
Washington State University
Pullman, WA

Chapter 1
Risk in Our Society

■ Overview

With this chapter you begin your study of risk management and insurance. This chapter provides a working definition of risk and a discussion of the various types of risk. Some risks that we face are uncertain losses caused by perils. Hazards are conditions that increase the chance that a loss will occur. Our concern in this course primarily will be pure risks—risks in which the possible outcomes are loss and no loss. As an individual, you face personal risks, property risks, and liability risks. There are a number of methods for handling risk: avoidance, retention, loss control, noninsurance transfers, and insurance.

■ Learning Objectives

After studying this chapter, you should be able to:

- Explain the meaning of risk.
- Distinguish between pure risk, speculative risk, and enterprise risk.
- Identify the major pure risks that are associated with financial insecurity.
- Understand how risk is a burden to society.
- Explain the major methods of handling risk.
- Define the following:

Avoidance	Moral hazard
Chance of loss	Morale hazard
Direct loss	Noninsurance transfers
Enterprise risk	Objective probability
Enterprise risk management	Objective risk
Financial risk	Particular risk
Fundamental risk	Peril
Hazard	Personal risks
Hedging	Physical hazard
Hold-harmless clause	Premature death
Human life value	Property risks
Incorporation	Pure risk
Indirect (or consequential) loss	Retention
Law of large numbers	Risk
Legal hazard	Speculative risk
Liability risks	Subjective probability
Loss control	Subjective risk

■ Outline

I.   Meaning of Risk
   A.   Objective Risk
   B.   Subjective Risk

II.   Chance of Loss
   A.   Objective Probability
   B.   Subjective Probability
   C.   Chance of Loss Distinguished from Risk

III. Peril and Hazard
   A.   Peril
   B.   Hazard
      1.   Physical Hazard
      2.   Moral Hazard
      3.   Morale Hazard
      4.   Legal Hazard

IV.   Basic Categories of Risk
   A.   Pure Risk and Speculative Risk
   B.   Fundamental Risk and Particular Risk
   C.   Enterprise Risk

V.   Types of Pure Risk
   A.   Personal Risks
   B.   Property Risks
   C.   Liability Risks

VI.   Burden of Risk on Society

VII. Methods of Handling Risk
   A.   Avoidance
   B.   Loss Control
   C.   Retention
   D.   Noninsurance Transfer
   E.   Insurance

■ Short Answer Questions

1. What is the difference between risk and chance of loss?

2. Explain why, from an economic standpoint, the impact of long-term disability can be more severe than the impact of premature death.

3. What is the difference between active and passive retention? Provide an example of each.

4. How do moral hazard and morale hazard increase the chance of loss?

5. How does objective probability differ from subjective probability?

6. Differentiate between the types of risk in the following pairs.
   (a) pure and speculative risks

   (b) fundamental and particular risks

7. What are "enterprise risk" and "enterprise risk management"?

8. What are the major costs of risk to society?

9. What are the potential advantages and disadvantages of using (a) retention and (b) avoidance to handle risk exposures?

10. What are the major characteristics of the risk-handling technique called insurance?

■ Multiple Choice Questions

Circle the letter that corresponds to the BEST *answer.*

1. Ben purchased fire insurance on his antique desk. While the desk was being moved, it was damaged. As "damage in transit" was not an insured peril, Ben set fire to the damaged desk. The desk was completely destroyed and Ben collected the insured value of the desk from his fire insurer. This scenario illustrates:
   (a) moral hazard.
   (b) subjective probability.
   (c) speculative risk.
   (d) morale hazard.

2. Which statement is true with regard to risk and insurance?
   I.   Most speculative risks can be privately insured.
   II. Insurance is a form of risk transfer.
   (a) I only
   (b) II only
   (c) both I and II
   (d) neither I nor II

3. The probability of drawing an ace from a thoroughly shuffled deck of playing cards is one-thirteenth (there are 4 aces out of 52 cards). This type of probability is known as:
   (a) subjective probability.
   (b) objective risk.
   (c) chance of loss.
   (d) objective probability.

4. When an earthquake occurred in California, a studio was filming a number of movies. In addition to the physical damage the studio sustained, the studio was forced to delay or cancel release of some films. The profits lost because of delay or cancellation illustrate:
   (a) consequential loss.
   (b) direct loss.
   (c) subjective probability.
   (d) objective probability.

5. Beth was late for work. As she rounded a curve, she hit a patch of oil that had been spilled on the road. She slid across the road and hit a guard rail. Beth was not hurt; however, her car was severely damaged. The presence of oil on the road is best described as a(n):
    (a) morale hazard.
    (b) objective risk.
    (c) moral hazard.
    (d) physical hazard.

6. In the preceding question, the collision between Beth's car and the guard rail is an example of a:
    (a) peril.
    (b) physical hazard.
    (c) morale hazard.
    (d) speculative risk.

7. All of the following are personal risks EXCEPT:
    (a) the risk of dying prematurely.
    (b) the risk of living too long (excessive longevity).
    (c) the risk of poor health.
    (d) the risk of damage to property.

8. Collins Van Lines requires each of their moving van drivers to complete a driver safety course each year. Requiring drivers to complete a driver safety course is an example of:
    (a) retention.
    (b) noninsurance transfer.
    (c) avoidance.
    (d) loss control.

9. Jack started a construction company. To protect his personal assets from the claims of creditors and plaintiffs, he decided to incorporate the business. Incorporating the business illustrates which method of risk treatment?
    (a) retention
    (b) noninsurance transfer
    (c) avoidance
    (d) loss control

10. The variation between actual and expected results is known as:
    (a) objective risk.
    (b) objective probability.
    (c) subjective probability.
    (d) subjective risk.

11. Which statement is true about hazard?
    I.   Morale hazard is a more severe problem than moral hazard.
    II. Peril and hazard are the same thing.

    (a) I only
    (b) II only
    (c) both I and II
    (d) neither I nor II

■ True/False

Circle the T if the statement is true, the F if the statement is false. Explain to yourself why a statement is false.

T   F   1. The risk associated with the purchase of common stock is a pure risk.

T   F   2. Indifference to loss because of the presence of insurance is called moral hazard.

T   F   3. Liability risks can be more severe than property risks.

T   F   4. As the sample size increases, the deviation between actual losses and expected losses also increases.

T   F   5. The presence of risk leads to a less than perfect allocation of productive resources.

T   F   6. Direct losses are the only type of losses associated with property risks.

T   F   7. Hedging price risks is an example of risk retention.

T   F   8. The subjective probability associated with an event is the same for all individuals.

T   F   9. There are both property risks and liability risks associated with operating an automobile.

T   F   10. Risk is the probability that a loss will occur.

T   F   11. Financial risk refers to the uncertainty of loss because of adverse price movements, changing interest rates, and similar exposures.

■ Case Applications

Case 1

Casinos and lotteries have increased in popularity in recent years. What type of risk (pure or speculative) is created when someone gambles at a casino or plays the lottery? The method of wagering at casinos is interesting. Most games of chance are designed to have repeated small bets rather than a single large bet. Why are the games designed in this way?

Case 2

Individuals who are in charge of handling loss exposures for corporations, municipalities, universities, etc., are called "Risk Managers." Why are the identification of hazards and the preparation for perils important in risk management? What types of physical hazards confront the Risk Manager of your College or University?

■ Solutions to Chapter 1

Short Answer Questions

1. Chance of loss is a probability concept. Risk is uncertainty concerning the occurrence of loss. The chance of loss (probability) may be the same for two events, but the risk could be very different. For example, two stocks may have the same expected return, 10%, and the distribution of their expected returns may be symmetric (50% probability of gain, 50% probability of loss). However, the standard deviation of the returns of the first stock may be 25%, while the standard deviation of the returns of the second stock may be only 10%. Thus the chance of loss for both stocks is 50%, but the first stock is of greater risk.

2. From an economic standpoint, long-term disability can be more severe than premature death. In either case, the income stream provided by the family breadwinner is interrupted. In the case of long-term disability, however, there are additional expenses that must be incurred by the disabled individual and his/her family.

3. Active retention involves the conscious decision to use retention to handle a risk after analysis of the risk. An example would be a business deciding to retain the risk of physical damage to vehicles in its delivery fleet rather than purchasing insurance. Passive retention occurs when risks are unknowingly retained. For example, a business may start to offer off-site day care as an employee benefit. The company may assume that its liability insurance will cover losses associated with the day care center. However, the coverage may include a "premises only" definition of insured locations. Thus the risk is passively retained because the company thought it was covered.

4. Morale hazard increases the chance of loss because the individual is indifferent to loss because of insurance. Thus proper loss control activities may not be undertaken. Moral hazard is more severe. Here an individual commits dishonest acts in an effort to collect from the insurer. Morale hazard is attitudinal; moral hazard involves dishonest acts.

5. Objective probability is a mathematical probability that can be determined by deduction or through statistical analysis. For example, based on pooled mortality data, we can estimate the probability that an individual will die before he or she reaches age 50. Subjective probability is an individual's own personal estimate of the chance of loss. As subjective probabilities are personal estimates, they are not identical across individuals and can be influenced by a number of factors.

6. (a) Pure risks have two possible outcomes: a loss or no loss. Speculative risks have three possible outcomes: loss, no loss, and gain. Pure risks are readily insurable, while most speculative risks are not privately insurable.
   (b) Fundamental risks affect the entire economy or large numbers of persons or groups within the economy. Inflation, drought, hurricanes, and epidemics are examples of fundamental risks. Particular risks are those risks that affect the individual only. The risk of damage to your auto or that you will get sick or injured are examples of particular risks.

7. Enterprise risk encompasses all major risks faced by a business firm, including pure risks, speculative risks, strategic risks, and operational risks. Enterprise risk management combines treatment of this broad range of risks into a single, unified, risk treatment program.

8. There are three major costs. First, emergency funds must be set aside to pay for losses when they occur. Second, because of risk, society may be deprived of needed goods and services. Finally, because of risk, society must bear the burden of fear and worry.

9. (a) The potential advantage of retention is that if the loss level is low, the expenditure to transfer the risk would not have been incurred. The potential disadvantage is that if the loss level is high, you will be responsible for all of the loss.

    (b) With avoidance, the probability of loss is reduced to zero. However, there may be some benefit that is foregone if avoidance is used. For example, the fear of liability may force discontinuation of operations and avoiding an exposure may mean the loss of profits that could have been earned if operations had continued.

10. Insurance has a number of important characteristics. First, insurance involves the transfer of risk. Second, insurance uses pooling to spread the cost of losses over the entire group that is insured. Third, insurance applies the law of large numbers to reduce objective risk.

Multiple Choice Questions

1. (a) As the original damage was not covered, Ben caused a greater loss in order to collect under his fire insurance policy. This fraudulent claim illustrates moral hazard.

2. (b) Speculative risks are not readily insurable. Insurance is a mechanism used to transfer risk to an insurer.

3. (d) Objective probability refers to the long-run relative frequency of an event based on an assumption of infinite observations with no changes in the underlying conditions. Given that the deck of cards is "fair," the objective probability of drawing an ace is one-thirteenth.

4. (a) A loss that occurs as a result of a direct loss is called an indirect, or consequential, loss.

5. (d) The oil on the road is a physical condition that increases the chance of loss. It is a physical hazard.

6. (a) Peril is the cause or source of loss. The collision between Beth's car and the guard rail is a peril.

7. (d) Personal risks are those that affect the individual—examples include premature death, poor health, living too long (excessive longevity), and unemployment. Property risks and liability risks are separate from personal risks.

8. (d) Loss control activities are undertaken to reduce the frequency and severity of losses. By requiring driver safety courses, Collins Van Lines is attempting to reduce the number of losses and limit the severity of those losses that do occur.

9. (b) Jack incorporated the business in order to transfer risk from himself to a legally created entity, the corporation. Business-related claims will be brought against the corporation, rather than against Jack and his personal assets. Jack is using incorporation as a noninsurance transfer of risk.

10. (a) The variation between actual losses and expected losses is called objective risk. Minimizing objective risk through the application of the law of large numbers is crucial for private insurers.

11. (d) Neither statement is true. Moral hazard is more severe than morale hazard. Morale hazard is attitudinal, while moral hazard involves committing dishonest acts. Peril and hazard are not the same thing. Hazard is a condition that increases the chance of loss. Peril is the cause or source of loss.

True/False

1. **F** This risk is a speculative risk because there are three possible outcomes: loss, breaking even, and gain. Loss and no loss are the possible outcomes with pure risks.

2. **F** Indifference to loss because of the presence of insurance is called morale hazard.

3. **T**

4. **F** When the sample size increases, the deviation between actual losses and expected losses declines. Private insurers rely on this principle, known as the law of large numbers.

5. **T**

6. **F** Indirect losses, such as continuing expenses and the loss of profits, are also associated with property risks.

7. **F** Hedging price risks illustrates the transfer of risk, not risk retention.

8. **F** Subjective probability is an individual's personal assessment of the chance of loss. Individuals may perceive the same situation differently, depending on their risk aversion, prior experience, age, education, and other factors.

9. **T**

10. **F** Chance of loss is the probability that a loss will occur. Risk is uncertainty concerning the occurrence of loss.

11. **T**

Case Applications

Case 1

The risk that is created when someone gambles is a speculative risk. In addition to the possibility of loss or no loss, there is also the potential for gain when one gambles. The reason that casino games are designed to include many repetitions is to reduce the level of objective risk for the casino. If a casino game is played four times for high stakes, the casino could lose four times in a row. However, if the casino game is played four hundred times at smaller stakes, the actual result will be far closer to the expected outcome. Although insurance is very different from gambling, insurers use the same mathematical principle (the law of large numbers) to reduce their objective risk by insuring large numbers of risks.

Case 2

By identifying hazards before losses occur, the Risk Manager may be able to reduce the likelihood that the hazard will lead to a loss. By preparing for losses caused by perils before they occur, Risk Managers are in a better position to respond when losses occur. Some physical hazards that may be important to the Risk Manager at your College or University include: hazardous materials in chemistry labs, crowded classrooms with limited building exits, ice on campus roads and sidewalks, unattended dormitory rooms, unattended vehicles in the parking lot, and unruly crowds at athletic events and concerts held on campus.

Chapter 2
Insurance and Risk

■ Overview

Insurance is an important method of transferring pure loss exposures to an entity better positioned to handle these risks. But what is insurance and how does insurance work? This chapter analyzes the insurance mechanism. You will learn the important characteristics of insurance and what conditions must be present for a risk to be privately insurable. This chapter also provides an overview of private and government insurance. Private insurance can be divided into two divisions: property and liability insurance and life and health insurance. Government insurance programs are designed to insure risks that may not be insurable on a private basis. Although insurance provides many benefits to society, there are some costs associated with the use of insurance. These costs and benefits are discussed at the conclusion of this chapter.

■ Learning Objectives

After studying this chapter, you should be able to:

- Explain the basic characteristics of insurance.
- Explain the law of large numbers.
- Describe the requirements of an insurable risk from the viewpoint of a private insurer.
- Identify the major insurable and uninsurable risks in our society.
- Describe the major types of insurance.
- Explain the social benefits and social costs of insurance.
- Define the following:

Adverse selection	Multiple-line insurance
Casualty insurance	Ocean marine insurance
Commercial lines	Personal lines
Expense loading	Pooling
Fidelity bonds	Property and liability insurance
Fortuitous loss	Reinsurance
Indemnification	Requirements of an insurable risk
Inland marine insurance	Risk transfer
Insurance	Social insurance
Law of large numbers	Surety bond
Life and health insurance	Underwriting

■ Outline

I.   Definition of Insurance

II.   Basic Characteristics of Insurance
    A. Pooling of Losses

    B. Payment of Fortuitous Losses

    C. Risk Transfer

    D. Indemnification

III. Requirements of an Insurable Risk
    A. Large Number of Exposure Units

    B. Accidental and Unintentional Loss

    C. Determinable and Measurable Loss

    D. No Catastrophic Loss

    E. Calculable Chance of Loss

    F. Economically Feasible Premium

IV.   Adverse Selection and Insurance

V.   Insurance and Gambling Compared

VI.   Insurance and Hedging Compared

VII. Types of Insurance
    A. Private Insurance
       1. Life and Health Insurance
       2. Property and Liability Insurance

    B. Government Insurance
       1. Social Insurance
       2. Other Government Insurance

VIII. Benefits of Insurance to Society

IX.   Costs of Insurance to Society

■ Short Answer Questions

1. What are the basic characteristics of insurance?

2. What is adverse selection? How do insurance companies attempt to avoid the problem of adverse selection?

3. Can individuals who have a higher-than-average probability of loss be insured without adverse selection occurring?

4. From the viewpoint of a private insurer, what conditions must be satisfied for a risk to be privately insurable?

5. Last night Ken and Ann Johnson's home burned to the ground. They were not insured. Clearly this was a catastrophic loss for the Johnsons; yet one of the characteristics of a privately insurable risk is that losses must not be catastrophic. Explain this apparent contradiction.

6. What is the law of large numbers? Why is the law of large numbers important to private insurers?

7. If a risk cannot be written by private insurers, does that mean that the risk cannot be insured?

8. Complete this outline:

    I.   Private Insurance

        A.

        B.

    II. Government Insurance

        A.

        B.

9. In what ways does insurance benefit society?

10. What are the costs of insurance to society?

11. How do insurance and gambling differ?

■ Multiple Choice Questions

Circle the letter that corresponds to the BEST *answer.*

1. All of the following are requirements of privately insurable risks EXCEPT:
    (a) losses must not be catastrophic.
    (b) losses must not be accidental.
    (c) there must be a large number of exposure units.
    (d) losses must be determinable and measurable.

2. Rhonda was concerned that her employees might steal money from the cash register. To provide protection against such losses, Rhonda should purchase:
    (a) workers compensation insurance.
    (b) fidelity bonds.
    (c) social insurance.
    (d) marine insurance.

3. Which statement(s) is (are) true with regard to insurance?
    I.   It involves the pooling of fortuitous losses.
    II. It involves transfer of risk and indemnification of loss.

    (a) I only
    (b) II only
    (c) both I and II
    (d) neither I nor II

4. Spreading of losses incurred by a few persons over the entire group so that in the process the average loss is substituted for the actual loss is called:
    (a) indemnification.
    (b) adverse selection.
    (c) underwriting.
    (d) pooling.

5. Insurance benefits society in all of the following ways EXCEPT:
    (a) it reduces fear and worry.
    (b) it provides indemnification when losses occur.
    (c) it leads to inflated claims.
    (d) it provides a source of investment funds.

6. All of the following risks are privately insurable EXCEPT:
    (a) the risk of premature death.
    (b) the risk of physical damage to your car.
    (c) the risk of unemployment.
    (d) the risk of poor health.

7. Ron was concerned that customers at his store might be injured while on the premises and file a lawsuit against him. To provide protection against such claims, Ron should purchase:
    (a) liability insurance.
    (b) social insurance.
    (c) surety bonds.
    (d) inland marine insurance.

8. Which statement(s) is (are) true with regard to the law of large numbers?

    I.   By applying the law of large numbers, insurers prevent losses from occurring.

    II. According to the law of large numbers, as the sample increases, objective risk declines.

    (a) I only

    (b) II only

    (c) both I and II

    (d) neither I nor II

9. A small property and liability insurance company concentrated its underwriting efforts in one city in Oklahoma. When tornadoes damaged a large number of structures in the city, the insurer did not have adequate financial resources to pay the losses and became insolvent. Which requirement of an insurable risk was violated in this scenario?

    (a) there must be a large number of exposure units

    (b) the loss should not be catastrophic

    (c) the loss must be accidental and unintentional

    (d) the loss must be determinable and measurable

10. Although insurance benefits society in many ways, there are some social costs associated with insurance. These social costs include all of the following EXCEPT:

    (a) insurers' cost of doing business.

    (b) inflated claims.

    (c) indemnification of losses.

    (d) fraudulent claims.

■ True/False

Circle the T if the statement is true, the F if the statement is false. Explain to yourself why a statement is false.

T   F   1. Marine insurance is used to insure goods in transit.

T   F   2. Multiple-line insurance provides several types of coverage in one contract.

T   F   3. There is no reason for the government to be involved in insurance.

T   F   4. Insurers play no role in capital formation in the U.S. economy.

T   F   5. Insurance benefits society by enhancing credit.

T   F   6. According to the law of large numbers, as the number of exposure units increases, the average size of loss declines.

T   F   7. Insurance and hedging are the same thing.

T   F   8. Market risks, financial risks, production risks, and political risks are generally uninsurable.

T   F   9. Pooling means that losses of a few are spread over the group and average loss is substituted for actual loss.

T   F   10. Social insurance programs are voluntary private insurance programs.

T   F   11. Purchasing insurance is simply a gamble that you will experience a loss.

T   F   12. A fortuitous loss is a loss that is expected to occur.

■ Case Applications

Case 1

An automobile club charges more for first-year memberships than for renewal memberships. When asked about this pricing policy, a club official said, "It costs something to put the new members' names on the books, and, more importantly, utilization of club services tends to be much higher for first-year members, so we must adjust our rates accordingly." Is a similar phenomenon observed in private insurance markets? Explain.

Case 2

The Feelings Mutual Insurance Company is considering writing two risks the company has not previously insured: windstorm and war. Considering the requirements of privately insurable risks, will The Feeling Mutual Insurance Company be able to write insurance for windstorm and war? Explain your answer.

■ Solutions to Chapter 2

Short Answer Questions

1. Insurance has a number of distinct characteristics. These characteristics include: pooling of losses, payment of fortuitous losses, risk transfer, and indemnification of losses.

2. Adverse selection is the tendency for persons who have a higher-than-average chance of loss to seek insurance at average rates, which if not controlled by underwriting, results in higher-than-expected loss levels. Insurance companies attempt to deal with the problem of adverse selection through careful underwriting and contractual provisions. Underwriting refers to the selection and classification of insureds. Underwriters determine if the policy should be written by the insurer, and if so, what premium should be charged and what restrictions should apply.

3. Yes. If these individuals are recognized as higher-than-average risks and charged a premium commensurate with the level of risk, adverse selection does not occur. There are auto insurers, for example, that specialize in insuring high-risk drivers.

4. From the viewpoint of a private insurer, there are six ideal requirements of an insurable risk:
   - there must be a large number of exposure units
   - the loss must be accidental and unintentional
   - the loss must be determinable and measurable
   - the loss should not be catastrophic
   - the chance of loss must be calculable
   - the premium must be economically feasible

5. There is no contradiction. Recall that we are considering whether the loss exposure can be insured from the viewpoint of a private insurer. The loss of the family home is a catastrophic loss from the homeowner's perspective; but from an insurer's perspective, the loss of one home is not catastrophic. Insurers are in the business of losses – they expect some losses to occur. It's only when loss levels are substantially higher than expected that insurers consider losses catastrophic.

6. The law of large numbers is a mathematical principle that states that as the sample size increases, the deviation between actual results and expected results declines. This principle is important to private insurers because through the application of the law of large numbers, insurers can reduce objective risk by increasing the number of loss exposures insured.

7. Just because the risk cannot be insured privately does not mean that the risk cannot be insured. Some risks that cannot be insured privately are covered by government insurers. For example, it is difficult for private insurers to write flood insurance and unemployment insurance. These coverages can be made available, however, through government insurance.

8. The two sub-categories under Private Insurance are:
   (a) Life and Health Insurance
   (b) Property and Liability Insurance

   The two sub-categories under Government Insurance are:
   (a) Social Insurance
   (b) Other Government Insurance

9. Insurance benefits society in a number of ways, including: indemnification of losses, less worry and fear, source of investment funds, loss-prevention incentives, and enhancement of credit.

0. Although insurance provides a number of benefits to society, there are a number of social costs attributable to the presence of insurance. First, there is the cost of insurance company operations. Second, there is a cost associated with fraudulent claims. Finally, claims may be inflated because of the presence of insurance.

1. Although insurance is often confused with gambling, there are two major differences between insurance and gambling. First, gambling creates a new speculative risk that was not present before, while insurance is a method of dealing with a pure risk that is already present. Second, gambling is socially unproductive, because the winner's gain comes at the expense of the loser. Insurance is socially productive, because both the insurer and the insured have a common interest in loss prevention and both parties benefit if a loss does not occur.

Multiple Choice Questions

1. (b) To be insurable, losses must be accidental and unintentional. If a loss is not accidental, it means that it is intentional.

2. (b) Fidelity bonds provide protection against the dishonest acts of employees, such as theft of cash.

3. (c) The four key characteristics stressed in the definition of insurance are covered in both statements. These characteristics include: pooling, fortuitous losses, transfer of risk, and indemnification of losses.

4. (d) Through pooling, the average loss of the group is substituted for the actual loss that individual members of the group may experience.

5. (c) The inflated claims that arise because of the presence of insurance are a cost of insurance to society, not a benefit.

6. (c) The risk of unemployment, as demonstrated in your text, generally is not privately insurable.

7. (a) Liability insurance provides protection against such lawsuits.

8. (b) The first statement is incorrect. The law of large numbers does not prevent losses from occurring. The law of large numbers addresses the predictability of losses. The second statement is correct. As the sample size increases, the variation between actual and expected losses (objective risk) declines.

9. (b) This insurer experienced catastrophic losses because it concentrated too much of the coverage it wrote in one area. Many of its exposure units were damaged at the same time, producing catastrophic losses for the insurer.

10. (c) Indemnification of losses is a benefit of insurance to society, not a cost.

True/False

1. T

2. T

3. F Some coverages that are deemed necessary by society are difficult, if not impossible, for private insurers to write. In such situations, the government is in a better position to provide the coverage than are private insurers.

4. **F** Insurers play an important role in capital formation in the U.S. economy. The premiums paid by policyowners are available for insurers to invest in the capital markets. Insurers are important investors in mortgages, corporate securities (stocks and bonds), and government securities.

5. **T**

6. **F** The law of large numbers does not address the average size of individual losses. As the sample size increases, the frequency of loss becomes more predictable.

7. **F** Insurance differs from hedging. Insurance transfers risks that are insurable. Hedging is used to transfer risks that are typically uninsurable, such as adverse price movements of a commodity. Secondly, insurance can reduce objective risk through the application of the law of large numbers. Hedging typically transfers risk only – it does not reduce risk.

8. **T**

9. **T**

10. **F** Social insurance programs are compulsory government insurance programs.

11. **F** There are two major differences between insurance and gambling. Insurance addresses a pure risk that already exists, while gambling creates a new speculative risk. Also, gambling is socially unproductive as a winner's gain comes at the expense of someone else. Insurance benefits both the insurer and the insured.

12. **F** A fortuitous loss is a loss that is unforeseen and unexpected.

Case Applications

Case 1

Auto clubs, like private insurers, are susceptible to adverse selection problems. Uninsured individuals are more likely to seek health insurance when they begin to have health problems. Drivers not enrolled in auto clubs are more likely to seek to join an auto club in anticipation of the need for club services (e.g., just before going on a long trip). Through underwriting, private insurers attempt to prevent higher-than-average risks from passing as average risks, leading to higher than anticipated losses. The auto club, aware that the utilization of club services will be higher than average for new club members, loads (charges extra) for a similar phenomenon.

Case 2

Is windstorm insurable?

- there would be a large number of exposure units
- losses would be accidental and unintentional
- losses would be determinable and measurable
- losses would not be catastrophic if the company diversified geographically or used reinsurance
- the chance of loss is calculable based on historical data
- the premium would be economically feasible

Windstorm meets the requisites of insurable risks. It should be noted, however, that it is difficult for insurers to cover damage caused by wind in certain areas (e.g., the Gulf Coast and property close to the ocean on the East Coast of the U.S.). In some states, "wind plans" help to make coverage for this type of damage available to property owners.

s war insurable?

- there would be a large number of exposure units

  losses would not be accidental and unintentional – in war you intend to destroy property

- losses may be difficult to determine and measure if widespread destruction occurred

- losses could very well be catastrophic; entire neighborhoods in London and Dresden were destroyed in World War II; if atomic weapons were used, such as the one used on Hiroshima, losses would indeed be catastrophic

- the chance of loss would not be calculable because the peril insured against is not a random event

  finally, because intentional catastrophic loss is possible and data are not available upon which premiums can be based, it is unlikely an affordable premium could be determined

War is not privately insurable.

Chapter 3
Introduction to Risk Management

Overview

You've probably practiced personal risk management without even realizing it. You may have decided to purchase auto insurance (risk transfer), decided not to drive on an icy road (risk avoidance), decided to use your seat belt (loss control), and your physical damage insurance may have a deductible (risk retention). Just as individuals practice risk management, so do small businesses, universities, municipalities, and corporations. This chapter provides an introduction to risk management in general and a discussion of personal risk management in particular. After defining risk management and discussing the objectives of risk management, the risk management process is examined. The risk management process consists of: identifying loss exposures, analyzing the loss exposures, selecting appropriate techniques for treating the loss exposures, and implementing and monitoring the risk management program.

Learning Objectives

After studying this chapter, you should be able to:

Define risk management and explain the objectives of risk management.

Describe the steps in the risk management process.

Explain the major risk control techniques, including: avoidance, loss prevention, and loss reduction.

Explain the major risk financing techniques, including retention, noninsurance transfers, and insurance.

Apply the principles of risk management to a personal risk management program.

Define the following:

Association or group captive	Maximum probable loss
Avoidance	Noninsurance transfer
Captive insurer	Personal risk management
Cost of risk	Retention
Deductible	Retention level
Excess insurance	Risk control
Loss exposure	Risk financing
Loss frequency	Risk management
Loss prevention	Risk management manual
Loss reduction	Risk management policy statement
Loss severity	Risk retention group
Manuscript policy	Self-insurance
Maximum possible loss	Single parent (pure) captive

■ Outline

I.   Meaning of Risk Management

II.   Objectives of Risk Management

    A. Preloss Objectives

    B. Postloss Objectives

III. Steps in the Risk Management Process

    A. Identifying Loss Exposures

    B. Analyze the Loss Exposures

    C. Select the Appropriate Techniques for Treating the Loss Exposures
       1. Risk Control
         a. Avoidance
         b. Loss Prevention
         c. Loss Reduction
       2. Risk Financing
         a. Retention
         b. Noninsurance Transfer
         c. Commercial Insurance
       3. Which Method Should be Used?

    D. Implement and Monitor the Risk Management Program
       1. Risk Management Policy Statement
       2. Cooperation with Other Departments
       3. Periodic Review and Evaluation

IV.   Benefits of Risk Management

V.   Personal Risk Management

■ Short Answer Questions

1. What are the steps in the risk management process?

2. What are the preloss and postloss objectives of risk management?

3. What conditions should be present if retention is used to handle a loss exposure?

4. What is a noninsurance transfer? List some examples of noninsurance transfers.

5. What is the relationship between loss control and insurance premiums?

6. Why might a manufacturing company establish a captive insurance company?

7. Complete the "Risk Management Matrix" by writing the name of the risk management technique that should be used with the various loss frequency/severity combinations.

	Severity	
	Low	High
Frequency Low		
High		

8. Why might the Risk Manager of a corporation interact with the Accounting Department and the Marketing Department?

9. What risk management technique is illustrated by each of the following?

   (a) Mid-South Van Lines requires each of their moving van drivers to complete a defensive driving course each year.

   (b) Linda purchased disability income insurance.

   (c) After tests revealed an experimental drug produced harmful side effects, Acme Drug Company discontinued development of the drug.

   (d) To protect his personal assets from the claims of creditors, Phil decided to incorporate his small business.

   (e) Towne and Country Dry Cleaners installed a sprinkler system in the laundering area.

10.   What type of information is included in a risk management policy statement?

11.   What is a manuscript policy and when are manuscript policies likely to be used?

12.   Name two personal loss exposures, two property loss exposures, and two liability loss exposures that may be considered in a personal risk management program.

■ Multiple Choice Questions

Circle the letter that corresponds to the BEST *answer.*

1. The first step in the risk management process is:
   (a) exposure analysis.
   (b) exposure identification.
   (c) implementation of the risk management program.
   (d) selection of the appropriate risk treatment technique.

2. The worst loss that could possibly occur is the:
   (a) maximum probable loss.
   (b) limit of liability.
   (c) maximum likely loss.
   (d) maximum possible loss.

3. Self-insurance is an example of which of the following risk management techniques?
   (a) loss control
   (b) noninsurance transfer
   (c) retention
   (d) avoidance

4. Which statement about risk management is true?
   I.   Risk management is concerned with the identification and treatment of loss exposures.
   II. Risk management is an ongoing process.

   (a) I only
   (b) II only
   (c) both I and II
   (d) neither I nor II

5. All of the following are methods of funding retained losses EXCEPT:
   (a) insurance.
   (b) borrowing.
   (c) current net income.
   (d) funded reserve.

6. Tom volunteered to build the stage for his community theater group. He asked each member of the group to sign a hold-harmless agreement absolving him of liability if the construction was defective and injuries occurred. Tom's use of the hold-harmless agreement illustrates which method of dealing with risk?
   (a) noninsurance transfer
   (b) insurance transfer
   (c) avoidance
   (d) retention

7. Jan purchased automobile physical damage insurance with a $500 deductible. This coverage illustrates which two risk management techniques?
   (a) loss control and avoidance
   (b) retention and transfer
   (c) transfer and loss control
   (d) avoidance and retention

8. All of the following are post-loss objectives of risk management EXCEPT:
   (a) survival of the firm.
   (b) reduction of anxiety.
   (c) continued operations.
   (d) stability of earnings.

9. Which statement about risk management techniques is true?
   I.   Using retention limits the liability of the firm to a specified amount.
   II. Risk transfer can be more expensive than risk retention.
   (a) I only
   (b) II only
   (c) both I and II
   (d) neither I nor II

10. All of the following are disadvantages of using insurance in a corporate risk management program EXCEPT:
    (a) premium payments are not tax-deductible.
    (b) insurance coverage may be expensive.
    (c) it may be time-consuming to negotiate the coverages and terms.
    (d) the presence of insurance may lead to less incentives to engage in loss control.

11. All of the following are reasons to form a captive insurance company EXCEPT:
    (a) the parent firm may have difficulty in obtaining some types of insurance.
    (b) premiums paid to a captive, under certain circumstances, may be tax-deductible.
    (c) the captive can serve as another profit center.
    (d) parent firms are allowed to take tax credits for losses paid by the captive.

12. In response to an increase in shoplifting losses, Higgins Department Store installed surveillance cameras and began to use magnetic tags on goods. These measures are examples of what risk management technique?
    (a) risk transfer
    (b) risk retention
    (c) risk avoidance
    (d) loss control

13. Jill lives in an area where driving conditions can be hazardous in winter months because of ice and snow. Jill purchased a four-wheel drive vehicle and she puts studded snow tires on her vehicle during the winter months. These measures are examples of:
    (a) risk transfer.
    (b) risk retention.
    (c) risk avoidance.
    (d) loss control.

■ True/False

Circle the T if the statement is true, the F if the statement is false. Explain to yourself why a statement is false.

T   F   1. Insurance management and risk management are the same thing.

T   F   2. Incorporating a business is a form of noninsurance transfer.

T   F   3. Passive retention occurs when you unknowingly retain a risk.

T   F   4. Risk management techniques can only be applied individually.

T   F   5. Risk management is useless if the loss has already occurred.

T   F   6. The risk management function must be performed in isolation. There is no need for interaction between the Risk Management Department and other departments.

T   F   7. Insurance should be the risk manager's first option, with the other techniques applied only if the loss exposures cannot be insured.

T   F   8. Retention has potential cash flow advantages.

T   F   9. A financially strong firm is in a better position to retain loss exposures than is a firm in a weaker financial position.

T   F   10. Past claims data are of no value to the risk manager.

T   F   11. The major advantage of avoidance as a risk management technique is that the chance of loss associated with a particular exposure can be reduced to zero.

T   F   12. Risk managers do not employ financial analysis in deciding upon the optimal risk treatment method.

T   F   13. Self-insurance is a form of retention.

■ Case Applications

Case 1

Valerie is President of Specialty Chemicals (SC). The company doesn't have a "Risk Manager"—insurance and loss control activities are handled by Steve, who is Treasurer. SC's commercial insurance is due to expire on June 30th. On June 26th, the agent servicing the account called Steve and said, "Our company has been forced to raise premiums. Your premium next year will be twice what you're paying now, and the coverage will be more limited." Steve was furious that the agent had not warned him earlier and Valerie ordered Steve to hire a risk management consultant to help them. Steve decided to hire you.

(a) Why did the agent wait so long to tell SC about the premium increase? Is SC also to blame for being surprised in this case?

(b)   As SC's risk management consultant, what would you do?

Case 2

John is Risk Manager for Universal Megatronics (UM). At UM, the Personnel Department is responsible for employee benefits and the Risk Management Department is concerned with property and liability exposures only. Late last year, UM added a new employee benefit, off-site day care, to UM employees who have children. No one bothered to tell John about this new benefit or its location. Why was John furious when he learned about the existence of the off-site day care center?

■ Solutions to Chapter 3

Short Answer Questions

1. The risk management process involves a series of logical steps. First, the exposures to loss must be identified. After identifying the loss exposures, they must be analyzed. Third, the appropriate risk management technique must be selected based on the potential frequency and severity of the loss exposures. After selecting the appropriate treatment techniques, the risk treatment plan must be implemented. Once implemented, the risk management program must be constantly monitored in case corrective action is needed.

2. Before losses occur, the objectives include: handling losses in the most economical way, reducing anxiety, and meeting externally imposed constraints.

    After losses occur, the objectives include: survival of the firm, continued operations, stability of earnings, continued growth, and social responsibility.

3. Retention may have to be used because no other technique may be available. Retention may also be used if the worst possible loss is not severe and if the losses are highly predictable.

4. Noninsurance transfer is a method of shifting the adverse consequences associated with risk to another party through some mechanism other than insurance. Examples of noninsurance transfers include: contracts, leases, incorporation of a business, and hold-harmless agreements.

5. The relationship between loss control activities and insurance premiums is an inverse relationship. The greater the efforts toward loss control, the less expensive the insurance coverage should be. For example, discounts are given for car bumpers that are better at handling collision. Another example is experience rating in commercial insurance. If a firm has an excellent track record in loss control and its insurer uses experience rating, premiums will be lower because of success in reducing frequency and severity of loss.

6. There are several reasons why a manufacturing company may decide to establish a captive insurer. The firm may face an insurance availability problem with regard to certain coverages; the firm may be seeking to stabilize earnings; the firm may need access to a reinsurer; the firm may want to establish the captive as a second profit center; and finally, under certain circumstances, the insurance premiums paid to the captive may be tax-deductible by the parent firm.

7. The following treatment methods go along with the loss frequency/severity combinations:

		Severity	
		Low	High
	Low	*Retention*	*Transfer (including insurance)*
Frequency	High	*Loss Control and Retention*	*Avoidance*

8. The Accounting Department may be of assistance in several ways. Obviously the Accounting Department would have lists and records of assets purchased, the Accounting Department would know to whom the firm owed money and how much was owed, and the income statement might be an excellent source of information regarding the business income loss exposure.

Interaction with the Marketing Department is important for several reasons. For example, a product improperly designed and advertised may lead to product liability litigation. Safe distribution of the product can reduce liability claims.

9. (a) The defensive driving course is an example of loss control. Hopefully, fewer losses will occur as a result.
   (b) Linda transferred the risk associated with disability to an insurer. The transfer of risk can be accomplished through insurance and noninsurance transfers. Disability income insurance, an insurance transfer, was used by Linda.
   (c) Discontinuing development of a hazardous drug is risk avoidance.
   (d) Incorporating a business transfers the risk from the individual to a legally created entity, the corporation. This method of dealing with risk is a noninsurance transfer of risk.
   (e) Installing a sprinkler system illustrates the use of loss control. If a fire starts, the sprinkler system will limit the damage the fire can cause.

10.   A risk management policy statement outlines the objectives of the organization with regard to how loss exposures are treated. The policy statement can also be used to educate other managers of the organization with regard to the risk management process and its objectives.

11.   A manuscript policy is an insurance contract written to address the specific needs of an insurance purchaser. Manuscript policies are used when there is no standard contract that is applicable to the situation or when the applicant is unwilling to accept the terms of the contract the insurer is offering.

12.   There are many examples that could be cited. Some personal loss exposures include the risk of premature death, the risk of poor health (sickness and disability), the risk of unemployment, and the risk of economic insecurity during retirement. Some property risks are the damage, destruction, or theft of property (e.g., a fire damaging the home, physical damage to an auto, theft of valuable property) and any consequential loss associated with the direct loss. Liability may arise from injuring someone, damaging someone's property, or personal injury, such as libel or slander. In addition to the risk of an adverse legal judgment, legal defense costs may be incurred defending the claim.

Multiple Choice Questions

1.   (b) The first step is exposure identification. The exposures cannot be analyzed and the proper risk treatment technique cannot be selected until the risk manager knows what loss exposures are present.

2.   (d) The maximum possible loss is the loss that could occur in the worst-case scenario.

3.   (c) Self-insurance is an example of retention. Rather than transferring the risk to a private insurer, as is done when insurance is purchased, the firm instead funds its own losses.

4.   (c) Both statements are true. Risk management is concerned with identifying and treating loss exposures. The risk management process is not a once-a-year or once-a-month activity. Individuals and businesses constantly face new loss exposures. These loss exposures must be analyzed and risk treatment plans must be formulated and implemented.

5.   (a) Borrowing, current net income, and a funded reserve are all methods of funding retained losses. Insurance is not a source of funds for retained losses. Insurance is a method of transferring risk, not retaining risk.

6.   (a) Tom used the hold-harmless agreement as a noninsurance risk transfer device.

7.   (b) Jan is using retention (she must pay the first portion of any physical damage loss to the vehicle because of the deductible) and transfer (physical damage insurance).

8.   (b) Reduction of anxiety is a pre-loss objective. In risk management lingo, reduction of anxiety is often referred to as "a quiet night's sleep." The other choices listed are post-loss objectives.

9.   (b) One of the problems of risk retention in isolation is that there are no caps and limits. If the firm has a "bad year," the company must pay for all of the losses. Insurance can be, and often is, more expensive than retention. Unfortunately, before the coverage period, you do not know which technique will be most cost-effective.

10.   (a) Premiums paid by a corporation for private insurance coverage are considered an ordinary cost of doing business. Private insurance premiums are a tax-deductible expense for a corporation.

11. (d) The parent firm is not permitted to take tax credits for losses paid by the captive insurer.

12. (d) These measures are loss control devices—the store is attempting to reduce the frequency of loss by catching shoplifters.

13. (d) These measures illustrate loss control. Using four-wheel drive and studded tires reduce the likelihood of being involved in an accident.

True/False

1. **F** Risk management is a broader field that encompasses insurance management.

2. **T**

3. **T**

4. **F** Many risk management techniques are applied together. Private insurance that includes a deductible combines retention and transfer. Loss control is commonly applied with retention, insurance, and non-insurance transfer.

5. **F** There are a number of post-loss risk management objectives.

6. **F** The Risk Manager does not work in isolation. Cooperation with other functional areas within the firm is needed for the Risk Manager to be successful.

7. **F** Insurance is expensive and by transferring risk for a fee, the company loses the use of the premiums paid. Insurance is but one of several risk management techniques, and is often employed in situations where retention would have been a better choice.

8. **T**

9. **T**

10. **F** Although past claims are no guarantee of future claims, past experience can help the risk manager to identify the types of claims that are likely to occur, as well as to assist in assessing the potential frequency and severity of future claims.

11. **T**

12. **F** Financial analysis is critical in the decision process. Consider, for example, the determination of the optimal deductible level. If the risk manager selects a higher deductible, a lower premium is required at the start of the coverage period. On the other hand, when losses occur, the company will have a greater cash outflow as the company has retained more of the loss. Financial analysis can assist in determining what deductible level is best. Financial analysis can be used to help decide between retention and transfer; and in determining whether an investment in loss control is financially justified.

13. **T**

Case Applications

Case 1

(a) It is likely that the agent was afraid that the account would be lost or at least "shopped" if SC officials were aware of the price increase. By informing the company of the rate hike and coverage limits when he did, the agent was hoping SC would be forced to renew the coverage under the insurer's terms. SC is culpable in this case, as well, for not monitoring insurance market conditions. SC officials should have been aware that coverage would be more expensive and more limited, and SC should have prepared for these problems in advance.

(b) As a consultant to SC, you should first ask the agent to extend coverage at a pro rata premium for a short period of time. During the extension, you should perform the steps in the risk management process. This analysis will tell you if SC has identified their exposures, properly assessed them, and if the company is employing the appropriate risk management techniques. The risk treatment methods must then be implemented. If insurance is part of the best treatment program, coverage should be put out for competitive bids. Even if the current agent is successful in retaining the account, the agent is put on notice that the company will shop the account if not satisfied with the service provided.

Case 2

Some insurance coverages list insured properties and locations. Because John did not know about the location of the day care operation, it could not have been listed. In addition, UM may not be covered for legal liability if a day care worker or a child is injured at the day care center. Even if the day care center was located at an insured location, the company's liability insurance might exclude liability for such an operation. If a child sustained a debilitating injury while under the care of the company-sponsored day care center, UM might face a large, uninsured, liability claim. This case underscores the importance of communication and cooperation between the Risk Management Department and other departments.

Chapter 4
Advanced Topics in Risk Management

■ **Overview**

In the previous chapter, you were introduced to the field of risk management and personal risk management. This second chapter on risk management covers some advanced risk management topics. The chapter discusses the evolution of corporate risk management to include financial risks and all risks facing the business. The impact of the underwriting cycle, insurance industry consolidation, and the securitization of risk are discussed, as well as loss forecasting, financial analysis in risk management decision making, and the application of some other risk management tools.

■ **Learning Objectives**

After studying this chapter, you should be able to:

- Explain the meaning of financial risk management and enterprise risk management.
- Describe the impact of the underwriting cycle and consolidation in the insurance industry on the practice of risk management.
- Explain the securitization of risk, including catastrophe bonds and weather options.
- Explain the methods that a risk manager employs to forecast losses.
- Show how financial analysis can be applied to risk management decision making.
- Describe other risk management tools that may be of assistance to risk managers.
- Define the following:

Capacity	Insurance brokers
Capital budgeting	Integrated risk program
Catastrophe bond	Interest rate risk
Catastrophe modeling	Internal rate of return (IRR)
Chief risk officer (CRO)	Intranet
Clash loss	Loss distribution
Combined ratio	Mutually exclusive events
Commodity price risk	Net present value (NPV)
Compounding	Regression analysis
Consolidation	Risk management information system (RMIS)
Currency exchange rate risk	Risk maps
Dependent events	Securitization of risk
Discounting	"Soft" insurance market
Double-trigger option	Surplus
Enterprise risk management	Time value of money
Financial risk management	Underwriting cycle
"Hard" insurance market	Value at risk (VAR) analysis
Independent events	Weather option

■ Outline

I.   The Changing Scope of Risk Management

    A.   Financial Risk Management

    B.   Enterprise Risk Management

II.   Insurance Market Dynamics

    A.   The Underwriting Cycle

    B.   Consolidation in the Insurance Industry

    C.   Securitization of Risk

III. Loss Forecasting

    A.   Probability Analysis

    B.   Regression Analysis

    C.   Forecasting with Loss Distributions

IV. Financial Analysis in Risk Management Decision Making

    A.   The Time Value of Money

    B.   Financial Analysis Applications

V.   Other Risk Management Tools

    A.   Risk Management Information Systems (RMIS)

    B.   Risk Management Intranets and Websites

    C.   Risk Maps

    D.   Value at Risk (VAR) Analysis

    E.   Catastrophe Modeling

■ Short Answer Questions

1.   What is financial risk management? What types of risk are considered in financial risk management?

2. How does enterprise risk management differ from traditional risk management and financial risk management?

3. What is the underwriting cycle? Be sure to discuss a "hard insurance market" and a "soft insurance market" in your answer.

4. How do (1) the level of surplus and (2) investment income impact the underwriting cycle?

5. What three types of insurance industry consolidations impact risk management?

6. What is securitization of risk and how does risk securitization increase the capacity of the insurance industry?

7. Differentiate between (1) independent, (2) dependent, and (3) mutually exclusive events.

8. What is meant by the phrase "time value of money"? Why is it important to apply time value of money analysis in risk management decision making?

9. What is capital budgeting? What does the net present value (NPV) of a loss control investment represent to the owners of an organization?

10. What is a risk management information system (RMIS)?

■ Multiple Choice Questions

Circle the letter that corresponds to the BEST *answer.*

1. Traditional risk management addressed all of the following loss exposures EXCEPT:
    (a) property risks.
    (b) financial risks.
    (c) personnel risks.
    (d) liability risks.

2. Second National Bank agreed to pay a high rate of return on long-term certificates of deposit. Shortly after several depositors opted for the long-term CDs, inflation plunged and rates of return dropped. Second National must continue to pay high rates on the long-term CDs even though interest rates have declined significantly. This scenario illustrates:
    (a) interest rate risk.
    (b) currency exchange risk.
    (c) business risk.
    (d) commodity price risk.

3. Which of the following are you LEAST LIKELY to observe when the property and liability insurance market is "hard"?
    (a) coverage availability problems
    (b) high premiums
    (c) tight underwriting standards
    (d) low premiums

4. Which of the following statements is true with regard to insurance market dynamics?
    I.   When the property and liability insurance industry is in a strong surplus position, insurers can cut premiums and loosen underwriting standards.
    II.   Insurance companies can lose money on their underwriting activities for the year, but still show a profit for the year.
    (a) I only
    (b) II only
    (c) both I and II
    (d) neither I nor II

5. ABC Insurance Company would like to begin offering depository and lending services to its policyowners. ABC Insurance Company purchased a small credit union, and through the credit union ABC offers these services to their policyowners. This scenario illustrates:
    (a) insurance company mergers and acquisitions.
    (b) formation of an enterprise risk management plan.
    (c) insurance broker mergers and acquisitions.
    (d) cross-industry consolidation.

6. A risk manager was considering the range of possible losses that her company might experience next year. She noted that major production facilities could only be destroyed once during the year, because the destruction of the production facility by one peril means that the facility could not be destroyed a second time. What is the situation called where the occurrence of one event precludes the occurrence of a second event?

(a) empty set events

(b) dependent events

(c) mutually exclusive events

(d) independent events

7. A risk manager was attempting to estimate how many physical damage claims would be reported for vehicles in the company's fleet the following year. He decided to perform a regression analysis using "number of vehicle claims" as the dependent variable. It would make sense to use each of the following variables as the independent variable EXCEPT:

(a) number of vehicles in the fleet.

(b) gallons of fuel used by fleet vehicles.

(c) number of people employed by the company.

(d) number of miles driven by fleet vehicles per year.

8. As a result of a court decision, XYZ Company must pay a claimant $100,000 two years from today. What is the present value of the $100,000 award that XYZ Company must pay in two years? Assume a 10 percent interest (discount) rate.

(a) $80,000

(b) $82,645

(c) $93,584

(d) $120,000

9. Which of the following statements is (are) true with respect to the time value of money?

I. One dollar received today is worth less than one dollar to be received three years from today.

II. The time value of money should be ignored in capital budgeting decisions.

(a) I only

(b) II only

(c) both I and II

(d) neither I nor II

10. Jenna is risk manager of LMN Company. Jenna was contacted by a vendor who was selling a computerized database that Jenna could use in LMN's risk management program. The database was capable of storing and analyzing risk management data and generating reports for Jenna. This computerized database is called a(n):

(a) risk management intranet.

(b) risk map.

(c) risk web.

(d) risk management information system.

■ True/False

Circle the T if the statement is true, the F if the statement is false. Explain to yourself why a statement is false.

T   F   1.   Enterprise management includes consideration of speculative financial risks.

T   F   2.   A dollar received today is less valuable than a dollar received a year from today.

T   F   3.   Contractual provisions and capital market instruments can be used to address financial risks.

T   F   4.   Chief risk officer is another name for risk manager.

T   F   5.   A combined ratio greater than one (or one hundred percent) indicates profitable underwriting

T   F   6.   A strong surplus position means that an insurance company is well-positioned to write coverage and take on risk.

T   F   7.   Insurance industry mergers have no impact upon the practice of risk management.

T   F   8.   If two events are dependent, the occurrence of one event affects the occurrence of the second event.

T   F   9.   The goal of regression analysis is to use the past relationship between variables to assist in predicting future results.

T   F   10. Time value of money analysis should be applied in capital budgeting decisions.

T   F   11. Risk management intranets are designed to provide information to the general public.

T   F   12. Catastrophe modeling can be employed by insurers, brokers, ratings agencies, and companies that have exposure to catastrophic loss.

■ Case Applications

Case 1

Universal Megatronics is a conglomerate comprised of three large divisions: HMR Bank and Mortgage Lending, International Construction Company, and The Cotton Apparel Company. When the three companies merged, the management team decided to centralize risk management. Ken Campbell, who was risk manager of the construction company, was named Risk Manager of Universal Megatronics. He has been asked to expand the traditional role of risk management to consider financial risks. Identify the types of financial risk inherent in each division and discuss how the risk could be addressed.

(a) HMR Bank and Mortgage Lending is in a very competitive business. Savers demand a competitive return on savings, while mortgage borrowers want the lowest rates possible. The majority of HMR mortgages are 30-year and 15-year fixed-rate loans.

b) U.S.-based International Construction Company engages in large projects in Europe and the Pacific Rim. Contracts are negotiated in advance, and all payments are made with local currency. International Construction requires payment of one-third of the cost of the project when construction begins, one-third when construction reaches the halfway point, and one-third upon completion of the project. Some projects require up to three years to complete.

(c) Cotton Apparel Company has contracts to deliver clothing to two national store chains. Buyers from the stores order apparel in desired styles and quantities, with delivery expected 6 to 9 months after the orders are placed. Cotton Apparel purchases "raw" cotton and converts it to fabric needed for the clothing its mills produce.

Case 2

Carla Powell is risk manager of LMN Industries. Several questions have arisen and she has asked for your assistance:

(a) A loss control investment will cost $30,000 today. The project will generate three cash flows: $10,000 one year from today, $20,000 two years from today, and $10,000 three years from today. What is this project's net present value (NPV) if the proper discount (interest) rate is 8 percent?

(b)   The probability that a fire will damage an LMN production facility (Location #1) is 4 percent in any given year. The annual probability that a wind storm will damage the same production facility is 6 percent. LMN has another production facility (Location #2) located 800 miles from the first facility. The probability that a fire will damage the second facility in any year is 5 percent. The annual probability that the second facility will experience a flood loss is 2 percent.

    1.   What is the probability that Location #1 will have *both* a fire loss and a wind loss in the same year?

    2.   What is the probability that Location #2 will have *at least one* flood loss or fire loss in a given year?

▪ Solutions to Chapter 4

Short Answer Questions

1.   Financial risk management is the identification, analysis, and treatment of speculative financial risks the organization faces. Such risks include commodity price risk, interest rate risk, and currency exchange rate risk. These risks differ from the traditional risks addressed by risk managers in that for these risks, there is also the possibility of a gain.

2.   Traditional risk management addressed property, liability, and personnel risks only. Financial risk management addresses speculative financial risks. Enterprise risk management is a broad concept that encompasses traditional pure risks and speculative financial risks. In addition, enterprise risk management addresses the organization's strategic and operational risks.

3. The underwriting cycle is an interesting phenomenon in property and liability insurance markets. Premium levels, underwriting stringency, and underwriting results exhibit a cyclical pattern over time. In a "hard insurance market," premiums are high and underwriting standards are tight. Business written during this time is usually profitable, helping the industry to build/restore surplus. When the industry is in a strong surplus position, a natural consequence is price competition and a "soft insurance market." In a soft market, insurers compete by lowering prices and loosening underwriting standards. This business is often unprofitable, and the insurer must draw upon the surplus to fund the losses. As surplus is eroded, rate hikes and a return to tighter underwriting standards are warranted, and the cycle repeats.

4. The level of surplus is a key determinant of underwriting cycle phases. When the industry and individual insurers are in a strong surplus position, they are able to withstand underwriting losses. Companies can lower premiums and loosen underwriting standards. If underwriting is unprofitable, these companies can draw upon the strong surplus position. As surplus is depleted through underwriting losses, a point may be reached where the company can no longer tolerate underwriting losses. At that time, premiums are raised and stricter underwriting is employed. As better business is written at higher premiums, underwriting profits are generated and the surplus is restored.

   Underwriting profits and losses do not occur in isolation. Investment income must also be considered. Insurers can lose money on underwriting and remain viable if there is sufficient investment income. Therefore, investment returns and anticipated investment returns have an impact upon the insurance marketplace. Insurers must charge higher premiums and employ tighter underwriting if they do not anticipate enough investment income to offset underwriting losses. Likewise, insurers can lower premiums and employ loose underwriting standards if anticipated investment returns will offset underwriting losses.

5. There are three types of consolidations that impact risk management. First, there are mergers between insurers. Second, there are mergers of insurance brokerages. Finally, there are cross-industry consolidations. The last category includes mergers and acquisitions between banks, insurers, brokerages, and other financial institutions.

6. Securitization of risk means that insurable risk is transferred to the capital markets through the issue of a financial security. A catastrophe bond issued by an insurer is a good example. This security pays interest and principal to the lender, just like other corporate bonds. If a catastrophic loss occurs, however, the issuer is not required to make some or all of the scheduled payments to the bondholder. The retained funds can be used to finance catastrophic losses. Through risk securitization, the financial resources of the capital markets can be used to finance catastrophic losses, rather than simply relying on the capacity of insurers and reinsurers.

7. If events are independent, the occurrence of one event has no impact upon the occurrence of the second event. A fire at a production facility in Toledo has no impact upon whether a fleet vehicle will be damaged on a highway in Arizona.

   If events are dependent, then the occurrence of one event can affect the occurrence of the second event. For example, if two buildings are located close together, the probability of the second building having a fire loss is greater if there is a fire at the first building.

   If events are mutually exclusive, the occurrence of one event means that the second event cannot occur. For example, if you have a small tract of land, it may only be large enough for one business. Building a gas station on the property precludes building a retirement home on the land, and vice versa.

8. The "time value of money" means that when cash flows are examined, it is important to consider the interest-earning capacity of money. The value of $1,000 to be received today is $1,000. The value of $1,000 to be received one year from today is less than $1,000. Why? If you had $1,000 today, you could invest the money and earn interest. One year from today your $1,000 would be worth more than $1,000. So in valuing cash flows, it is important to consider the timing of the cash flows. The same amount of money in different time periods is of different value once the interest-generating capacity of the money is considered.

9. Capital budgeting is the analysis of investments in plant and equipment. Individual projects are analyzed to determine whether the project should be undertaken by considering the cost of the project relative to the benefit provided by the project. Only projects that will make the organization better of (increase value) should be adopted.

    Net present value (NPV) is one method of evaluating investment projects. The net present value of a project is equal to the present value of the future cash flows that the project will generate minus the cost of the project. A loss control project may benefit the organization by reducing losses and by providing a cost reduction in insurance premiums. However, there is a cost involved if the loss control project is undertaken. As the present value of the future cash flows is "netted" against the cos of the project, the NPV demonstrates the value of the project to the owners of the firm.

10. A risk management information system (RMIS) is a computerized database that a risk manager uses to store and analyze risk management data. The database can be used to prepare reports and to predic future loss levels. Such systems are marketed by a number of vendors, or an organization may develop its own RMIS.

Multiple Choice Questions

1. (b)   Traditionally, risk management was limited to property, liability, and personnel risks. The inclusion of financial risks is a relatively recent development. Many companies still use "financ people" to address such risks.

2. (a)   Second National is obliged to pay the higher interest rate even though Second National may ear a lower rate of return on "new money" that it loans or invests. The scenario illustrates interest rate risk.

3. (d)   Low premiums are not characteristic of a "hard" insurance market. In a hard insurance market, premiums are high, underwriting standards are tight, and some coverages may not be offered.

4. (c)   Both statements are true. A healthy surplus position means that the company can withstand pric competition and potential losses. In addition, just because an insurer loses money on its underwriting activities, it does not mean that the company is unprofitable for the year. The company's total income represents underwriting results plus investment results. An insurer can lose money on the underwriting side of the business, but offset the underwriting loss with investment income.

5. (d)   As the merger in this case is between two different financial services segments (banking and insurance), the acquisition represents "cross-industry" consolidation.

6. (c)   Events are mutually exclusive if the occurrence of one event means that a second event cannot occur.

7. (c)   The number of people employed by the company would be a bad predictor of vehicle claims because many of the people employed have nothing to do with the fleet of vehicles. Fuel consumed, miles driven, and number of vehicles would be far better predictors of vehicle claims.

8. (b)   The present value of the award is \$82,645. This value is obtained using the discounting formula:

$$\text{Present Value} = \frac{\$100,000}{(1+0.10)^2} = \$82,645$$

9. (d)   Neither statement is correct. One dollar received today is worth more than one dollar received three years from today. A dollar received today can earn interest immediately and will be worth more than one dollar three years from today. Time value of money must be considered in capital budgeting decisions. Capital expenditures are likely to generate cash flows in the future, and these cash flows must be valued according to the time when they will be received.

10. (d)   The vendor was selling a risk management information system (RMIS). These systems can be used to store and analyze risk management data.

True/False

1. **T**

2. **F** A dollar received today is worth more than a dollar received a year from today. The dollar received today can be used to earn interest immediately. One year from today you would have one dollar plus the interest earned on the one dollar.

3. **T**

4. **F** The role of the chief risk officer is broader than that of a traditional risk manager. The chief risk officer is responsible for a wider range of risks facing the organization than the risks for which a risk manager is responsible.

5. **F** The combined ratio is the ratio of losses plus expenses to premiums. If the combined ratio exceeds one (or one hundred percent), it means that for every dollar collected in premiums, the insurer paid more than one dollar in losses and expenses. A combined ratio greater than one indicates unprofitable underwriting results.

6. **T**

7. **F** In the case of insurance company mergers, the consolidation means there will be fewer but larger insurance companies in the marketplace. In the case of insurance brokers, in the past risk managers could get quotes from several large independent brokerages. With consolidation, however, there are fewer large independent organizations. The text mentions three "top 10" brokers that merged and are now part of a large, single entity.

8. **T**

9. **T**

10. **T**

11. **F** Risk management intranets are websites with search capabilities that are designed for internal, rather than external, use.

12. **T**

Case Applications

Case 1

(a) HMR Bank and Mortgage Lending presents the classic interest rate problem. Borrowers have borrowed money at fixed rates for long periods (30 years and 15 years). If short-term rates increase significantly, the company will have a significant portion of its loan portfolio earning a lower rate of interest. One solution may be greater use of variable interest rate loans so the interest rate fluctuation over time with current market rates. Incentives could be offered for borrowers to accept variable rate loans. Another possibility is to "swap" the fixed-rate loans with another financial institution that has too much exposure to variable loan rate loans.

(b) International Construction Company's payment terms present an interesting currency exchange rate risk problem. The company receives one-third of costup front, and there is the risk that currency paid at later stages of construction may have lost value. The Risk Manager could try to get more of the money upfront, or use currency futures to hedge this exchange rate risk.

(c) The financial risk with Cotton Apparel Company is a commodity price risk. The company enters into agreements to deliver clothing at an agreed-upon price today, with delivery in the future. In the meantime, something might happen that would cause the price of cotton to increase significantly, altering the profitability of the transaction. The risk could be hedged through cotton futures contracts.

Case 2

(a) The Net Present Value (NPV) is equal to the sum of the present value of the future cash flows less the cost of the project:

$$\frac{\$10,000}{(1+0.08)} + \frac{\$20,000}{(1+0.08)^2} + \frac{\$10,000}{(1+0.08)^3} - \$30,000 = \text{Net Present Value}$$

$$\$9,259 + \$17,147 + \$7,938 - \$30,000 = \$4,344$$

The NPV is $4,344. As the NVP is positive, the project is acceptable.

(b) 1. There is only a slight chance that *both* of the events will occur, as the probability that either event will occur is small. The probability that both events will occur is the product of the individual probabilities:

$$0.04 \times 0.06 = 0.0024 \text{ or } 0.24\%$$

2. As the events are not mutually exclusive (both could occur), the probability that at least one will occur is the probability that either will occur minus the probability that both will occur (to avoid double counting):

$$0.05 + 0.02 - (0.05 \times 0.02) = 0.069 \text{ or } 6.9\%$$

Chapter 5
Types of Insurers and Marketing Systems

Overview

There are a number of types of insurance organizations: mutual companies, stock companies, fraternals, reciprocals, Lloyd's of London, Blue Cross/Blue Shield plans, and health maintenance organizations (HMOs). There are also a variety of marketing systems. The individual marketing insurance may be an independent agent, an exclusive agent, a direct writer, or a general agent. Coverage also may be purchased through an employer-based group plan or in response to phone or mail solicitation. The prospective purchaser might enlist the services of an insurance broker to purchase insurance. In this chapter, we examine the types of private insurers, distinctions between agents and brokers, and types of marketing systems employed by property and liability insurers and life and health insurers.

Learning Objectives

After studying this chapter, you should be able to:

- Describe the major types of private insurers, including the following: stock insurers, mutual insurers, reciprocal exchanges, Lloyd's of London, Blue Cross and Blue Shield plans, and health maintenance organizations (HMOs).
- Explain why some life insurers have demutualized or formed holding companies in recent years.

  Explain the difference between an agency building system and a nonbuilding agency system as life insurance marketing systems.
- Describe the direct response system for selling life insurance.
- Describe the marketing systems in property and liability insurance, including: independent agency system, exclusive agency system, direct writers, direct response system, and mixed systems.
- Define the following:

Advance premium mutual	Independent agency system
Agency building system	Lloyd's of London
Agent	Managerial system
Assessment mutual	Mass merchandising
Broker	Multiple distribution system
Contingent or profit-sharing commission	Mutual insurer
Demutualization	Nonadmitted insurer
Direct-response system	Nonbuilding agency system
Direct writer	Personal-producing general agent
Exclusive agency system	Reciprocal exchange
Expirations or renewal rights to business	Savings bank life insurance
Fraternal insurer	Stock insurer
General agency system	Surplus lines broker
Holding company	

■ Outline

I.   Overview of Private Insurance in the Financial Services Industry

II.   Types of Private Insurers

    A.   Stock Insurers

    B.   Mutual Insurers

    C.   Reciprocal Exchanges

    D.   Lloyd's of London

    E.   Blue Cross and Blue Shield Plans

    F.   Health Maintenance Organizations (HMOs)

III. Agents and Brokers

    A.   Agents

    B.   Brokers

IV.   Types of Marketing Systems

    A.   Life Insurance Marketing Systems

        1. Agency Building System

        2. Nonbuilding Agency System

        3. Direct Response System

    B.   Property and Liability Insurance Marketing Systems

        1. Independent Agency System

        2. Exclusive Agency System

        3. Direct Writer

        4. Direct Response System

        5. Multiple Distribution System

V.   Group Insurance Marketing

■ Short Answer Questions

1. List the different types of mutual insurers.

2. The financial services sector in recent years has been characterized by consolidation and convergence. What is the meaning of these terms with respect to the financial services sector?

3. How do stock insurance companies and mutual insurance companies differ?

4. How does an advance premium mutual differ from an assessment mutual?

5. What are the distinctive characteristics of Lloyd's of London?

6. What are the differences between insurance agents and brokers?

7. If you need a specific type of insurance, and none of the insurers licensed to operate in your state market that type of insurance, how do you obtain the coverage?

8. What are the primary methods of marketing life insurance coverage?

9. What are the primary methods of marketing property and liability insurance coverage?

0. What are the characteristics of mass merchandising?

■ Multiple Choice Questions

Circle the letter that corresponds to the BEST *answer.*

1. Cindy sells property and liability insurance. She is a salaried employee of the one company that she represents. Cindy is a(n):
   - (a) independent agent.
   - (b) general agent.
   - (c) exclusive agent.
   - (d) direct writer.

2. Which statement(s) about mutual insurers is(are) true?
   - I. They are owned by their policyowners.
   - II. Some mutual insurers are permitted to assess policyowners if losses are higher than anticipated.
   - (a) I only
   - (b) II only
   - (c) both I and II
   - (d) neither I nor II

3. All of the following methods are used to distribute life insurance EXCEPT:
   - (a) independent agency system.
   - (b) general agency system.
   - (c) managerial system.
   - (d) direct response system.

4. Some mutual companies have gone through a conversion process and have become stock insurance companies. All of the following are advantages of the stock form of organization relative to the mutual form of organization EXCEPT:
   - (a) the ability to offer stock options may make it easier to attract and retain key personnel.
   - (b) it's easier to raise capital as a stock organization.
   - (c) stock insurance companies are exempt from state premium taxes and federal income taxes.
   - (d) stock insurers have great flexibility to expand by acquiring other companies.

5. A plan for providing property and liability insurance to individuals in a group under a single program of insurance at reduced rates is called:
   - (a) surplus lines insurance.
   - (b) direct response.
   - (c) direct writing.
   - (d) mass merchandising.

6. John would like to start a business raising race horses. When he inquired about insurance coverage for race horses, he learned that none of the insurers operating in his state sell that particular type of coverage. In his state, insurance on race horses would be described as a(n):
   - (a) monocline.
   - (b) expired line.
   - (c) surplus line.
   - (d) multiple line.

7. All of the following channels are used to distribute property and liability insurance EXCEPT:
   (a) general agency system.
   (b) independent agency system.
   (c) direct writers.
   (d) exclusive agency system.

8. What type of insurer can be defined as an unincorporated mutual in which each member insures the other members and, in turn, is insured by the other members?
   (a) stock insurer
   (b) assessment mutual
   (c) reciprocal exchange
   (d) fraternal insurer

9. Which statement is true with regard to agents and brokers?
   I. Life insurance agents typically have greater authority to bind coverage than do property and liability insurance agents.
   II. Brokers legally represent insurance purchasers, not insurers.
   (a) I only
   (b) II only
   (c) both I and II
   (d) neither I nor II

10. Which statement is true with regard to independent insurance agents?
    I. They are compensated through a salary paid by the insurers they represent.
    II. They represent only one insurer.
    (a) I only
    (b) II only
    (c) both I and II
    (d) neither I nor II

11. Bruce obtained health insurance coverage from a nonprofit prepayment plan that provides coverage for physicians' and surgeons' fees and hospital services. Bruce obtained this coverage from a:
    (a) Blue Cross and Blue Shield plan.
    (b) mutual insurer.
    (c) stock insurer.
    (d) health maintenance organization (HMO).

12. Because demutualization is a slow and cumbersome process, some states have enacted legislation that allows the mutual company to be reorganized so that it may own or acquire control of stock companies that can issue additional shares of common stock. The reorganized mutual company is called a(n):
    (a) mutual holding company.
    (b) captive insurance company.
    (c) shell insurance company.
    (d) fronting insurance company.

True/False

Circle the T if the statement is true, the F if the statement is false. Explain to yourself why a statement is false.

T   F   1. Mutual insurers guarantee dividend payments to their policyowners.

T   F   2. A captive insurance company is a mutual insurance company that is owned by a stock insurance company.

T   F   3. The managerial system is a distribution system for property and liability insurance.

T   F   4. Exclusive agents represent only one insurer or a group of insurers under common ownership.

T   F   5. Mass merchandising refers to selling life and health insurance through the mail, newspapers, or other media.

T   F   6. Surplus lines brokers are authorized to place coverage with nonadmitted insurers.

T   F   7. Lloyd's of London restricts its underwriting to heterogeneous loss exposures, such as a star quarterback's arm or a famous dancer's legs.

T   F   8. Mutual insurance companies may only write life and health insurance.

T   F   9. Stock insurance companies frequently issue assessable insurance policies.

T   F   10. Fraternal insurance companies are one type of mutual insurer.

T   F   11. An independent agent, rather than the company he or she represents, owns expiration rights to the coverage the independent agent has sold.

T   F   12. Blue Cross/Blue Shield organizations stress service benefits rather than cash benefits.

T   F   13. Demutualization makes raising new capital more difficult.

T   F   14. Personal-producing general agents are hired to sell insurance and not to recruit new agents.

■ Case Applications

Case 1

For many years, Sarah Jane was a successful independent insurance agent. Recently, she was recruited by two insurance companies. With the first company, Sarah Jane would be an exclusive agent. With the second company, she would be a direct writer. What changes would Sarah Jane observe if she switched from being an independent agent to an exclusive agent or direct writer?

Case 2

Benson Insurance gives an award each year to the agent who sells the most insurance coverage. In three of the last five years, this award was won by Clark Edwards. In an effort to determine what makes Clark such a successful agent, Benson Insurance Company decided to examine the business he produced. In the examination, the company learned that insureds solicited by Clark had 50 percent more claims than business solicited by other Benson Insurance agents. Benson Insurance is rethinking how the company compensates and rewards its agents. How might compensation and rewards be restructured to obtain better underwriting results?

Solutions to Chapter 5

Short Answer Questions

1. The types of mutual insurers include: assessment mutuals, advance premium mutuals, and fraternal insurers.

2. Consolidation means that the number of firms operating in the financial services market has declined over time because of mergers and acquisitions. Announcements of bank mergers and insurance company mergers have become commonplace. The obvious result is fewer, but on average larger, financial services organizations.

   Convergence means that financial institutions can now sell a wide variety of products outside their core business area. Prior to the passage of the Gramm-Leach-Bliley Act (The Financial Modernization Act of 1999), a financial services company had limited ability to operate outside of its core area—banks concentrated on banking, insurers sold insurance, and securities firms handled investments. Today, we see convergence—for example, one large personal lines insurance company now offers mutual funds, depository operations (banking), and extends mortgage loans.

3. Stock insurance companies are owned by their stockholders who participate in the profits and losses of the insurer. Stock companies cannot issue assessable policies. Mutual companies are owned by their customers, the policyowners. If the experience of the mutual insurer is favorable, the company may refund a portion of the premiums paid to the policyowners through dividend payments.

4. Advance premium mutuals charge a premium upfront that is expected to be sufficient to pay all claims and expenses. If premiums are not sufficient, any deficit is made up through the surplus of the organization, which is the difference between the insurer's assets and liabilities. Assessment mutuals reserve the right to levy an additional charge against policyowners if the premiums originally charged are not sufficient to cover claims and expenses.

5. Lloyd's of London has several distinctive characteristics. First, Lloyd's of London is technically not an insurance company but rather an association providing services to its members. Second, the insurance coverage is actually written through syndicates that belong to Lloyd's of London. Third, new "names" have limited liability with respect to the insurance they write as individuals. Fourth, corporations with limited liability can also join Lloyd's of London. Fifth, individual members must meet stringent financial requirements. Finally, Lloyd's of London is licensed only in a small number of jurisdictions in the United States.

6. An insurance agent is someone who legally represents the insurer and has the authority to act on the insurer's behalf. Brokers legally represent insurance buyers who are seeking coverage. Brokers don't have authority to bind an insurer. Both agents and brokers are compensated through commissions.

7. In this situation, you would obtain coverage through a nonadmitted insurer. As such an insurer has not been admitted to operate in the state, the insurer will not have sales representatives in your state. To obtain coverage with a nonadmitted insurer, a specialist known as a surplus lines broker may be used. Surplus lines brokers are authorized to place coverage with nonadmitted insurers.

8. The primary methods of marketing life insurance coverage include: the agency building system (which includes the general agency system and managerial system), the nonbuilding agency system, and the direct response system.

9. The primary methods of marketing property and liability insurance coverage include: the independent agency system, the exclusive agency system, through direct writers, the direct response system, and the multiple distribution system.

10. Mass merchandising has a number of distinctive characteristics. First, property and liability insurance is sold to individual members of a group. Second, individual underwriting is employed. Third, rates are lower because of lower commissions and lower administrative expenses. Finally, employees usually fund all of the coverage without contributions from employers.

Multiple Choice Questions

1. (d) Cindy is a direct writer. Direct writers and exclusive agents are both affiliated with only one company. Direct writers are salaried employees while exclusive agents are compensated through commissions.

2. (c) Both statements are true. Mutual insurers are owned by their policyowners and have no stockholders. Assessment mutuals can assess policyowners if losses are higher than anticipated.

3. (a) The independent agency system is used to market property and liability insurance. The other methods listed are used to market life insurance.

4. (c) Stock companies are not exempt from state premium taxes and federal income taxes. The other statements are true with respect to stock companies compared to mutual companies.

5. (d) Mass merchandising has all of the characteristics described.

6. (c) Surplus lines are those coverages for which there is no market in the state. John would have to obtain coverage from a nonadmitted insurer using the services of a surplus lines broker.

7. (a) General agency is a marketing system used to distribute life insurance coverage.

8. (c) A reciprocal exchange has the characteristics described.

9. (b) Property and liability insurance agents typically have greater authority to bind the insurer than do life insurance agents. Brokers represent insurance buyers, not insurers.

0. (d) Neither statement is true. Independent agents are not employees of insurance companies and are not paid salaries. Independent agents are independent business men and women who represent more than one insurer. They are compensated through commissions.

1. (a) Blue Cross and Blue Shield plans are typically nonprofit prepayment plans that provide coverage for hospital services and physicians' and surgeons' fees.

2. (a) The mutual insurance company is reorganized as a holding company that can own or acquire stock companies.

True/False

1. **F** Although mutual companies may pay dividends to policyowners, the dividend payments are not guaranteed.

2. **F** A captive insurance company is an insurance company that is owned by a parent company for the purposes of insuring the parent company's loss exposures. A petroleum company, for example, may establish a captive insurance company to provide pollution liability coverage for the parent firm.

3. **F** The managerial (branch office) system is a life insurance distribution system, not a property and liability insurance distribution system.

4. **T**

5. **F** What is described here is direct response, not mass merchandising. Mass merchandising refers to selling property and liability insurance to individual members of groups.

6. **T**

7. **F** Although Lloyd's of London receives notoriety for writing heterogeneous risks like these, Lloyd's of London is also important in ocean marine insurance, reinsurance, and other areas.

8. **F** There are many mutual insurance companies that write property and liability insurance. Liberty Mutual Insurance Company and State Farm Insurance Company are two excellent examples of mutual insurance companies that market property and liability coverage.

9. **F** Only certain types of mutual insurers can issue assessable policies. Stock companies cannot issue assessable policies.

0. **T**

1. **T**

2. **T**

3. **F** Demutualization makes it easier to raise new capital. Under the mutual ownership structure, there are no publicly traded ownership rights. If a stock company (e.g., a demutualized insurer) wishes to raise more capital, it can sell shares of stock.

4. **T**

Case Applications

Case 1

As an independent agent, Sarah Jane is an independent businessperson representing more than one insurer. She owns the expiration rights to the coverage she sells and her renewal commissions are equal to the commissions earned on new business. As an exclusive agent, Sarah Jane would still be an independent businessperson, however she would represent only one company. The company, rather than Sarah Jane, would own the expiration rights and a higher commission would be paid on new business than on renewal business. If she takes the job as a direct writer, Sarah Jane will be an employee rather than an agent. She will be paid a salary and will represent only one insurer.

Case 2

If Clark is being compensated on a straight commission basis, he has an incentive to sell as much insurance coverage as possible. To do this, he may be soliciting bad risks, and some of these bad risks may be slipping past the company's underwriters and producing an above-average number of claims. Rather than only considering the quantity of coverage sold, Benson Insurance could also consider the quality of the applicants solicited by its agents. Benson Insurance could, for example, consider the ratio of losses paid to premium dollars written by Benson Insurance agents, and award commissions that consider the loss ratio of business generated by the agent (profit-sharing commissions). The annual award could be changed from an award based on quantity only to an award recognizing quantity and quality of coverage sold.

Chapter 6
Insurance Company Operations

■ Overview

Up until now, your contact with individuals who work in the insurance industry has most likely been with sales and claims personnel. Both of these important operations require interaction with the general public and these functions are performed away from the company's headquarters. Have you ever seen an insurance company home office or regional office? In case you haven't, these buildings tend to be very large structures. Insurance companies need this space because there are many other vital operations that go on "behind the scenes." In addition to discussing the claims and marketing operations of insurance companies, this chapter discusses other important functional areas of insurance companies, including: rate making, underwriting, reinsurance, investments, loss control, and a number of other functions. There are many interesting job opportunities available in the insurance industry.

■ Learning Objectives

After studying this chapter, you should be able to:

- Explain the rate-making function of insurers.
- Explain the steps in the underwriting process.
- Describe the sales and marketing activities of insurers.
- Describe the steps in the process of settling a claim.
- Explain the reasons for reinsurance and the various types of reinsurance treaties.
- Explain the importance of insurance company investments and identify the various types of investments of insurers.
- Define the following:

Actuary	Excess-of-loss treaty
Adjustment bureau	Facultative reinsurance
Catastrophe bonds	Independent adjustor
Ceding commission	Line underwriter
Ceding company	Loss control
Certified Financial Planner (CFP)	Medical Information Bureau (MIB) report
Certified Insurance Counselor (CIC)	Producers
Cession	Production
Chartered Financial Consultant (ChFC)	Public adjustor
Chartered Life Underwriter (CLU)	Quota-share treaty
Chartered Property and Casualty Underwriter (CPCU)	Rate making
	Reinsurance
Claims adjustor	Reinsurance pool
Class underwriting	Reinsurer
Company adjustor	Retention limit (net retention)
Electronic data processing (EDP)	Retrocession

Retrocessionaire   Treaty reinsurance
Securitization of risk   Underwriting
Surplus-share treaty   Unearned premium reserve

■ Outline

I.   **Rate Making**

II. **Underwriting**

    A.   Statement of Underwriting Policy

    B.   Basic Underwriting Principles

    C.   Steps in Underwriting

    D.   Other Underwriting Considerations

III. **Production**

    A.   Agency Department

    B.   Professionalism in Selling

IV. **Claims Settlement**

    A.   Basic Objectives in Claim Settlement

    B.   Types of Claims Adjustors

    C.   Steps in Settlement of a Claim

V.   **Reinsurance**

    A.   Definitions

    B.   Reasons for Reinsurance

    C.   Types of Reinsurance
        1. Facultative Reinsurance
        2. Treaty Reinsurance

    D.   Alternatives to Traditional Reinsurance

VI. **Investments**

    A.   Life Insurance Investments

    B.   Property and Liability Insurance Investments

VII. **Other Insurance Company Functions**

    A.   Electronic Data Processing

    B.   Accounting

    C.   Legal Function

    D.   Loss Control Services

■ Short Answer Questions

1. What is the role of actuaries? Why is their job more difficult than pricing products in other industries?

2. What is the role of underwriters in the insurance industry?

3. Where do underwriters obtain the information they need to make their decisions?

4. In the context of insurance, what is meant by the term "production"?

5. What are the insurer's basic objectives in settling claims?

6. What are the steps in the claims settlement process?

7. What is reinsurance and why would an insurance company use reinsurance?

8. What is the distinction between facultative reinsurance and treaty reinsurance?

9. Why are investments important to insurance companies?

10. Why does an insurance company need a legal department?

11. If a manufacturing company has its own risk management department, why would this company need loss control services provided by an insurer?

12. HELP WANTED! Fill in the name of the insurance-related position beside the description of the job.

JOB DESCRIPTION	JOB TITLE
Great earnings potential! We give you authority to represent our company and products. You market our insurance coverage. We pay you a commission for each policy you sell.	a.
Immediate Opening! Someone to verify reported losses have occurred and determine the amount of any covered loss. Applicant must possess strong "people skills."	b.
We seek a highly skilled individual to determine rates for life insurance. Must possess a strong math and statistics background. Excellent pay and benefits!	c.
WE'RE VERY SELECTIVE about the risks we insure and the people we hire! We need applicants with strong analytical skills to review applications and to select and classify insureds.	d.
We're seeking an individual with an engineering background to help us service our insureds. The person we hire will perform factory inspections and make safety recommendations to our policyowners.	e.

Multiple Choice Questions

Circle the letter that corresponds to the BEST *answer.*

1. Which statement is true with regard to insurance rate making?
   I. Rates are calculated by people known as adjustors.
   II. An insurer doesn't know when insurance is sold if the premium charged is adequate.
   (a) I only
   (b) II only
   (c) both I and II
   (d) neither I nor II

2. Individuals who have a higher-than-average probability of experiencing a loss often try to pass as average risks in order to obtain insurance at more favorable rates. What functional area at insurance companies attempts to detect such individuals?
   (a) rate making
   (b) claims settlement
   (c) accounting
   (d) underwriting

3. All of the following are reasons for using reinsurance EXCEPT:
   (a) reinsurance increases underwriting capacity.
   (b) reinsurance provides protection against catastrophic loss.
   (c) reinsurance reduces the number of claims.
   (d) reinsurance reduces the unearned premium reserve.

4. Integrity Insurance entered into a reinsurance agreement with Omega Reinsurance. Under terms of the agreement, Omega receives 40 percent of the premiums and is responsible for 40 percent of the losses, regardless of the size of the policy written by Integrity. What type of reinsurance is illustrated in this scenario?
   (a) facultative reinsurance
   (b) surplus-share treaty
   (c) quota-share treaty
   (d) excess-of-loss treaty

5. Which statement is true with regard to insurance company investments?
   I. Investment income helps to reduce the cost of insurance.
   II. Pooled premiums of insurance companies are an important source of funds in the economy.
   (a) I only
   (b) II only
   (c) both I and II
   (d) neither I nor II

6. Insurance companies need a legal department for all of the following reasons EXCEPT:
    (a) to review policy terminology before the coverage is marketed.
    (b) to prepare the insurance company's financial statements.
    (c) to help in the collection of subrogation recoveries.
    (d) to defend liability claims against their policyowners.

7. Kevin's background is market research. He was hired by Alpha Insurance to perform an analysis of consumers in a certain geographic region. His research indicated that although these consumers were fairly affluent, most did not have large amounts of life insurance. Kevin's position at the insurance company would fall under which functional area?
    (a) claims settlement
    (b) production
    (c) underwriting
    (d) rate making

8. All of the following are usual sources of information for an underwriter EXCEPT:
    (a) secretly taped phone conversations.
    (b) the agent's report.
    (c) results of a physical exam.
    (d) an inspection report.

9. Ken lives in a sparsely populated area of western Nebraska. Some insurers that write coverage in this area cannot afford to have a full-time claims adjustor on their payroll. Instead, when a policyowner reports a claim, insurance companies hire Ken to investigate the claim. Ken is a(n):
    (a) independent adjustor.
    (b) agent.
    (c) company adjustor.
    (d) public adjustor.

10. All of the following are important underwriting principles EXCEPT:
    (a) selection of risks that can be written at standard rates.
    (b) selection according to the company's underwriting standards.
    (c) proper balance within each rate classification.
    (d) equity among policyowners.

11. As an alternative to reinsurance, some insurers transfer insurable risk to the capital markets through the creation of a financial instrument, such as a catastrophe bond. Such transfers are called:
    (a) immunization of risk.
    (b) avoidance of risk.
    (c) securitization of risk.
    (d) indexation of risk.

■ True/False

Circle the T if the statement is true, the F if the statement is false. Explain to yourself why a statement is false.

T   F   1. Property and liability insurance company investments tend to be of longer duration than do life insurance company investments.

T   F   2. Underwriters select and classify insurance applicants.

T   F   3. With surplus-share treaty reinsurance, the proportions of premiums and losses shared by the ceding company and the reinsurer depend on the amount of coverage written.

T   F   4. Electronic data processing is not used by insurers.

T   F   5. Reinsurance can be used to provide protection against catastrophic loss.

T   F   6. The individuals who determine the rate to charge for insurance coverage are called "producers."

T   F   7. One goal of underwriters is to prevent adverse selection from occurring.

T   F   8. Company adjustors are independent contractors who insurance companies hire on an as-needed basis.

T   F   9. It is impossible for a property and liability insurance company to grow too fast.

T   F   10. If an insurance company is using facultative reinsurance, it must look for a reinsurer each time the company uses reinsurance.

T   F   11. Insurance companies may limit the amount of coverage they are willing to write on certain exposures.

T   F   12. There are many diverse employment opportunities available in the insurance industry.

T   F   13. Catastrophe bonds are issued by insurance companies to help fund payments for catastrophic losses.

■ Reinsurance Problems

1. Kellwood Insurance entered into a quota share treaty reinsurance arrangement with Jackson Reinsurance. Under the terms of the agreement, Kellwood was responsible for 40 percent of the losses and Jackson was responsible for 60 percent of the losses. Kellwood wrote a $100,000 property insurance policy and the insured suffered a $20,000 loss. How will this claim be settled?

2. Reliable Security Insurance Company entered into a surplus share treaty reinsurance agreement with Ventura Reinsurance. Reliable Security set a retention limit (line) of $150,000; and Ventura agreed to reinsure up to six lines ($900,000). For what portion of the following losses will Reliable Security and Ventura Reinsurance be responsible?

    (a) Reliable Security wrote an $80,000 property insurance policy and a $25,000 loss occurred.

    (b) Reliable Security wrote a $450,000 property policy and a $60,000 loss occurred.

    (c) Reliable Security wrote a $750,000 property insurance policy and a $90,000 loss occurred.

3. Superior Insurance was concerned that the loss experience of their new all-risk coverage would be unfavorable. They entered into an excess-of-loss treaty reinsurance agreement with ACME Reinsurance, setting a retention limit of $2 million in cumulative losses for the policy year.

    (a) If losses for the policy year total $1.4 million, what is the liability of each insurer?

    (b) If losses for the policy year total $3.6 million, what is the liability of each insurer?

■ Case Applications

Case 1

When Betty, an underwriter, returned from lunch one day, she discovered a sign had been placed on her desk. The sign featured the word "SALES" in large black letters, with a red circle drawn around the word and a line drawn through it. Another underwriter told Betty that Alan, an agent, placed the sign on her desk. Why would Alan leave this sign on Betty's desk? Hint—what are the functions of producers and underwriters, and how are producers compensated?

Case 2

Although each of the insurance company operations was discussed separately in this chapter, there is interaction between and among these functional areas. For each of the pairs of functional areas listed below, explain why there might be a need for interaction between the areas.

(a)   rate making and production

(b)   claims and underwriting

■ Solutions to Chapter 6

Short Answer Questions

1. Actuaries are rate makers—they determine the premium to charge for insurance coverage. The pricing of insurance is more difficult than pricing products in other industries. With other products, the cost of goods sold is known in advance. With insurance, the cost is not known until total losses and expenses are known, which may be months or years in the future.

2. Underwriters are charged with selecting and classifying the applicants for insurance. Just because an agent forwards an application to a home office or a regional office does not mean that the coverage will be written. The underwriter may reject the applicant. If the applicant is acceptable, the underwriter must assign the applicant to the appropriate rating category. The classification of acceptable risks is designed to assure equity in the rating classes. Thus riskier applicants must pay more for their coverage than insureds who are less risky.

3. Underwriters obtain information from a variety of sources, including: the application, the agent's report, an inspection report, physical inspection, physical exams and physician's report, and the Medical Information Bureau (MIB).

4. Production refers to the sales and marketing activities of insurers. Agents who sell coverage are known as "producers." In addition to agents who are visible in the field, there is a production department at the insurer's home or regional office.

5. The basic objectives of an insurer in settling claims include: verification that the loss occurred and was covered under the terms of the insurance contract, fair and prompt payment of covered claims, and personal assistance to insureds.

6. Before a claim can be settled, the insured must notify the insurance company (or their agent) that a loss has occurred. Upon notification, the insurance company will investigate the claim. Next, the insured must file proof of loss. Finally, the adjustor must make a decision about whether the claim will be paid and if so, the amount of the settlement.

7. Reinsurance refers to the shifting of part or all of the insurance originally written by one insurer to another insurer. The company originally writing the coverage may wish to transfer part or all of the risk to a reinsurer for a number of reasons: to increase underwriting capacity, to stabilize profits, to reduce the unearned premium reserve, and to provide protection against catastrophic loss.

8. Facultative reinsurance is an optional, case-by-case method of reinsurance. The ceding company has no preestablished relationship with a reinsurer. When reinsurance is needed, the ceding company shops for it. With treaty reinsurance, the ceding company and reinsurer have a preexisting agreement Any coverage written falling within the scope of the agreement is automatically reinsured.

9. In insurance, the phrase "two sides of the ledger" is often heard. This phrase refers to the fact that insurance companies have two major sources of income. First, insurers have the insurance products they market. This portion of the business is called the underwriting side of the ledger. Premium income may or may not be sufficient to pay losses and cover expenses. Second, insurers have an opportunity to make money through investments. As premiums are paid in advance, insurance companies can invest these funds and generate investment income. Investment income helps to hold premiums lower and offset any losses the insurer may sustain on the underwriting side of the ledger.

10. A legal department is needed by private insurers for a number of reasons. As part of the liability coverage provided to the insured, the insurer may agree to provide a legal defense. Lawyers are needed to review policy forms before they are introduced, to review advertising copy, and to provide legal advice regarding taxes, marketing, insurance laws, and investments. In addition, lawyers are needed to help collect subrogation recoveries.

11. Loss control services provided by an insurer may be invaluable to the manufacturing company. Loss control engineers are specialists in their area. While the risk management department may be effective in some loss control activities, the services of loss control specialists can help to further prevent and reduce losses. Using loss control services provided by the insurer also may reduce the cost of insurance coverage.

12. (a) The insurer placing this ad is looking for an AGENT to market coverage. Most agents are compensated through commissions on the coverage sold.

   (b) CLAIMS ADJUSTORS verify that losses have occurred and assist in settling covered claims. "People skills" are needed as adjustors deal with people who have suffered a loss.

   (c) ACTUARIES are highly skilled mathematicians and statisticians who determine insurance rates.

   (d) The very selective people this insurer seeks are called UNDERWRITERS. Underwriters select who will be insured by the company, and classify those who they select by placing them in an underwriting classification based on the level of risk.

   (e) This insurer is looking for someone to join their LOSS CONTROL department. In this case, a loss control engineer is needed to help the insurer service its insureds.

Multiple Choice Questions

1. (b) Insurance rates are calculated by individuals known as actuaries, not adjustors. Insurers are not sure whether rates charged are adequate when coverage is sold. Rate adequacy depends on claims and expenses, and insurers can only estimate these values before selling coverage.

2. (d) Underwriters select and classify insurance applicants. The problem described can lead to adverse selection against the insurer unless the underwriters detect these higher-than-average risk applicants and classify them appropriately.

3. (c) The number of claims is independent of whether the coverage has been reinsured. Reinsurance arrangements determine how liability for claims will be apportioned between the ceding company and the reinsurer.

4. (c) Quota-share reinsurance is illustrated in this scenario. Regardless of the size of the risk written by the ceding company, Omega receives 40 percent of premiums and pays 40 percent of losses. It is not facultative reinsurance because Integrity has a prearranged reinsurance agreement with Omega.

5. (c) Both statements are true. In the absence of income from investments, insurance premiums would have to be higher. Secondly, pooled premiums are an important source of investment funds. Insurance companies invest in government securities, corporate stocks and bonds, mortgage-backed securities, real estate, and other investments.

6. (b) The insurance company legal staff does not prepare the insurer's financial statements. The insurance company's accounting department is charged with that function.

7. (b)   Production covers many facets of marketing, not simply sales. Kevin's market research will help Alpha Insurance target the company's sales efforts.

8. (a)   Obtaining information this way would be expensive and a violation of privacy rights.

9. (a)   Independent adjustors are not employees of an insurance company. They are hired when needed to adjust claims.

10. (a)   Just because the risk cannot be written at standard rates does not mean the risk is uninsurable. Insurers often write coverage on risks that are not standard and charge these insureds higher premiums and/or include coverage restrictions.

11. (c)   The method of risk transfer described is known as securitization of risk.

True/False

1. **F** Property and liability insurance company investments tend to be of shorter duration than life insurance company investments.

2. **T**

3. **T**

4. **F** Given the volume of data that insurers must manage, electronic data processing is essential for insurers.

5. **T**

6. **F** It is actuaries, not producers, who calculate rates. Producers are involved in the marketing activities of the insurer.

7. **T**

8. **F** Company adjustors are employees of insurance companies. Independent adjustors are hired on an as-needed basis.

9. **F** Given that property and liability insurers must incur expenses when coverage is written, but can only realize premiums as earned with the passage of time, it is possible for insurance companies to grow too fast. Reinsurance can be used to reduce the unearned premium reserve and provide surplus relief.

10. **T**

11. **T**

12. **T**

13. **T**

Reinsurance Problems

1. Under this quota-share treaty, Kellwood agreed to pay 40 percent of the losses and Jackson agreed to pay 60 percent of the losses. If a $20,000 loss occurred, Kellwood be responsible for $8,000 (.40 × $20,000) and Jackson would be responsible for $12,000 (.60 × $20,000).

2. (a) Reliable Security would be responsible for the entire loss as the coverage written ($80,000) did not exceed the company's retention limit ($150,000).

   (b) Reliable Security would retain one line, $150,000, and shift two lines ($300,000) to Ventura. Reliable Security is responsible for one-third ($150,000/$450,000) of any loss, and Ventura is responsible for two-thirds ($300,000/$450,000) of any loss. So Reliable Security would be responsible for $20,000 of the loss, and Ventura would be responsible for $40,000 of the loss.

   (c) In the case of a $750,000 property policy, Reliable Security would retain one line ($150,000) and shift four lines ($600,000) to Ventura. Reliable Security is responsible for one-fifth of any loss because Reliable Security is providing one-fifth of the coverage ($150,000/$750,000). Ventura is responsible for four-fifths of any loss as they are providing four-fifths of the coverage ($600,000/$750,000). Reliable Security would pay $18,000 of the loss and Ventura would pay $72,000 of the loss.

3. (a) Superior Insurance would pay all of the losses because total losses did not exceed the company's retention limit.

   (b) If the losses for the policy year were $3.6 million, Superior Insurance would be responsible for losses up to the retention limit of $2 million. Losses in excess of this amount would be the responsibility of ACME. So ACME would pay the remaining $1.6 million of losses.

Case Applications

Case 1

While it is the job of agents to solicit applications for coverage, it is the job of underwriters to determine if the applicants are insurable and, if so, at what rate. Many insurance agents are compensated through commissions, and commissions are only earned when coverage is actually sold. Based on the description provided, it is likely that Alan has submitted a number of applications that Betty either rejected or classified as "riskier than average." Perhaps the "riskier than average" applicants sought insurance coverage with another company. Alan is displeased with Betty's underwriting decisions. He is trying to earn commissions while she is finding deficiencies with the applicants that he brings forward.

Case 2

(a) Rate making may have a direct impact upon production. For example, if the rate makers determine a rate for a product that is not competitive with other insurers, it will be difficult for the company's agents to sell the coverage. Agents may also provide input to help price a risk, especially in commercial insurance.

(b) The claims personnel adjust losses—they see the types of losses that occur and the extent of the damage. An underwriter may have difficulty evaluating an insurance application because he or she may not be aware of the types of losses that could occur or the potential severity of these losses. The underwriter might call upon someone from the claims area to assist in evaluating loss exposures.

Chapter 7
Financial Operations of Insurers

■ Overview

This chapter examines the financial operations of insurance companies. In the first portion of the chapter, two important financial statements, the balance sheet and the income and expense statement, are discussed. Important entries on these financial statements are examined, as well as profitability measures. The remainder of the chapter is devoted to rate making. After a discussion of business and regulatory rate making objectives, rate making methods used in the property and casualty insurance industry are examined. Life insurance rate making is covered in the appendix to Chapter 13.

■ Learning Objectives

After studying this chapter, you should be able to:

● Understand the three major sections of the balance sheet for a property and casualty insurance company: assets, liabilities, and policyholders' surplus.

● Identify the sources of revenue and types of expenses incurred by a property and casualty insurer.

● Explain how profitability is measured in the property and casualty insurance industry.

● Understand the balance sheet and income and expense statement of a life insurance company, and explain how profitability is measured in the life insurance industry.

● Explain the objectives of rate making in the property and casualty insurance industry and discuss the basic rate making methods, including judgment rating, class rating, and merit rating.

● Define the following:

Annual pro rata method	Loss adjustment expenses
Asset valuation reserve	Loss ratio
Balance sheet	Loss ratio method (loss reserves)
Case reserves	Loss ratio method (of rating)
Class rating (manual rating)	Loss reserve
Combined ratio	Merit rating
Earned premiums	Net gain from operations
Expense ratio	Overall operating ratio
Experience rating	Policyholders' surplus
Exposure unit	Pure premium
Gross premium	Pure premium method (of rating)
Gross rate	Rate
Income and expense statement	Reserve for amounts held on deposit
Incurred-but-not-reported loss reserve (INBR)	Retrospective rating
Investment income ratio	Schedule rating
Judgment rating	Unearned premium reserve
Loading	

■ Outline

I.   Property and Casualty Insurers

   A.   Balance Sheet

      1.   Assets

      2.   Liabilities

      3.   Policyholders' Surplus

   B.   Income and Expense Statement

      1.   Revenues

      2.   Expenses

   C.   Measuring Profit or Loss

   D.   Recent Underwriting Results

II.   Life Insurance Companies

   A.   Balance Sheet

      1.   Assets

      2.   Liabilities

      3.   Policyholders' Surplus

   B.   Income and Expense Statement

      1.   Revenues

      2.   Expenses

   C.   Measuring Financial Performance

III.   Ratemaking in Property and Casualty Insurance

   A.   Objectives in Rate Making

      1.   Regulatory Objectives

      2.   Business Objectives

   B.   Basic Rate Making Definitions

   C.   Rate Making Methods

      1.   Judgment Rating

      2.   Class Rating

      3.   Merit Rating

IV.   Rate Making in Life Insurance

■ Short Answer Questions

1.   What are the three major sections of a balance sheet, and what is the balance sheet equation?

2. How do an insurance company's assets differ from the assets of other business firms? What are the two major liabilities of property and casualty insurance companies?

3. What are the two major sources of income for an insurance company?

4. What is the "combined ratio" for a property and casualty insurance company, and what does the combined ratio measure?

5. Two assets commonly listed on a life insurance company's balance sheet are "contract loans" and the "separate account." Explain what these two assets represent.

6. State insurance departments have regulatory objectives with respect to rate making. What are these objectives? What are an insurance company's business objectives in rate making?

7. The gross premium that an insurer charges consists of the pure premium and the loading. Explain each of these components of the gross premium.

8. What are the three basic rating methods used in property and liability insurance?

9. Explain the two methods of determining class rates.

0. What is the difference between experience rating and retrospective rating?

Multiple Choice Questions

Circle the letter that corresponds to the **BEST** *answer.*

1. Under one type of property and liability insurance rate making, exposures with similar characteristics are placed in the same underwriting category, and each is charged the same rate. This type of rating is called:
    (a) class rating.
    (b) judgment rating.
    (c) retrospective rating.
    (d) merit rating.

2. All of the following are assets that you might find on the balance sheet of a property and casualty insurance company EXCEPT:
    (a) corporate bonds.
    (b) common stock.
    (c) policy loans.
    (d) real estate securities.

3. Which statement(s) is(are) true with regard to property and casualty insurance rate making?
    I.   Under the pure premium method, the pure premium is the rate charged insureds.
    II. Judgment rates are determined largely by the underwriter's judgment.
    (a) I only
    (b) II only
    (c) both I and II
    (d) neither I nor II

4. All of the following are methods of estimating the size of the reserve for reported property and liability losses EXCEPT the:
    (a) schedule rating method.
    (b) average value method.
    (c) loss ratio method.
    (d) tabular value method.

5. The gross insurance premium consists of the pure premium plus the:
   (a) net single premium.
   (b) policy reserve.
   (c) loading.
   (d) unearned premium.

6. Under one form of merit rating, the insured's loss experience during the current policy period determines the actual premium for that period. This type of merit rating is called:
   (a) experience rating.
   (b) judgment rating.
   (c) schedule rating.
   (d) retrospective rating.

7. All of the following are rating methods used in property and casualty insurance EXCEPT:
   (a) judgment rating.
   (b) class rating.
   (c) Best's rating.
   (d) merit rating.

8. Which statement(s) is(are) true with regard to property and casualty insurance profitability?
   I.   The combined ratio compares an insurer's losses and expenses to its premiums.
   II. A combined ratio in excess of 1 (or 100 percent) indicates underwriting profitability.
   (a) I only
   (b) II only
   (c) both I and II
   (d) neither I nor II

9. States have rating laws that require insurance rates to meet certain standards. These standards includ all of the following EXCEPT:
   (a) rates should not be unfairly discriminatory.
   (b) rates must provide large profits to insurers.
   (c) rates must be adequate.
   (d) rates must not be excessive.

10. Which statement(s) is(are) true with regard to a life insurance company's balance sheet?
    I.   Assets are equal to liabilities plus policyholders' surplus.
    II. Policy reserves are a major liability of a life insurance company.
    (a) I only
    (b) II only
    (c) both I and II
    (d) neither I nor II

True/False

Circle the T if the statement is true, the F if the statement is false. Explain to yourself why a statement is false.

T F   1. Under experience rating, the insured's prior loss experience determines the actual premium for this period.

T F   2. A property and liability premium can be described as earned as soon as it is paid to the insurance company.

T F   3. The two major sources of revenue for a property and casualty insurance company are premiums and investment income.

T F   4. Under class rating, exposures with similar characteristics are placed in the same underwriting class and each is charged the same rate.

T F   5. The rating system should be independent of loss control efforts.

T F   6. Case reserves are loss reserves established for each individual claim when the claim is reported.

T F   7. Policy reserves are considered an asset of the insurance company.

T F   8. The balance sheet is prepared for a specified period, the income and expense statement is prepared for a specific date.

T F   9. Once insurers calculate rates for a given exposure, the rates are never adjusted.

T F   10. The loss ratio is the ratio of incurred losses plus loss adjustment expenses to earned premiums.

T F   11. Under schedule rating, each exposure is rated individually with a basic rate that is adjusted for desirable and undesirable physical features.

Calculations

1. Secured Property Insurance Company estimates that 250,000 structures they insure will generate incurred property losses and loss adjustment expenses of $50 million during the next year. If Secured Property's expense ratio is 25 percent, what is the gross premium for this property insurance?

2. Jackson Casualty had incurred losses and loss adjustment expenses of $375,000 and earned premiums of $500,000 for one line of coverage last year. The expected loss ratio was 70 percent. According to the loss ratio method, by what percentage must Jackson Casualty increase the premium for this line of coverage?

■ Case Applications

Case 1

Based on the life insurance rate making discussion in this chapter and in the appendix to Chapter 13, Dan, age 32, computed the net level premium for a 10-pay whole life policy purchased by a man age 32. Then he called a number of agents to get price quotes for 10-pay whole life for a 32 year-old man. All of the agents quoted premiums that were higher than those Dan calculated. Dan rechecked his calculations twice and is sure that he did not make any mistakes in his calculations. What is the best explanation for the difference between the net level premiums Dan calculated and the premiums quoted by the agents?

Case 2

Barbara Jorgenson is President of Jorgenson Chemical, a company that manufactures industrial chemicals including highly flammable acids. Her company has outgrown its present facility, and Barbara is considering moving to a larger building. She has found two acceptable buildings. The first is a brick building located in a run-down section of the city. The building was constructed in 1936 and all of the internal fixtures have been removed. The building shares common walls with a vacant building and a warehouse. The second building is located eight miles outside the city limit. It is a free-standing wood frame building constructed two years ago. According to the building code, a sprinkler system was mandatory. What are the positive and negative features of these buildings from a schedule rating perspective?

Solutions to Chapter 7

Short Answer Questions

1. The major sections of a balance sheet are the assets, the liabilities, and owners' equity. Assets are items of value that are owned by the business. Liabilities are obligations (debts) of the business. Owners' equity is the difference between the assets and liabilities of the business. The balance sheet equation is:

$$\text{Assets} = \text{Liabilities} + \text{Owners' Equity}$$

2. The assets of an insurance company are primarily financial assets. The assets for other types of businesses often consist of plant and equipment. Insurance companies use premiums and retained earnings to invest in financial assets. Insurers use these invested assets to generate investment income.

   Property and liability insurers are required to maintain two principal types of reserves: the unearned premium reserve and the loss reserve. The unearned premium reserve is a liability reserve that represents the unearned portion of gross premiums on all outstanding policies at the time of valuation. The fundamental purpose of the unearned premium reserve is to pay for losses that occur during the policy period. The loss reserve is another important liability reserve for property and liability insurers. A loss reserve is the estimated cost of settling claims that have occurred but that have not been paid as of the valuation date.

3. The two major sources of income for an insurance company are premiums paid by policyowners and income generated from investments. Property and casualty insurance companies will sometimes lose money on their underwriting activities, but offset the loss with investment income, and still post a profit for the accounting period.

4. The combined ratio is the sum of two ratios, the expense ratio and the loss ratio. The expense ratio is the ratio of underwriting expenses to premiums written. The expense ratio is often in the 20 to 35 percent range. The loss ratio is the ratio of losses and loss adjustment expenses incurred to premiums earned. The loss ratio is often in the 60 to 75 percent range. If an insurance company's expense ratio was 30 percent and the loss ratio was 72 percent, the combined ratio would be 102 percent. This ratio means that for every dollar of premiums, the insurer paid out a dollar and two cents in expenses and claims. The combined ratio measures the profitability of underwriting activities. A combined ratio less than 1 (or 100 percent) indicates underwriting profitability. A combined ratio greater than 1 (or 100 percent) indicates an underwriting loss.

5. The savings reserve in a cash value life insurance can be borrowed by the policyowner. These loans are similar to an account receivable, as policy loans must be repaid prior to the death of the insured or the loan balance is subtracted from the death benefit payment. Policyowners are required to pay interest on policy loans as life insurers forego the investment income they could have earned by investing the funds the policyowner borrowed.

   Separate account assets are the assets backing interest-sensitive/investment-oriented products marketed by life insurers. State insurance rules restrict the investments backing traditional life insurance products. The separate account is a way of separating the assets backing the products marketed by the life insurer.

6. The regulatory objectives in rate making include: rate adequacy, making sure rates are not excessive, and assuring that rates are not unfairly discriminatory.

   The business objectives of rate making are: simplicity, responsiveness, stability, and encouragement of loss control.

7. The pure premium is the portion of the gross premium that is needed to pay the expected losses and the costs to adjust the losses. The loading is an allowance added to the pure premium to cover other expenses, a profit for the insurer, and a margin for other contingencies (e.g., adverse investment experience, higher than anticipated losses, etc.).

8. The three basic rating methods used in property and liability insurance are judgment rating, class rating, and merit rating. Types of merit rating include schedule rating, experience rating, and retrospective rating.

9. The two methods of determining class rates are the pure premium method and the loss ratio method. The pure premium is determined by dividing the dollar amount of incurred losses and loss-adjustmen expenses by the number of exposure units. The pure premium is divided by one minus the expense ratio to determine the gross rate.

    Under the loss ratio method, the actual loss ratio is compared to the expected loss ratio, and the rate i adjusted accordingly. This method determines the rate adjustment (increase or decrease) necessary.

10. Under an experience rating plan, the class or manual rate is adjusted upward or downward based on past loss experience. Thus the experience from earlier periods is used to determine the current premium. Under a retrospectively rated plan, the insured's loss experience during the current period determines the actual premium paid for the period.

Multiple Choice Questions

1. (a) This type of rating is called class rating. Under class rating, the rate charged reflects the average loss experience of the class as a whole.

2. (c) Some life insurance policies develop a savings reserve (the cash value) that can be borrowed by policyowners. As property and casualty coverages do not develop a savings reserve, there are no such loans in property and casualty insurance. The other choices are typical investments of a property and casualty insurance company.

3. (b) Only the second statement is true. Insurers must add a loading to the pure premium to cover expenses. Judgment rates are determined by the underwriter's judgment.

4. (a) Schedule rating is a form of merit rating, not a method of estimating loss reserves.

5. (c) The gross premium is equal to the pure premium plus a loading. The loading covers expenses, contingencies, and profit.

6. (d) Under retrospective rating, the premium for the current period is determined by the actual experience during the current period.

7. (c) Best's rating is a rating assigned to an insurance company based on the company's financial strength. The A.M. Best Company assigns the rating. The other three choices are property and casualty insurance rating methods.

8. (a) Only the first statement is true. The combined ratio is the sum of the expense ratio, which compares underwriting expenses and premiums written, and the loss ratio, which compares losses and loss adjustment expenses to premiums earned. If the combined ratio is less than one (or 100 percent), the insurer is profitable.

9. (b) Rating standards do not guarantee that insurers will earn large profits.

0. (c) Both statements are true. The first statement restates the balance sheet equation. Policy reserves are a major liability of life insurers. Policy reserves represent an obligation of the insurer to pay future policy benefits.

True/False

1. **T**

2. **F** When the premium is paid to the insurer, it is placed in the unearned premium reserve. With the passage of time, these unearned premiums become earned premiums.

3. **T**

4. **T**

5. **F** The rating system should provide incentives for loss control. Experience rating, for example, bases premiums upon past loss experience. If loss control is effective, loss levels are reduced, which in turn reduces future premiums.

6. **T**

7. **F** Policy reserves are considered a liability because they represent an obligation of the insurer to pay future benefits to policyowners.

8. **F** The balance sheet shows asset and liability values on a specific date. The income and expense statement reflects income and expenses for a specified period, such as a quarter or a year.

9. **F** One business objective of a rating system is that the system should be responsive. There may be a need to adjust rates because of interest rate changes, changes in loss experience, changes in legal interpretations, etc.

0. **T**

1. **T**

Calculations

1. To calculate the gross premium, it is first necessary to calculate the pure premium. The pure premium is equal to the incurred losses and loss-adjustment expenses per exposure unit. The pure premium is:

$$\frac{\$50,000,000}{250,000} = \$200 \text{ per structure}$$

The pure premium is then loaded for expenses, underwriting profit, and other contingencies. The gross premium is:

$$\frac{\text{Pure Premium}}{1 - \text{Expense Ratio}} = \frac{\$200}{1 - .25} = \$266.67$$

2. As the actual loss ratio, .75 ($375,000/$500,000), exceeded the expected loss ratio (.70), a rate increase is needed. Under the loss ratio method, the rate change needed is the percentage by which the actual loss ratio exceeded the expected loss ratio. The indicated rate change is:

$$\frac{\text{Actual Loss Ratio} - \text{Expected Loss Ratio}}{\text{Expected Loss Ratio}} = \frac{.75 - .70}{.70} = 7.14\%$$

Case Applications

Case 1

Dan calculated the net level premium. The insurance agents were quoting the gross premiums charged by their companies. The difference between the net premium and the gross premium is the loading added to the net level premium. Three major types of expenses are reflected in the loading: production, distribution and maintenance expenses. The loading also reflects a margin for contingencies and a contribution to company profits. If Dan were to "load" the premium he calculated, it would be close to the rates the agent quoted.

Case 2

Under schedule rating, each building is rated individually based on a number of factors. The pros and con of each building are discussed below:

- Construction: The older brick structure is more fire resistant than a wood frame structure. A major concern is loss caused by fire. Brick, other masonry, and metal construction are superior to wood frame from a fire-damage rating perspective. The age of the brick structure (constructed in 1936) might also be an issue.

- Occupancy: The occupancy would be the same for either building: chemical (acid) manufacturing. As noted, the occupancy would be less risky from a fire perspective in the brick structure.

- Protection: The brick building in the city has no internal fire safety system. Given when it was constructed, no sprinkler system may be present. On the positive side, however, the building is in an urban area. Given this location, there may be a fire hydrant on the corner and a fire station located clos to the building. The wood frame building has a sprinkler system installed. On the negative side, there i probably no source of water for a fire department to use given the rural location, and fire department response time may be higher.

- Exposure: The brick structure faces additional risk from the adjacent buildings. A fire could start in the warehouse next door and spread to the structure. The vacant building is also a concern. Given that thes structures are in a "run-down" part of the city, vagrants may use the vacant structure. The wood frame building is free-standing, so it faces no risk of fire spreading from an adjacent structure; however it is exposed to the elements on all four sides.

- Maintenance: Neither building is occupied. Underwriters may consider Jorgenson's past safety record when rating the new structure for maintenance.

Chapter 8
Government Regulation of Insurance

Overview

You've probably heard of the Food and Drug Administration (FDA), the Security and Exchange Commission (SEC), and the Environmental Protection Agency (EPA). Federal boards, agencies, and departments are charged with regulating various aspects of commerce in the United States. Which federal regulatory body is charged with regulation of the insurance industry? The answer is . . . NONE! For a number of reasons, states are the primary regulators of insurance, and federal regulation applies only to the extent that state regulation does not apply. In this chapter we examine why insurance is regulated, the history of insurance regulation, the methods of regulating insurers, the areas that are regulated, the objectives of insurance regulation, and some current issues in the regulation of insurance.

Learning Objectives

After studying this chapter, you should be able to:

Explain the major reasons why insurers are regulated.

Identify key legal cases and legislative acts that have had an important impact on insurance regulation.

Identify the major areas that are regulated.

Explain the objectives of rate regulation and the different types of rating laws.

Explain the major arguments for and against state regulation of insurance.

Define the following:

Admitted assets

Alien insurer

Assessment method

Credit-based insurance score

Domestic insurer

File-and-use law

Financial Modernization Act of 1999

Flex-rating law

Foreign insurer

Guaranty funds

McCarran-Ferguson Act

Modified prior approval law

National Association of Insurance
    Commissioners (NAIC)

Open-competition

Paul v. Virginia

Policyowners' surplus

Prior-approval law

Rebating

Reserves

Retaliatory tax laws

Risk-based capital (RBC)

South-Eastern Underwriters
    Association (SEUA) case

Twisting

Use-and-file law

■ Outline

I.   Reasons for Insurance Regulation

   A.   Maintain Insurer Solvency

   B.   Compensate for Inadequate Consumer Knowledge

   C.   Ensure Reasonable Rates

   D.   Make Insurance Available

II.   Historical Development of Insurance Regulation

   A.   Early Regulatory Efforts

   B.   *Paul v. Virginia*

   C.   South-Eastern Underwriters Association Case

   D.   McCarran-Ferguson Act

   E.   Financial Modernization Act of 1999

III. Methods of Regulating Insurers

   A.   Legislation

   B.   Courts

   C.   State Insurance Departments

IV.   What Areas are Regulated?

   A.   Formation and Licensing of Insurers

   B.   Solvency Regulation

   C.   Rate Regulation

   D.   Policy Forms

   E.   Sales Practices and Consumer Protection

   F.   Taxation of Insurers

V.   State Versus Federal Regulation

   A.   Advantages of Federal Regulation

   B.   Advantages of State Regulation

   C.   Shortcomings of State Regulation

   D.   Repeal of the McCarran-Ferguson Act

VI. Current Issues in Insurance Regulation

    A. Bid Rigging by Brokerage Firms

    B. Questionable Accounting Practices

    C. Unauthorized Entities Selling Insurance

    D. Modernizing Insurance Regulation

    E. Insolvency of Insurers

    F. Credit-Based Insurance Score

Short Answer Questions

1. Why is regulation of the insurance industry necessary?

2. What are the three principal methods of regulating insurers?

3. What areas are regulated by insurance regulators?

4. What is meant by the terms: admitted assets, reserves, and policyowners' surplus?

5. How do risk-based capital requirements help to reduce the risk of insurance company insolvencies?

6. What are the various types of rating laws that are used by the states?

7. How are consumers protected through the regulation of insurer sales practices?

8. What are the advantages of state regulation of insurance?

9. What are the arguments in support of federal regulation of insurance?

10. One current insurance regulatory issue is bid rigging by brokerage firms. How were contingent commissions allegedly used to rig insurance coverage bids?

11. What is finite reinsurance? How does finite reinsurance help the company purchasing finite reinsurance?

12. What are the principal methods that can be employed to ensure the solvency of insurance companies

■ Multiple Choice Questions

Circle the letter that corresponds to the BEST *answer.*

1. In a certain state, all insurance rates must be approved by the state insurance department before the rates can be used. This type of rating law is called:
    (a) file-and-use.
    (b) open-competition.
    (c) flex-rating.
    (d) prior-approval.

2. Which statement is true with regard to insurance regulation?
    I. The federal government plays absolutely no role in regulating insurance.
    II. Insurance is regulated primarily by the states.

    (a) I only
    (b) II only
    (c) both I and II
    (d) neither I nor II

3. Regulators are concerned with a number of financial characteristics of insurers. One measure is the difference between an insurer's assets and its liabilities. This measure is known as an insurer's:

   (a) policyowners' surplus.
   (b) reserves.
   (c) risk-based capital.
   (d) admitted assets.

4. Assume that the premium tax rate is 2.5 percent in Florida and 3.0 percent in Georgia. If insurers domiciled in Florida are required to pay a 3.0 percent tax on premiums written in Georgia, Florida requires insurers domiciled in Georgia to pay a 3.0 percent premium tax on business written in Florida even though the premium tax rate in Florida is 2.5 percent. This scenario illustrates a(n):

   (a) retaliatory tax law.
   (b) prior-approval law.
   (c) insurance guaranty fund.
   (d) open-competition law.

5. The amount of new business an insurer can write is limited by the insurer's:

   (a) nonadmitted assets.
   (b) policyowners' surplus.
   (c) common stock investments.
   (d) premium tax rate.

6. Why are insurance companies regulated?

   I. To ensure reasonable rates.
   II. To make insurance available.

   (a) I only
   (b) II only
   (c) both I and II
   (d) neither I nor II

7. Insurance companies are subject to many laws and regulations. The principal areas regulated include all the following EXCEPT:

   (a) sales practices and consumer protection.
   (b) rate regulation.
   (c) the number of policies sold.
   (d) formation and licensing of insurers.

8. Cathy is a life insurance agent. She was trying to sell a policy to Frank. In an effort to "close the deal," Cathy offered to give Frank a share of her commission if he purchased the policy. This practice, which is illegal in almost all states, is called:

   (a) rebating.
   (b) collateral estoppel.
   (c) twisting.
   (d) churning.

9. All of the following are advantages of state regulation of insurance EXCEPT:
    (a) greater opportunity for innovation.
    (b) uniformity of laws.
    (c) greater responsiveness to local needs.
    (d) decentralization of political power.

10. Mutual of Omaha is domiciled in Nebraska and has been admitted to write coverage in Tennessee. I Tennessee, Mutual of Omaha is considered a(n):
    (a) domestic insurer.
    (b) foreign insurer.
    (c) captive insurer.
    (d) alien insurer.

11. The landmark court decision that established the right of states to regulate insurance was:
    (a) the South-Eastern Underwriters Association case.
    (b) the McCarran-Ferguson Act.
    (c) *Metropolitan Life Insurance Company v. The Commissioner.*
    (d) *Paul v. Virginia.*

12. The Financial Modernization Act of 1999 (Gramm-Leach-Bliley, Act):
    (a) made it clear that states were to be the primary regulators of insurance.
    (b) deregulated commercial insurance lines.
    (c) removed barriers separating financial services fields.
    (d) repealed the McCarran-Ferguson Act and shifted insurance regulation to the federal government

■ True/False

Circle the T if the statement is true, the F if the statement is false. Explain to yourself why a statement is false.

T F   1. Insurance is regulated primarily at the state level.

T F   2. The primary purpose of the premium tax is to raise revenues for the state, not to provide fund for insurance regulation.

T F   3. If the National Association of Insurance Commissioners (NAIC) drafts a model law, all state must adopt the law.

T F   4. Insurance guaranty funds provide for the payment of unpaid claims of insolvent insurers.

T F   5. If a state is using a file-and-use rating law, state regulatory officials must approve the rates before an insurer can use them.

T F   6. Just as auto makers often offer rebates to car purchasers, rebating in insurance is a widesprea sales practice in all states.

T F   7. Federal regulation of insurance would provide greater uniformity of laws from state to state.

T   F   8.   Life insurance rates are not directly regulated by the states.

T   F   9.   The decision in the South-Eastern Underwriters Association Case affirmed the right of states to regulate insurance.

T   F   10.   While insurers are exempt from income taxes, they are required to pay a tax on premiums written that averages about 10 percent.

T   F   11.   Some automobile and homeowners insurers are using an applicant's credit record for the purposes of underwriting and rating.

T   F   12.   Requiring insurers to satisfy risk-based capital requirement helps to reduce the risk of insurer insolvencies.

■ Case Applications

Case 1

Tom is a life insurance agent with E-Z Pay Life Insurance Company. He met with Jenny who purchased a life insurance policy from another company six years earlier. Tom compared the competitor's policy with a comparable E-Z Pay Life policy. The E-Z Pay policy requires a significantly lower premium and offers a higher rate of return. Tom was honest and forthright about the policy comparison, and Jenny surrendered her old policy and purchased a new policy through Tom. Has Tom done anything wrong? Explain your answer.

Case 2

Although domiciled in South Carolina, Palmetto Casualty Company is licensed to sell insurance in twelve states. In eight states, prior-approval of rates is required. Two states use a file-and-use rating law, one state uses open-competition, and the remaining state has adopted a flex-rating law. Explain what is required of Palmetto Casualty Company under each of these rating laws.

■ Solutions to Chapter 8

Short Answer Questions

1. Regulation of the insurance industry is necessary to maintain insurer solvency, to protect consumers who have inadequate knowledge of insurers and insurer practices, to ensure reasonable rates, and to make insurance available.

2. Insurers are primarily regulated through legislation, court decisions, and through state insurance departments.

3. The principal areas regulated include: formation and licensing of insurers, solvency regulation, rate regulation, policy forms, and sales practices and consumer protection.

4. Admitted assets are those assets that state law allows an insurer to list on its statutory balance sheet in determining the insurer's financial condition. Reserves are liabilities that reflect obligations that the insurer must satisfy in the future, such as payments for future losses. Policyowners' surplus is the difference between an insurer's assets and its liabilities.

5. Risk-based capital requirements mean that insurers must have a certain amount of capital depending on the riskiness of their investments and insurance operations. The risk-based capital standards give regulators an early warning with respect to insurer financial problems. The standards also discourage insurers from investing too heavily in risky investments.

6. The various types of rating laws include: prior-approval laws, modified prior approval laws, file-and-use laws, use-and-file laws, flex-rating laws, state-made rates, and open competition.

7. Consumers are protected in a number of ways. In order to represent an insurer or the insured, agents and brokers must be licensed by the state. Licensing usually requires that the agent or broker pass a written examination. To assure agents and brokers remain "current" in their field, states have enacted continuing education requirements. In addition, states have promulgated laws to protect consumers against twisting, rebating, and other unfair trade practices. Policy forms used by insurers must be readable. State insurance departments have a complaint division, and some states provide a variety of publications and brochures for consumers.

8. The major advantages of state regulation include: greater responsiveness to local needs, uniformity of laws promoted by the National Association of Insurance Commissioners (NAIC), greater opportunity for innovation, unknown consequences of federal regulation, and decentralization of political power.

9. Proponents of federal regulation of insurance assert that federal regulation will lead to uniformity of insurance laws, greater efficiency, and more competent regulators.

10. Insurance brokers receive commissions from insurers for the business placed with the insurers. Some agents and brokers also receive contingent commissions based on premium volume, loss ratios, and other factors. Contingent commissions provide an incentive to place business with specific insurers. However, the insurer offering the contingent commission may not be offering the best coverage for the client of the broker. It is alleged that some brokers placed business with specific insurers to earn contingent commissions to the detriment of their clients. The net effect is that insurance purchasers paid more for their insurance coverage than they should have paid. Some brokers were charged with rigged bids, false bids, price fixing, and pressure tactics.

11. Finite reinsurance is a complex reinsurance arrangement through which a limited amount of reinsurance is transferred to a reinsurer. The total premiums paid are close to the total maximum coverage provided. In many cases, the loss reinsured has already occurred. As the loss is spread over several years, the net effect of finite insurance is smoothing loss payments over time, rather than taking a large financial hit immediately.

12. Several methods of ensuring the solvency of insurers are employed. The methods include: financial requirements relating to capital and surplus and other variables, risk-based capital standards, submission and analysis of annual financial statements, field examinations of insurers, the NAIC's "early warning system" using the IRIS ratios, and the NAIC's FAST (Financial Analysis Solvency Tracking) solvency screening system.

Multiple Choice Questions

1. (d) The rating law described is a prior-approval law. Under prior-approval, state regulators must approve the rates before they can be used.

2. (b) While insurers are primarily regulated at the state level, federal law applies to the extent that state law does not apply.

3. (a) The difference between an insurer's assets and liabilities is known as the policyowners' surplus.

4. (a) A retaliatory tax law is illustrated in this scenario. Florida is "retaliating" against Georgia's treatment of Florida insurers doing business in Georgia by charging the higher tax rate.

5. (b) The amount of new business an insurer can write is limited by the amount of policyowners' surplus. A conservative rule of thumb specifies that a property and liability insurer can safely write $2 in new net premiums for each $1 of policyowners' surplus.

6. (c) Insurance companies are regulated to make insurance available, to make sure insurance is affordable, and for a number of other reasons.

7. (c) The number of policies sold is not regulated. State regulators will, however, consider the ability of the insurer to discharge any liabilities that may arise from the policies sold.

8. (a) Cathy is offering a rebate as a financial inducement to purchase the coverage. Rebating is an illegal sales practice in almost every state.

9. (b) State regulation of insurance does not promote uniformity of laws. Indeed, what may be legal in one state may be illegal in a neighboring state.

10. (b) Mutual of Omaha would be considered a foreign insurer in Tennessee. In Nebraska, Mutual of Omaha is considered a domestic company. A foreign insurer is an insurer domiciled in another state that has been licensed to do business in your state.

11. (d) The landmark court decision that established the right of states to regulate insurance was *Paul v. Virginia*.

12. (c) The Financial Modernization Act of 1999 repealed rules that prevented banks, insurers, and investment firms from making full entry into each other's markets.

True/False

1. **T**

2. **T**

3. **F** The NAIC can only recommend adoption of a model law. Although the NAIC has no legal authority to force states to adopt their recommendations, many model laws drafted by the NAIC have been adopted by states or adopted in a modified form.

4. **T**

5. **F** Under a file-and-use rating law, insurers are required only to file their rates with state regulators. Once filed, the rates can be used immediately; however, insurance regulators may later not approve the rates.

6. **F** Rebating in insurance is an illegal sales practice in almost all states.

7. **T**

8. **T**

9. **F** The decision in the South-Eastern Underwriters Association case said that insurance was interstate commerce when conducted across state lines, therefore was subject to federal anti-trust laws.

10. **F** Insurers are not exempt from state and federal income taxes. In addition, insurers are taxed on the premiums they write. Premium tax rates are usually between 2 and 3 percent.

11. **T**

12. **T**

Case Applications

Case 1

Tom has done nothing wrong. If he had used incomplete or inaccurate information when comparing the policies, he would have been guilty of an illegal sales practice known as twisting. Based on the description provided, the replacement of Jenny's old policy with an E-Z Pay Life policy appears to be justified.

Case 2

In the eight states that have prior-approval laws, the rates must be filed with state regulators and approved before the rates can be used. Under a file-and-use law, the insurer is required to file rates with the state insurance department, however the rates can be used immediately. The regulators have the right to disapprove the rates later. Open competition is the most liberal form of rating law. Under open competition, insurers are not required to file their rates with state regulators. Under this type of rating law, it is assumed that market forces will determine the appropriate price and availability of insurance coverage. Finally, under flex-rating, prior approval is only required if the rate increase or decrease exceeds a specific, predetermined, range.

Chapter 9
Fundamental Legal Principles

■ Overview

Insurance contracts are complex documents embodying years of industry tradition, case law, and general practices. This chapter examines the legal environment of insurance contracts, including: fundamental legal principles, requirements to form an insurance contract, legal characteristics of insurance contracts, and insurance law as it applies to agency. Although you may have been introduced to some of these concepts in a Business Law course, there are unique aspects of insurance contracts that you should know.

■ Learning Objectives

After studying this chapter, you should be able to:

- Explain the fundamental legal principles reflected in insurance contracts, including: principle of indemnity, principle of insurable interest, principle of subrogation, and principle of utmost good faith.
- Explain how the legal concepts of representations, concealment, and warranty support the principle of utmost good faith.
- Describe the basic requirements for the formation of a valid insurance contract.
- Show how the nature of insurance contracts differs from that of other contracts.
- Explain the law of agency and how it affects the actions and duties of insurance agents.
- Define the following:

Actual cash value	Legal purpose
Agency agreement	Legally competent parties
Aleatory contract	Material fact
Apparent authority	Offer and acceptance
Binder	Pecuniary (financial) interest
Broad evidence rule	Personal contract
Commutative contract	Principle of indemnity
Concealment	Principle of insurable interest
Conditional contract	Principle of reasonable expectations
Conditional premium receipt	Principle of utmost good faith
Conditions	Replacement cost insurance
Consideration	Representations
Contract of adhesion	Subrogation
Estoppel	Unilateral contract
Express authority	Valued policy
Fair market value	Valued policy law
Implied authority	Waiver
Innocent misrepresentation	Warranty

■ Outline

I.   Fundamental Legal Principles

   A.   Principle of Indemnity

   B.   Principle of Insurable Interest

   C.   Principle of Subrogation

   D.   Principle of Utmost Good Faith

II.   Requirements of an Insurance Contract

   A.   Offer and Acceptance

   B.   Consideration

   C.   Competent Parties

   D.   Legal Purpose

III.   Distinct Legal Characteristics of Insurance Contracts

   A.   Aleatory Contract

   B.   Unilateral Contract

   C.   Conditional Contract

   D.   Personal Contract

   E.   Contract of Adhesion

IV.   Law and the Insurance Agent

   A.   General Rules of Agency

   B.   Waiver and Estoppel

■ Short Answer Questions

1.   How do actual cash value settlements support the principle of indemnity? What are the exceptions to the principle of indemnity?

2. How does the principle of insurable interest help to reduce moral hazard?

3. How does the principle of subrogation support the principle of indemnity?

4. Distinguish between concealment and misrepresentation.

5. What four elements must be present to form a binding insurance contract?

6. For each pair of terms, circle the characteristic that applies to insurance contracts.

Bilateral	or	Unilateral
Aleatory	or	Commutative
Conditional	or	Unconditional
Personal	or	Impersonal

7. Differentiate between waiver and warranty.

8. What are the three sources of an agent's authority to bind the principal?

9. What are the three general rules of agency that govern the actions of agents and their relationships with insureds?

10. What elements are necessary to invoke the doctrine of estoppel?

■ Multiple Choice Questions

Circle the letter that corresponds to the BEST *answer.*

1. If there is ambiguity in an insurance contract, it is construed in favor of the insured because of which legal characteristics of insurance contracts?
    (a) principle of indemnity
    (b) contract of adhesion
    (c) aleatory contracts
    (d) doctrine of concealment

2. To collect for a covered loss under a property insurance contract, when must an insurable interest exist?
    I.   At the inception of the contract
    II. At the time of the loss

    (a) I only
    (b) II only
    (c) both I and II
    (d) neither I nor II

3. Sandy purchased renter's insurance that covered personal property on an actual cash value basis. She paid $2,000 for a living room set 3 years ago. When the living room set was destroyed by fire, it was 20 percent depreciated. A comparable new living room set will cost $2,400. How much will Sandy collect from her insurer?
    (a) $2,000
    (b) $2,400
    (c) $1,600
    (d) $1,920

4. Brad's homeowners insurance excludes losses if there is a "material increase in hazard." After buying the policy, Brad started to make fireworks in the basement. A spark from a wood stove ignited some gunpowder, and the home burned to the ground. Which legal characteristic of insurance contracts may prevent Brad from collecting under his policy?
    (a) conditional contracts
    (b) personal contracts
    (c) contracts of adhesion
    (d) aleatory contracts

5. Insurable interest is required for all of the following reasons EXCEPT:
    (a) to prevent gambling.
    (b) to measure the extent of loss.
    (c) to reduce premiums.
    (d) to reduce moral hazard.

6. Which statement(s) is/are true about subrogation?
   I. Subrogation supports the principle of indemnity.
   II. Subrogation helps to keep insurance premiums lower.
   (a) I only
   (b) II only
   (c) both I and II
   (d) neither I nor II

7. When Ellen completed her life insurance application, she answered "No" to the question, "Have you ever had hepatitis?" She had hepatitis two years ago. If Ellen dies shortly after the policy is issued, the insurer may be able to deny the claim because of the doctrine of:
   (a) concealment.
   (b) insurable interest.
   (c) warranty.
   (d) misrepresentation.

8. All of the following are exceptions to the principle of indemnity EXCEPT:
   (a) actual cash value insurance.
   (b) replacement cost insurance.
   (c) life insurance.
   (d) valued policies.

9. All of the following conditions must be met to form a binding property insurance contract EXCEPT:
   (a) contract must be in writing.
   (b) exchange of consideration.
   (c) competent parties.
   (d) offer and acceptance.

10. Insurance contracts have which of the following legal characteristics?
    I. They are bilateral contracts.
    II. They are aleatory contracts.
    (a) I only
    (b) II only
    (c) both I and II
    (d) neither I nor II

11. Kate completed a life insurance application. Her agent forwarded the application to the insurer. The insurer issued the policy. The agent delivered the policy to Kate. When Kate received the policy, she paid the premium. When was the offer accepted in this case?
    (a) when Kate completed the application
    (b) when the agent forwarded the application to the insurer
    (c) when the insurer issued the policy
    (d) when Kate received the policy and paid the first premium

12. Which statement about the principle of indemnity is correct?

    I.   The principle of indemnity reduces moral hazard.

    II. Replacement cost insurance supports the principle of indemnity.

    (a) I only

    (b) II only

    (c) both I and II

    (d) neither I nor II

13. Bill called his insurance agent to check whether his auto insurance would apply to a rental car. The agent said, "No sweat, you're covered." Bill was involved in an accident while driving the rental car. The claim submitted to his insurer was denied. Bill may be able to collect because of the doctrine of:

    (a) reasonable expectations.

    (b) estoppel.

    (c) waiver.

    (d) conditional contracts.

14. Ted owns an auto parts store. In exchange for a premium discount from his insurer, he promised that no cash would be kept on the premises overnight and that two guard dogs would patrol the grounds at night. Ted's promises were incorporated into the insurance contract. His promises are:

    (a) representations.

    (b) warranties.

    (c) waivers.

    (d) expressed powers.

■ True/False

Circle the T if the statement is true, the F if the statement is false. Explain to yourself why a statement is false.

T   F   1. Actual cash value coverage on your personal property will cost more than replacement cost coverage.

T   F   2. If you knowingly withhold information that will affect the underwriting decision, you have committed misrepresentation.

T   F   3. In property insurance, you can purchase insurance coverage based on the expectation of an insurable interest.

T   F   4. A principal is responsible for the acts of an agent when the agent is acting within the scope of his or her authority.

T   F   5. It's better for insurance applicants to have their statements construed as warranties rather than as representations.

T   F   6. In general, property insurance agents have greater authority to bind the companies they represent than do life insurance agents.

T   F   7. While the applicant for insurance coverage gives consideration in the form of the premium, the insurance company does not give any consideration.

T   F   8. If an insurer voluntarily waives a legal right under the contract, it cannot later deny payment of a claim on the grounds that the legal right was violated.

T   F   9. If you interfere with your insurer's subrogation rights against a third party, you jeopardize your right to collect from your insurer.

T   F   10. Insurance contracts are characterized by an equal exchange of value by the parties to the contract.

T   F   11. If an individual claims to represent an insurer but gives no proof of an agency relationship, you should not presume the individual is an agent for the insurer.

T   F   12. The cover page of an insurance contract is called a binder.

■ Case Applications

Case 1

Kate was trying to sell her home. In listing the many positive features of the home, Kate said, " . . . and I just paid for my homeowners insurance for another year. If you buy the house, I'll throw in free homeowners insurance for a year!" What do you think of Kate's offer?

Case 2

An employee considered terminating employment. When he asked his employer about health insurance coverage if he quit his job, he was told that his group health insurance plan (which included major medical insurance) could be converted to identical individual coverage. The coverage would also apply to his wife and children. The employee converted the coverage and quit his job. Shortly thereafter, his wife gave birth to a child who was born with a serious medical condition. When the former employee sought reimbursement of the child's medical expenses, he learned that the conversion policy did not include major medical insurance. He brought suit against the former employer. Will his suit be successful?

■ Solutions to Chapter 9

Short Answer Questions

1. An actual cash value settlement supports the principle of indemnity because through such a settlement, an insured is restored to the pre-loss positions. If a partially depreciated asset is destroyed, the depreciated value of a replacement asset is paid, rather than the full value of a replacement asset.

   There are four exceptions to the principle of indemnity: life insurance, replacement cost coverage, valued policies, and valued policy laws.

2. In the absence of insurable interest, there would be a severe moral hazard problem. Individuals could purchase life insurance on strangers or property insurance on property they did not own. Then they would have an incentive to bring about a loss in order to collect the insurance settlement. The insurable interest requirement prevents such losses.

3. Subrogation supports the principle of indemnity because through subrogation, an insured collects only once for a loss covered by insurance. When an insurer pays its insured, the insured surrenders his or her right of action against the negligent third party to the insurer. Thus the insured collects from the insurer only, not from the insurer and the third party.

4. Misrepresentation occurs when an applicant for insurance lies about something. If the lie involves something material, it is grounds for the insurer to void the contract. Concealment is silence when there is an obligation to disclose information. If the information that is not disclosed is material, it is grounds for the insurer to void the policy.

5. To form a binding insurance contract, there must be a valid offer and acceptance, the contract must be for a legal purpose, the parties to the contract must be competent, and there must be an exchange of consideration between the parties to the contract.

6. Insurance contracts have the following characteristics: they are unilateral, aleatory, conditional, and personal.

7. In the context of insurance contracts, waiver refers to the voluntary relinquishment of a legal right. Warranty refers to a promise made by an insured that must be satisfied for an insurer to be held liable under the contract.

8. The three sources of authority are express authority, implied authority, and apparent authority.

9. There is no presumption of an agency relationship. An agent must have authority to bind the principal. A principal is responsible for the acts of an agent when the agent is acting within the scope of his or her authority.

10. For estoppel to be invoked, three conditions are necessary. First, there must be a representation of fact. Second, this representation of fact must be reasonably relied upon by another party. Finally, harm would occur to the party who relied upon the representation if the representation was retracted, therefore the person who made the representation cannot take it back.

ultiple Choice Questions

1. (b) Insurance contracts are contracts of adhesion. While the contract must be accepted in its entirety, ambiguity in the contract is construed in favor of the insured.

2. (b) Property contracts can be purchased based on an expectation of insurable interest. It is only necessary to demonstrate insurable interest when the loss occurs in order to collect under the policy.

3. (d) As the coverage is written on an actual cash value (ACV) basis, the insurer will make an adjustment to take depreciation into consideration. ACV is replacement cost less depreciation:

$$ACV = \$2,400 - (\$2,400 \times .20)$$
$$ACV = \$1,920$$

4. (a) In an insurance contract, the insurer makes a conditional promise to indemnify. Here the conditions were not satisfied as Brad significantly increased the chance of loss.

5. (c) Insurable interest helps to prevent gambling, assists in determining extent of the loss, and helps to reduce moral hazard. Insurable interest does not reduce premiums.

6. (c) Subrogation supports the principle of indemnity because the insured is only permitted to collect once for the loss. When the insurer pays the insured, the insured surrenders his or her right to proceed against a negligent third party. As insurers are able to recoup part or all of the loss settlements paid to their policyowners, subrogation helps reduce premiums.

7. (d) Ellen's lie about hepatitis is a material misrepresentation. If Ellen dies during the first or second year that the life insurance contract is in force, her insurer may be able to deny the claim because of the material misrepresentation.

8. (a) Actual cash value insurance supports the principle of indemnity by restoring the insured to his or her pre-loss position. The other choices are all exceptions to the principle of indemnity.

9. (a) It is not necessary for a property insurance contract to be in writing. As property agents have greater authority, it is not uncommon for coverage to be bound over the phone. The other element of valid insurance contracts missing from the list is the legal purpose requirement.

10. (b) Insurance contracts are unilateral, not bilateral. Only the insurer makes a legally enforceable promise. They are aleatory as the values exchanged by the parties to the contract are unequal due to chance.

11. (d) As Kate did not pay the premium when her application was submitted, the offer was made by the insurer when the contract was issued. Kate accepted this offer by paying the first premium and accepting delivery of the policy.

12. (a) The principle of indemnity reduces moral hazard as it prevents you from collecting more than the actual amount of the loss. Replacement cost insurance violates this principle, as you are "better off" after the settlement because no allowance for depreciation is made.

13. (b) The doctrine of estoppel may be invoked in this case. There was a representation of fact made by the agent. Bill reasonably relied upon the representation. Harm would clearly result if the agent were allowed to retract the statement, so the agent may not be permitted to do so.

14. (b) Ted's promises are warranties. He is promising that certain conditions must be met (no cash on the premises overnight and guard dogs on site) before the insurer will be liable for losses.

True/False

1. **F** As actual cash value coverage allows the insurer to reduce the loss settlement because of depreciation, it costs less than replacement cost coverage.

2. **F** Failure to divulge material information is concealment, not misrepresentation.

3. **T**

4. **T**

5. **F** Under common law, materiality is not considered with regard to warranty. If a statement is false, regardless of whether the fact is material, it can be used to defeat a claim against the insurer. Misrepresentation considers whether the fact was material.

6. **T**

7. **F** The insurer's consideration is in the form of a conditional promise. Should a loss occur, the insurer will provide indemnity if the conditions stated in the policy are satisfied.

8. **T**

9. **T**

10. **F** There is an unequal exchange of values because chance is involved. Because of this characteristic, insurance contracts are described as aleatory.

11. **T**

12. **F** A binder is temporary evidence of insurance until a formal insurance contract can be drafted.

Case Applications

Case 1

Although Kate's offer sounds generous, insurance contracts are personal in nature. An insurance company will want to consider the insurability of the new homeowner. While underwriters consider the property that will be covered, they also consider the character of the property owner. The purchaser, for example, may have several arson convictions or may be close to declaring bankruptcy. The purchaser of Kate's home should secure his or her own homeowners insurance.

Case 2

The suit filed by the former employee will be successful because of the doctrine of estoppel. The employer made a statement of fact. The employee reasonably relied upon this representation of fact. Clearly harm would result if the employer were allowed to retract the representation after it had been reasonably relied upon by the former employee.

Chapter 10
Analysis of Insurance Contracts

■ Overview

In this chapter we turn our attention to insurance contracts. Even though many insurance contracts are offered, there are certain elements that are common to all insurance contracts. This chapter examines the basic parts of an insurance contract, endorsements and riders, deductibles, coinsurance, and loss settlement when more than one insurance policy covers the loss. The material presented in this chapter will be of great assistance to you as you begin to examine individual insurance contracts. In addition to the "usual" exercises, a problem set and a review of coinsurance are provided.

Learning Objectives

After studying this chapter, you should be able to:

Identify the basic parts of any insurance contract.

Explain the meaning of an "insured" in an insurance contract.

Describe the common types of deductibles that appear in insurance contracts, including straight deductibles and calendar-year deductibles.

Explain how coinsurance works in a property insurance contract.

Show how coinsurance works in a health insurance contract.

Explain how losses are paid when more than one insurance contract covers the same loss.

Define the following:

Aggregate deductible	Exclusions
"All-risks" policy	Insuring agreement
Calendar-year deductible	Large-loss principle
Coinsurance clause	Named insured
Conditions	Named-perils policy
Contribution by equal shares	Open-perils policy
Coordination-of-benefits provision	Other-insurance provisions
Corridor deductible	Percentage participation clause (coinsurance)
Declarations	Primary and excess insurance
Deductible	Pro rata liability
Elimination (waiting) period	Special coverage policy
Endorsements and riders	Straight deductible
Equity in rating	

■ Outline

I. **Basic Parts of an Insurance Contract**

    A. Declarations

    B. Definitions

    C. Insuring Agreement

    D. Exclusions

    E. Conditions

    F. Miscellaneous Provisions

II. **Definition of the "Insured"**

III. **Endorsements and Riders**

IV. **Deductibles**

    A. Purposes of Deductibles

    B. Deductibles in Property Insurance

    C. Deductibles in Health Insurance

V. **Coinsurance**

    A. Nature and Purpose of Coinsurance

    B. Coinsurance Problems

VI. **Coinsurance in Health Insurance**

VII. **Other-Insurance Provisions**

    A. Pro Rata Liability

    B. Contribution by Equal Shares

    C. Primary and Excess Insurance

■ Coinsurance Revisited

Most property losses are not total losses. Effective risk management helps to prevent losses from occurring and reduces the severity of losses that occur. For example, a fire may start in a storage building, but the heat or smoke may trigger a sprinkler system. The sprinkler system may extinguish the fire before it has a chance to spread. Given that most losses are partial losses, there is a disincentive to insure for full value. Not insuring for full value creates a problem in determining loss settlements, as can be shown through the following example:

Assume there are three identical buildings, each valued at $1 million. Building A is insured for $500,000; Building B is insured for $800,000; and Building C is insured for $1 million. Also assume that a total loss occurs. The insurer's liability, respectively, is $500,000, $800,000, and $1 million.

How will partial losses be handled, however? Assume, instead, that a $200,000 loss occurs. Obviously each of the buildings is insured for more than $200,000. Even though two of the buildings are only partially insured, the owners will expect to be fully indemnified because the loss was less than the amount of coverage carried. However, it clearly would be inequitable to provide full indemnification to all of the property owners as each purchased a different amount of insurance. How can partial losses be settled equitably when less than full insurance coverage is carried?

One solution is coinsurance. Coinsurance requires the property owner to purchase insurance equal to a specified percentage of value if the insured wants to collect in full for a partial loss. If less than the prescribed amount of coverage is carried, the insured must bear a portion of the loss. The coinsurance formula is:

$$\frac{\text{Amount of Insurance Carried}}{\text{Amount of Insurance Required}} \times \text{Loss} = \text{Loss Payment}$$

Suppose in our previous example that the property insurance policy included an 80% coinsurance requirement. Thus to be fully reimbursed for any partial loss, $800,000 in insurance coverage (80% × $1 million) must be purchased. The owner of Building A insured for $500,000. If a $200,000 loss occurred, the owner would receive:

$$\frac{\$500,000}{\$800,000} \times \$200,000 = \$125,000$$

Because the building was not insured for 80% of its value, the additional portion of the loss must be absorbed by the owner.

If the building were insured for $800,000; the fraction in the formula is ($800,000/$800,000) which equals one. Thus the entire $200,000 loss would be covered by the insurer. Note, however, that the maximum liability of the insurer is $800,000.

The building owner who insured for $1 million would collect the full value of any partial loss and $1 million if a complete loss occurred.

Short Answer Questions

1. List and explain the six parts of an insurance contract.

2. What is the difference between an insuring agreement that provides named-perils coverage and an insuring agreement that provides all-risk (open-perils) coverage?

3. Why are exclusions used in insurance contracts?

4. Why do insurers include definitions of terms in the insurance contract?

5. Why are endorsements and riders used in insurance contracts?

6. Why is coinsurance used in property insurance and what is the coinsurance formula?

7. Why are deductibles used in insurance?

8. Why are "other insurance" provisions necessary in insurance contracts?

9. In what ways can the "insured" be defined in an insurance contract?

10. What types of information would be included in the miscellaneous provisions of an insurance contract?

■ Multiple Choice Questions

Circle the answer that corresponds to the BEST answer.

1. The part of an insurance contract that can be written on a named-perils or all-risk basis is the:
    (a) insuring agreement.
    (b) conditions.
    (c) exclusions.
    (d) declarations.

2. A written provision that adds to, deletes from, or in some other way alters an insurance contract is called a(n):
    (a) deductible.
    (b) endorsement or rider.
    (c) binder.
    (d) coinsurance provision.

3. Carson Company purchased a commercial property insurance policy. Under one provision of the policy, Carson would pay all covered losses until the sum paid reached $50,000; then the insurer would cover all future losses. This provision is a(n):
    (a) corridor deductible.
    (b) percentage participation clause.
    (c) coinsurance clause.
    (d) aggregate deductible.

4. Which statement is true about the conditions section of an insurance policy?
    I. It contains a description of the property or life that is insured.
    II. It explains what types of perils, losses, and property are not covered under the contract.
    (a) I only
    (b) II only
    (c) both I and II
    (d) neither I nor II

5. Tom was disabled and unable to work. Before he was able to collect under his disability income insurance policy, he was required to serve a two-week period during which no benefits were paid. This two-week period is called a:
    (a) franchise deductible.
    (b) waiting period.
    (c) corridor deductible.
    (d) percentage participation clause.

6. Bert purchased fire insurance on his dwelling. Shortly thereafter, he began to manufacture fireworks in the basement, near the furnace. When a fire severely damaged his home, the insurer denied liability because the policy stated, "we will not be liable for any losses directly attributable to a material increase in hazard." This clause is an example of a(n):
    (a) condition.
    (b) declaration.
    (c) definition.
    (d) insuring agreement.

7. Which statement is true with regard to deductibles?
    I. Property insurance premiums are unrelated to deductibles.
    II. Deductibles help to eliminate small claims.
    (a) I only
    (b) II only
    (c) both I and II
    (d) neither I nor II

8. Exclusions are used in insurance contracts for all of the following reasons EXCEPT:
    (a) to provide a physical description of the property to be insured.
    (b) to prevent moral hazard from occurring.
    (c) to eliminate the duplication of coverage.
    (d) to avoid coverage of uninsurable perils.

9. One other-insurance provision assesses liability of an insurer in relation to the proportion that the company's insurance bears to the total amount of insurance in force. This other-insurance provision is:
   (a) pro rata liability.
   (b) contribution by equal shares.
   (c) percentage participation.
   (d) primary and excess.

10. Which statement is true with regard to endorsements?
    I. If there is a conflict between the endorsement and the underlying contract, the endorsement usually takes precedence.
    II. An endorsement can be used to add coverage for additional perils to a named-perils contract.
    (a) I only
    (b) II only
    (c) both I and II
    (d) neither I nor II

■ True/False

Circle the T if the statement is true, the F if the statement is false. Explain to yourself why a statement is false.

T F   1. Insurance policies written on an all-risk basis cover all perils.

T F   2. Coinsurance in property insurance and coinsurance (percentage participation) in health insurance operate in the same way.

T F   3. Riders and endorsements are used to amend insurance contracts.

T F   4. Life insurance is an example of a named-perils coverage.

T F   5. A straight deductible requires the insured to bear a portion of each loss before the insurer has any liability.

T F   6. Cancellation rights and subrogation provisions are miscellaneous provisions in insurance contracts.

T F   7. Deductibles are not used in life insurance.

T F   8. Under a primary and excess other insurance settlement, it is possible that only one insurer will be required to pay for a loss.

T F   9. Individuals must be mentioned by name in order to be covered under insurance contracts.

T F   10. To determine if a peril is covered under an all-risk policy, you have to read the list of covered perils.

T F   11. Other-insurance provisions are designed to prevent profiting from insurance and violating the principle of indemnity.

T F   12. An aggregate deductible may be based on losses that occur during a calendar year.

Problems

1. Harold owns a building valued at $400,000. He purchased $280,000 in property insurance on the building, and the property insurance contract includes an 80% coinsurance clause.

    (a) If an $80,000 covered loss occurs, how much will Harold collect from his insurer?

    (b) If a $340,000 covered loss occurs, how much will Harold collect from his insurer?

    (c) How would your answers to part (a) and part (b) change if, instead of $280,000, Harold insured the building for $320,000?

2. Although still married, Mike and Beth Harris are legally separated. Mike insured their vacation home for $200,000. Unaware that Mike purchased coverage, Beth insured the vacation home for $300,000. While both policies were in force, a $90,000 covered loss occurred. How will the loss be settled if:

    (a) pro rata liability is used?

    (b) contribution by equal shares is used?

(c) primary and excess insurance is used, with Mike's coverage deemed primary?

3. Janice's health insurance includes an 80-20 coinsurance (percentage participation) provision, after a $250 deductible is satisfied. Janice needed medical attention and the covered medical expenses totaled $25,250. How will this claim be settled?

4. Bob's insurance coverage started at the beginning of the year. Given the following losses: January 1, $500 loss; March 27, $1,200 loss; and August 6, $800 loss; how much will Bob have to pay if:

(a) the losses were auto collision losses and Bob carried a $250 straight deductible?

(b) the losses are health-related claims, and Bob carries a $1,000 aggregate deductible based on the calendar-year?

Case Applications

Case 1

Part of ABC Insurance Company's training program for new employees is an analysis of insurance contracts. After the training program is completed, each new employee is given an "Insurance Skills Test." One question from the test requires employees to identify sections of an insurance policy. The test provides short excerpts from ABC policies. Employees are asked to identify the excerpt as a(n): (1) declaration, (2) definition, (3) insuring agreement, (4) exclusion, (5) condition, or (6) miscellaneous provision.

Part of the test is reproduced here. Identify the section of the policy from which the excerpt was taken.

a) "The property is a wood frame building located at 852 Pine Street in Metro City. It was constructed in 1979 and is currently valued at $60,000. The building has smoke detectors and a sprinkler system."

b) "If there has been a material increase in hazard or if the building is left vacant or unoccupied beyond 30 days, this coverage is suspended."

c) "We will not be responsible for losses that are intentionally caused. . . . Nor will we be responsible for the loss of money, stocks, or bonds."

d) "This policy covers direct physical damage to your property that is not specifically excluded."

(e) "In this policy, an "occurrence" will mean a loss that develops over time as well as sudden and accidental losses."

(f) "If the insurer and insured cannot agree on the value of the insured loss, each party will name an appraiser, and the two appraisers will jointly appoint an umpire. A decision by any two of the three (appraisers and umpire) is binding upon the insured and the insurer."

Case 2

Henry and Carol Green filed two insurance claims. Determine the insurer's liability in each case.

(a) The Greens purchased a storage building in another city two years ago. They insured the building fo $64,000 under a property insurance policy that included an 80 percent coinsurance requirement. At the time the building was damaged by a covered peril, the building was valued at $90,000. The damage was $9,000. How much will the Greens collect from their insurer?

(b) The Greens purchased a cabin in the mountains together with their friends, Guy and Ruby Blake. Th Greens and Blakes periodically use the cabin. The Greens insured the cabin for $50,000. Unaware that the Greens had insured the cabin, Guy and Ruby insured the cabin for $75,000. Recently the cabin sustained a $15,000 loss that was covered by both policies. If the insurers agree to settle the claim on a pro rata basis, how much of the claim will be paid by the Greens' insurer?

Solutions to Chapter 10

Short Answer Questions

1. Declarations: Statements about the property or life to be insured; used for underwriting and rating purposes as well as identification of the property or life insured.

   Definitions: Section of the policy in which the insurer explains the meaning of key words or phases in the contract. Definitions help to reduce disputes between the insurer and insured because key words and phrases are clearly defined as part of the contract.

   Insuring Agreement: Part of the insurance contract that states the major promises of the insurer. The insuring agreement can be written on an all-risk ("open perils") or named-perils basis.

   Exclusions: Listing of perils, losses, and property that are not covered under the insurance contract.

   Conditions: Provisions that qualify or place limitations on the insurer's promise to perform.

   Miscellaneous Provisions: General provisions common to insurance contracts that address the relationship between the insurer and the insured, and the responsibilities of the insurer toward third parties.

2. Named-perils coverage lists causes of loss that are covered under the policy. If the peril causing a loss is not named, the loss is not covered. All-risk coverage provides protection against all risks, except those that are specifically excluded. If the peril causing the loss is not excluded, the loss is covered.

3. Exclusions are used in insurance contracts for a number of reasons. Some risks (e.g., war) are not privately insurable. Some exposures are too hazardous to insure. Coverage may be provided elsewhere so it does not need to be provided under the contract. Exclusions are also needed to protect against losses attributable to moral hazard. Finally, some coverages may not be needed by a typical insured.

4. Insurers have an incentive to make contracts more readable and more easily understood. As we learned in Chapter 9, ambiguity in an insurance contract is construed against the insurer. To provide clarity, insurers specifically define the meaning of certain key words or phrases.

5. The purpose of endorsements and riders is to add to, delete from, or in some other way modify an insurance contract. For example, a renter can change the personal property coverage in his or her policy from actual cash value coverage to replacement cost coverage by adding a replacement cost endorsement to the renter's insurance policy.

6. Coinsurance is used to achieve equity in rating. It requires insureds to purchase property coverage for a specified percentage of value if they wish to collect in full for a partial loss. If they have not satisfied the coinsurance requirement, they must bear a portion of the loss.

   The coinsurance formula is:

   $$\frac{\text{Amount of Insurance Carried}}{\text{Amount of Insurance Required}} \times \text{Loss} = \text{Insurer's Liability}$$

7. Deductibles are used for a number of reasons. It costs something to process a claim, regardless of the size of the claim. Deductibles reduce the number of small claims filed. Secondly, deductibles reduce premiums. The more of the loss the insured is willing to retain through the deductible, the lower the premium. Finally, deductibles reduce moral and morale hazard because the insured is required to bear a portion of the loss.

8. Other insurance provisions are needed because in some situations more than one insurance policy covers a loss. In the absence of other insurance provisions, the loss settlement would not be coordinated, and more than the value of the loss might be paid, violating the principle of indemnity.

9. The insured can be defined in a number of ways. One way, as is done in life insurance, is to name on specific person by name. A second practice is to insure the person mentioned in the declarations and others who satisfy the definition of a "named insured." For example, the personal liability coverage of the homeowners contract covers the purchaser named in the declarations, as well as his or her spouse and children. Finally, the coverage may extend to persons not specifically named in the contract. For example, business auto coverage does not list the name of every employee. If the employer hires a new delivery driver, he or she is covered.

10. Some miscellaneous provisions address disputes relating to valuation. Other common miscellaneous provisions pertain to subrogation, cancellation, loss notification, and claim settlement practices.

Multiple Choice Questions

1. (a) The insuring agreement can be written on an all-risk or named-perils basis.

2. (b) Endorsements and riders are added to insurance contracts to amend the underlying policy.

3. (d) The provision described is an aggregate deductible.

4. (d) Neither statement is true with regard to conditions. The first statement describes the declarations section; the second statement describes the exclusions section.

5. (b) A waiting or elimination period is an initial period at the start of a covered disability during which no benefits are paid. It is really a deductible expressed in time, rather than dollars.

6. (a) This clause states a condition that must be satisfied (no material increase in hazard) for the insurer to provide indemnity. If the insured has violated the condition, as was the case here, the insurer can deny coverage of the claim.

7. (b) The level of the deductible will affect the premium that is charged for the coverage. The lower the deductible, the higher the premium. Deductibles help to reduce the number of small claims submitted to insurers.

8. (a) A physical description of the property insured is found in the declarations section of the policy. Exclusions are used for the reasons listed in the other choices.

9. (a) Pro rata settlements fit this description. If an insurer has written 75 percent of the total coverage in force when a loss occurs, the insurer must pay 75 percent of the loss.

10. (c) Both statements are true. The endorsement takes precedence unless it is in violation of the law. Endorsements are commonly used to broaden coverage by adding perils.

True/False

1. **F** All risks are covered except those risks that are specifically excluded.

2. **F** Coinsurance in property insurance requires the policyowner to insure for a specified percentage o value in order to collect in full for a partial loss. Coinsurance (percentage participation) in health insurance determines loss sharing after the deductible is satisfied.

3. **T**

4. **F** Life insurance is all-risk coverage, with very few exclusions.

5. **T**

6. **T**

7. **T**

8. **T**

9. **F** Often times a description of an insured is used (e.g., spouse of the insured, children of the insured, employee of the insured).

10. **F** You would have to read the list of exclusions. If the peril is not excluded, the peril is covered.

11. **T**

12. **T**

Problems

1. (a) Harold carries $280,000 in coverage. However, $320,000 (.80 × $400,000) was required to satisfy the coinsurance provision. Therefore Harold will receive:

$$\frac{\$280,000}{\$320,000} \times \$80,000 = \$70,000$$

(b) According to the coinsurance formula, $297,500 should be paid:

$$\frac{\$280,000}{\$320,000} \times \$340,000 = \$297,500$$

However, recovery is limited to the face amount of the coverage. The insurer will be liable for $280,000.

(c) If Harold had insured the building for $320,000; the first loss would have been paid in full:

$$\frac{\$320,000}{\$320,000} \times \$80,000 = \$80,000$$

Although the coinsurance requirement is also satisfied in the second case, the settlement is limited by the face amount of the coverage. The maximum the insurer will pay if a $340,000 loss occurs is $320,000, the amount of coverage purchased.

2. (a) Under pro rata liability, each insurer is responsible for the proportion of the loss that its coverage bears to the total insurance in force. Mike's insurer has written 40% of the coverage in force ($200,000/$500,000); and Beth's insurer has written 60% of the coverage in force ($300,000/$500,000). Therefore the $90,000 loss would be settled in this manner:

$$\frac{\$200,000}{\$500,000} \times \$90,000 = \$36,000 \text{ (Mike's Insurer)}$$

$$\frac{\$300,000}{\$500,000} \times \$90,000 = \$54,000 \text{ (Beth's Insurer)}$$

(b) Under contribution by equal shares, each insurer contributes equally until the loss is paid in full or the limit of liability of the insurer is reached. In this case, each insurer would contribute $45,000 to settle the claim.

(c) Under primary and excess insurance, one insurer pays first, and if its limit of liability is not high enough to cover the entire claim, then the other insurer pays the remainder. In this case, Mike's insurer would pay the entire claim. If the claim had been larger, $220,000 for example, Mike's insurer would pay $200,000 and Beth's insurer would pay the balance.

3. The claim would be settled in the following manner:

$25,250	Total Claim
– $250	Janice Pays the Deductible
$25,000	Balance of Claim

The insurer pays 80% of the $25,000 balance, which is $20,000.

Janice pays 20% of the $25,000 balance, which is $5,000.

So Janice would pay a total of $5,250 of the claim.

4. (a) An auto insurance collision deductible is an example of a straight deductible. Thus Bob would have to pay the first $250 of each of the three losses.

(b) Under a calendar-year deductible, covered losses are totaled until they reach a specified level, and then the insurer pays the remaining claims. In this case, Bob would be responsible for the $500 claim in January. He would also be responsible for $500 of the $1,200 claim in March. That amount, plus the $500 he paid in January, satisfies the calendar-year deductible. The insurer would be responsible for the $700 balance of the March claim and the entire $800 claim in August.

Case Applications

Case 1

1. (a) Declarations: A description of the insured property (location, value, construction, age, and protection) is provided.

(b) Conditions: The insurer provides a conditional promise of indemnity. The insurer will pay for damage to the property. However, if the hazard has been materially increased or the building was vacant or unoccupied before a loss occurred, the insurer will not pay the claim.

(c) Exclusions: Here the insurer is excluding coverage for a type of loss (intentional acts) and for certain types of property.

(d) Insuring Agreement: The major promises of the insurer are summarized in a simple sentence. The insurer will pay for direct physical damage to the insured property, unless the loss is excluded.

(e) Definitions: What is an occurrence? The insurer here defines the term broadly to include not only damage that occurs over time, but also sudden and accidental losses.

(f) Miscellaneous Provisions: This answer is arrived at through the process of elimination. It's not a definition, or a declaration, or a condition, or an exclusion, or part of the insuring agreement. Therefore, it is assigned to the catch-all category "miscellaneous provisions."

2. (a) To collect in full for a partial loss, the Greens would have needed to carry $72,000 in coverage at the time of loss (80 percent of $90,000 is $72,000). As this requirement was not met, the coinsurance formula must be applied. The Greens will receive $8,000 from the insurer:

$$\frac{\$64,000}{\$72,000} \times \$9,000 = \$8,000$$

(b) As the policies will respond on a pro rata basis, the percentage for which each insurer is responsible must be determined. A total of $125,000 worth of coverage was in force at the time of the loss ($50,000 plus $75,000). Of this amount the Greens' coverage was $50,000 of the total of $125,000, or 40 percent. The Blakes' coverage was $75,000 out of the total of $125,000, or 60 percent. Therefore, the Greens' insurer will pay 40 percent of the loss, which is $6,000:

$$\$15,000 \times .40 = \$6,000$$

The Blakes' insurer will pay 60 percent of the loss, which is $9,000:

$$\$15,000 \times .60 = \$9,000$$

Chapter 11
Life Insurance

◼ Overview

This chapter begins a block of material on several important personal risks: premature death, poor health, and excessive longevity. This chapter examines premature death and the financial services products designed to address this risk. We will consider the economic impact of premature death upon various types of families, methods of determining how much life insurance to purchase, and the various life insurance products available to address this important personal risk, including: term insurance, whole life insurance, universal life insurance, variable life insurance, and other life insurance products.

◼ Learning Objectives

After studying this chapter, you should be able to:

- Explain the meaning of premature death.
- Describe the financial impact of premature death on different types of families.
- Explain the needs approach for estimating the amount of life insurance to own.
- Explain the basic characteristics of term life insurance.
- Explain the basic characteristics of ordinary life insurance.
- Describe the following variations of whole life insurance: variable life insurance, universal life insurance, and variable universal life insurance.
- Describe the basic characteristics of current assumption whole life insurance.
- Define the following:

Blackout period	Needs approach
Capital retention approach	Net amount at risk
Cash-surrender value	Ordinary life insurance
Cash value life insurance	Preferred risks
Convertible	Premature death
Current assumption whole life	Readjustment period
Dependency period	Reentry term insurance
Endowment insurance	Renewable
Estate clearance fund	Savings bank life insurance
Group life insurance	Second-to-die life insurance
Human life value	Single-premium whole life insurance
Indeterminate-premium whole life	Term insurance
Industrial (home service) life insurance	Universal life insurance
Legal reserve	Variable life insurance
Limited-payment policy	Variable universal life insurance
Modified life policy	Whole life insurance

■ Outline

I. Premature Death

A. Meaning of Premature Death

B. Costs of Premature Death

C. Declining Problem of Premature Death

D. Economic Justification of Life Insurance

II. Financial Impact of Premature Death on Different Types of Families

A. Single People

B. Single-Parent Families

C. Two-Income Earners with Children

D. Traditional Families

E. Blended Families

F. Sandwiched Families

III. Amount of Life Insurance to Own

A. Human Life Value Approach

B. Needs Approach

C. Capital Retention Approach

D. Adequacy of Life Insurance for American Families

E. Opportunity Cost of Buying Life Insurance

IV. Types of Life Insurance

A. Term Insurance

B. Whole Life Insurance

C. Endowment Insurance

V. Variations of Whole Life

A. Variable Life Insurance

B. Universal Life Insurance

C. Variable Universal Life Insurance

D. Current Assumption Whole Life Insurance

E. Indeterminate-Premium Whole Life Insurance

VI. Other Types of Life Insurance

■ Short Answer Questions

1. What costs are associated with premature death?

2. How can the purchase of life insurance be justified from an economic standpoint?

3. How do the typical life insurance needs of a single adult who has no children differ from the typical life insurance needs of a single parent?

4. What is the difference between a blended family and a sandwiched family?

5. What are the steps in calculating the human life value of the breadwinner?

6. What basic family needs are considered in the application of the needs approach?

7. How does the needs approach of determining the amount of life insurance to purchase differ from the capital retention approach?

8. Why do yearly renewable term insurance premiums increase each year? Why is yearly renewable term insurance inappropriate for providing lifetime insurance protection?

9. Many term insurance policies are "renewable" and "convertible." Explain what is meant by these two characteristics of term insurance.

10. What is the difference between the "legal reserve" and the "cash value"?

11. How does variable life insurance differ from traditional whole life insurance?

12. What are the major characteristics of universal life insurance? How does variable universal life insurance differ from universal life insurance?

13. How does current assumption whole life differ from indeterminate-premium whole life?

■ Multiple Choice Questions

Circle the letter that corresponds to the BEST *answer.*

1. Which statement is true with regard to the human life value approach?
   - I.   It crudely measures the economic value of a human life.
   - II. It considers the specific needs of the family in determining the amount of life insurance to purchase.
   - (a) I only
   - (b) II only
   - (c) both I and II
   - (d) neither I nor II

2. Which of the following $100,000 yearly renewable term (YRT) policies would require the LOWEST premium?
   - (a) YRT purchased by a man age 30
   - (b) YRT purchased by a woman age 30
   - (c) YRT purchased by a man age 60
   - (d) YRT purchased by a woman age 60

3. Which statement is true with regard to yearly renewable term insurance?
   - (a) premiums remain level from year to year
   - (b) premiums increase at an increasing rate from year to year
   - (c) the insured must demonstrate insurability to renew the coverage
   - (d) yearly renewable term premiums are unrelated to the probability of death

4. An important consideration in determining the amount of life insurance to purchase is the need for income during the one- or two-year period after the death of the breadwinner. This period is called the:
   - (a) blackout period.
   - (b) readjustment period.
   - (c) accumulation period.
   - (d) dependency period.

5. All of the following are costs associated with premature death of the breadwinner EXCEPT:
   - (a) loss of the family's share of the deceased breadwinner's future income.
   - (b) personal maintenance expenses of the deceased.
   - (c) a reduction in the family's standard of living.
   - (d) additional expenses, such as funeral expenses and uninsured medical bills.

6. All of the following are characteristics of variable life insurance EXCEPT:
   - (a) the premium payments are flexible.
   - (b) the cash value is not guaranteed.
   - (c) the policyowner selects where the savings reserve is invested.
   - (d) a minimum death benefit is guaranteed, but the death benefit can be higher if the investment performance is favorable.

7. Julie purchased a life insurance policy with these characteristics: the policy was nonparticipating, the maximum premium that the insurer could charge was stated in the policy, and the insurer is permitted to adjust the premium based on anticipated future experience. What type of life insurance did Julie purchase?

   (a) current assumption whole life insurance

   (b) indeterminate-premium whole life insurance

   (c) variable universal life insurance

   (d) industrial life insurance

8. In addition to caring for their young children, Lyle and Lynn Thomas also support Lyle's father and Lynn's mother. This type of family is called a:

   (a) sandwiched family.

   (b) blended family.

   (c) nuclear family.

   (d) traditional family.

9. Which statement about universal life insurance is true?

   I. Universal life allows the policyowner to vary premium payments.

   II. Universal life allows the policyowner to earn a market-based rate of return on the cash value.

   (a) I only

   (b) II only

   (c) both I and II

   (d) neither I nor II

10. The difference between the face amount of a life insurance policy and the legal reserve of the policy is called:

    (a) the human life value.

    (b) the net amount at risk.

    (c) the level premium.

    (d) the cash value.

11. One form of life insurance has a reduced premium for the first three to five years, with premium increased after this initial period. This type of whole life insurance is called:

    (a) variable life insurance.

    (b) indeterminate-premium whole life insurance.

    (c) current assumption whole life insurance.

    (d) modified life insurance.

12. Which $50,000 life insurance policy, if purchased at age 32, would have the highest cash value when the insured was 50 years old?

    (a) whole life paid-up at age 65

    (b) 10-year level term insurance

    (c) continuous premium whole life insurance

    (d) 10-payment whole life insurance

3. Bill purchased a nonparticipating life insurance policy. The cash value was based on the insurer's present mortality, expense, and investment experience. His premium was guaranteed for an initial period, and is "redetermined" after three years. Bill purchased:

(a) universal life insurance.

(b) variable life insurance.

(c) current assumption whole life insurance.

(d) indeterminate-premium whole life insurance.

14. Which statement about second-to-die life insurance is true?

I. Second-to-die life insurance is often used in estate planning.

II. Second-to-die life insurance costs less than purchasing two separate policies.

(a) I only

(b) II only

(c) both I and II

(d) neither I nor II

■ True/False

Circle the T if the statement is true, the F if the statement is false. Explain to yourself why a statement is false.

T   F   1. Premature death is defined as death before reaching life expectancy.

T   F   2. Yearly renewable term insurance premiums increase at an increasing rate as the insured grows older.

T   F   3. Industrial life insurance is group term coverage sold to industrial workers.

T   F   4. The dependency period refers to the period until the youngest child reaches age 18.

T   F   5. A blended family is one in which a son or daughter with children is also supporting an aged parent or parents.

T   F   6. Each family head needs exactly five times his or her annual salary in life insurance.

T   F   7. Coverage ceases after the last premium is paid on a limited-payment whole life policy.

T   F   8. Preferred risks have a lower-than-average probability of death.

T   F   9. The difference between the face amount of a life insurance policy and the legal reserve is the cash value.

T   F   10. Under the level premium method of providing life insurance protection, premiums paid during the early years are lower than what is needed to pay death claims.

T   F   11. Financial dependency is a major justification for the purchase of life insurance.

T   F   12. The blackout period is the one- or two-year period following the death of the breadwinner.

■ Problem Set: Determining How Much Life Insurance to Purchase

1. Tom, age 32, is a bookkeeper. Tom believes that he will have average annual earnings of $80,000 per year up until he retires in 30 years. Roughly 50 percent of Tom's average annual earnings are used to pay taxes, insurance premiums, and for self-maintenance; with the balance available for family support. Assuming a 6% interest rate, what is Tom's human life value?

2. Janine would like to use the needs approach to determine if she should purchase additional life insurance. Janine's employer provides two times each employee's salary in group life insurance. Janine's salary is $45,000 per year. She has the following needs that she would like to satisfy upon her death: cost of funeral/final illness ($15,000); income support for her daughter ($60,000); income support for her dependent father ($70,000) and educational funds for her daughter ($40,000). Her current assets include $6,000 in a checking account and $14,000 in a mutual fund. Janine also estimates about $25,000 in Social Security survivor benefits would be payable if she died. How much additional life insurance should Janine purchase, according to the needs approach?

3. Toby is attempting to determine how much life insurance he should purchase according to the capital retention approach. Toby's goal is to provide $20,000 in income per year before taxes to his heirs. Toby's real estate investments currently generate $6,000 per year before taxes. His preferred stock pays $2,500 in dividends annually; and he has a $50,000 certificate of deposit locked in at an interest rate of 8 percent. All of these investments will pass to Toby's heirs upon his death. The balance of the desired cash flow will be funded through life insurance proceeds, which can be invested to yield 5 percent. How much additional life insurance is required?

Case Applications

Case 1

Kelly Richards is a 35 year-old investment banker. She is single and has no dependents. While she knows a great deal about stocks and bonds, she knows little about life insurance. She met with two life insurance agents. The first agent calculated Kelly's human life value and recommended that she purchase a $350,000 life insurance policy. The second agent used the needs approach and recommended that she purchase a $50,000 life insurance policy. Kelly is confused. Explain to Kelly how two methods of determining the appropriate amount of life insurance could produce such divergent results.

Case 2

Ron Feldman, age 24, would like to purchase life insurance. He met with an agent who handed him a schedule of premiums. As Ron started to review the premiums per thousand dollars of coverage, he noticed they increased slightly each year. After reviewing the premiums for the first ten years, Ron mentioned he needed permanent, lifetime protection. The agent replaced the first schedule with a second schedule. On the second schedule, premiums were level annual amounts, but higher than the premiums on the first schedule. Ron believes the agent is trying to take advantage of his lack of knowledge of life insurance to sell him a higher priced policy. What would you say to Ron?

■ Solutions to Chapter 11

Short Answer Questions

1. A number of costs are associated with premature death. These costs include: loss of the family's share of the breadwinner's future earnings, costs associated with death itself (unpaid hospital bills, funeral expenses, probate and estate costs, and taxes), possible reduction in the standard of living, an noneconomic costs such as emotional distress and loss of a parental role model.

2. The purchase of life insurance can be justified economically based on financial dependency. If an individual is earning an income, and others are dependent upon the income for their well-being, life insurance can be used to replace the income.

3. A single adult with no children likely has no one financially dependent upon him or her. If no one is financially dependent, death of the single person will not create financial hardship for others. Other than a small amount of life insurance to cover costs associated with death (funeral, estate clearance, uninsured medical bills, etc.), large amounts of life insurance usually are not needed by single adults Premature death of the family head in a single-parent family can cause severe economic insecurity fo the surviving children. There is a need for large amounts of life insurance on the family head in mos single parent families.

4. A blended family is one in which a widowed or divorced spouse with children remarries, and his or her new spouse also has children. A sandwiched family is one in which a son or a daughter with children is also supporting an aged parent or parents. Such a family is "sandwiched" between an older and younger generation, both financially dependent upon them.

5. A number of steps are involved in calculating the human life value. First, the individual's average annual earnings over the wage-earning years are estimated. Next, personal maintenance expenses, taxes, and insurance premiums are deducted in order to determine the net cash flow the individual would make available to his or her family. Then, the number of years that the individual would make this cash flow available is determined. Finally, the estimated future net cash flows are discounted back to present value and summed to determine the human life value.

6. The most important family needs that are considered include: estate clearance fund, income during the readjustment period, income during the dependency period, life income to the surviving spouse, special needs (e.g., mortgage redemption, educational fund, and emergency fund), and a retirement fund.

7. Under the needs approach, an amount of life insurance is purchased such that unfunded needs are me after the death of the breadwinner. Under this approach, the life insurance proceeds are liquidated to satisfy the needs of the surviving family members.

   The capital retention approach, as the name implies, emphasizes preservation of capital. In this approach, the income needs of the survivors are determined. These needs are then compared to the income that could be generated from the assets of the breadwinner if he or she died. If sufficient income is not available from present assets, life insurance proceeds are used to fund the difference. Enough life insurance is purchased such that the invested life insurance proceeds will provide the additional income required. Under the capital retention approach, the capital is not liquidated—only the income generated from the invested capital is used.

8. Yearly renewable term insurance premiums increase each year because the premium is determined by the probability of death at each attained age. As this form of insurance is only for one year, individual insureds must pay their pro rata share of the death claims of those who die during the year. As the probability of death increases each year, premiums must increase so the insurer has enough funds to satisfy the death claims. At older ages, the probability of death is so great that the coverage becomes unaffordable. Many insurers do not permit renewal of term insurance past a specified age, such as 65.

9. Renewable term insurance, as the name implies, permits the coverage to be put back in force again at the end of the coverage period. A major benefit of renewable term insurance is that the coverage can be placed in force again without the insured having to prove that he or she is still insurable. If term insurance is convertible, it means that the term insurance can be switched to permanent life insurance. Conversion does not require the insured to prove that he or she is still insurable. Conversion can be based on the insured's attained age or the original age at which the term coverage was purchased.

10. The legal reserve is a liability item reflecting the excess premiums paid during the early years of a level-premium policy. The reserve steadily increases over the life of the contract. The purpose of the legal reserve is to provide lifetime protection. Because of the legal reserve, cash values become available. Cash values are a by-product of the premium payment method. Because the policyowner has paid more than actuarially required during the early years of the policy, he or she should receive something back from the insurer if the policy is surrendered.

11. Variable life insurance is fixed-premium life insurance in which death benefit and the cash value vary according to the investment experience of a separate account maintained by the insurer. With variable life insurance, the cash value is not guaranteed, as it is with traditional whole life insurance. If investment experience is favorable, the face amount of insurance is increased. If the investment experience is poor, the amount of life insurance is reduced, but it can never fall below the original face amount.

12. Universal life insurance has a number of distinguishing characteristics. These distinguishing characteristics include: unbundling of protection and savings components, two forms of coverage available, considerable flexibility concerning premiums and face value, cash withdrawals permitted, and favorable income tax treatment.

Variable universal life insurance is also called universal variable life insurance. It possesses all of the characteristics of universal life insurance, but with two major exceptions. With universal variable life insurance, the policyowner determines where the premiums are invested. Second, the policy does not guarantee a minimum interest rate on the cash value.

13. Current assumption whole life insurance is nonparticipating life insurance in which the cash values are based on the insurance company's current mortality, investment, and expense experience. The death benefit is level, there's a minimum guaranteed cash value, and the premiums vary based on the insurer's experience. There is a guarantee that the premium will not exceed a specified amount.

Indeterminate-premium whole life insurance is also nonparticipating life insurance. This type of life insurance permits the insurer to adjust the premium based on anticipated future experience. The maximum premium that can be charged by the insurer is stated in the policy. The initial premium is lower than the maximum premium and is guaranteed for an initial period. After the initial guaranteed period expires, the insurer can increase the premium.

Multiple Choice Questions

1. (a) The human life value is a crude estimate of the economic value of a human life. It does not, however, consider specific family needs (e.g., mortgage payments, number of children, etc.) in determining the amount of life insurance to purchase.

2. (b) Yearly renewable term insurance premiums vary with the age and gender of the insured. Younger individuals pay less per-thousand for term life insurance than do older individuals. Women pay less for life insurance than men of the same age, given that women, on average, live longer than men.

3. (b) Yearly renewable term premiums track the probability of death. As individuals grow older, the probability of death increases at an increasing rate, hence yearly renewable term insurance premiums also increase at an increasing rate.

4. (b) The one- or two-year period following the death of the breadwinner is known as the readjustment period.

5. (b) The personal maintenance expenses of the deceased are not a cost of premature death. Indeed, following premature death, the personal maintenance expenses of the deceased individual are no longer incurred.

6. (a) Premium payments are fixed, not flexible, with variable life insurance. The other choices listed are characteristics of variable life insurance.

7. (b) Julie purchased an indeterminate-premium whole life policy. These nonparticipating policies permit the insurer to adjust premiums (within limits) based on anticipated future experience.

8. (a) This type of family is called a sandwiched family. A middle generation is supporting both younger and older dependents.

9. (c) Both statements are true. Premium payment flexibility is a characteristic of universal life insurance. This form of life insurance also permits the policyowner to earn a rate of return tied to some market-based index.

10. (b) The net amount at risk is the difference between the face amount and the legal reserve.

11. (d) The type of life insurance described is called modified life insurance.

12. (d) The 10-payment life whole life insurance policy is paid up. All the premiums required for the 10-payment, whole life insurance policy have been paid by the time the insured is 42 years old. Paid-up policies of the same face value have a higher cash value than policies of the same face value that are not paid up.

13. (c) Bill purchased current assumption whole life insurance. The premium is based on the current experience of the insurer. This policy is somewhat similar to indeterminate-premium whole life, however indeterminate-premium policies base the premium on anticipated future experience rather than actual current experience.

14. (c) Both statements are true. Estate liquidity is often needed upon the death of the second spouse, and this type of life insurance is well-suited for this contingency. As only one death benefit is paid, the insurance costs less than purchasing two separate policies.

True/False

1. **F** Premature death can be defined as death of the family head with outstanding, unfulfilled financial obligations.

2. **T**

3. **F** Industrial life insurance is individual, cash value, life insurance. The coverage is sold in low face amounts, with the premiums collected at the insured's home.

4. **T**

5. **F** A blended family is one in which a divorced or widowed spouse with children remarries, and the new spouse also has children.

6. **F** Each family head needs an amount of life insurance necessary to provide financial security in case of premature death. For some families, that amount is significant. Other families may need little, if any, life insurance.

7. **F** Coverage remains in force for all of life. For example, if someone purchases a 20-payment whole life policy at age 30, the coverage remains in force past age 50, when the last premium payment is due.

8. **T**

9. **F** The difference between the face amount of a life insurance policy and the legal reserve is called the net amount at risk.

10. **F** Under the level premium method, premiums paid in early years are greater than what is needed to pay death claims. This overpayment in early policy years is used to help pay death claims in later policy years while holding the premium level.

11. **T**

12. **F** The one- or two-year period following the death of the breadwinner is called the readjustment period.

Problem Set

1. Tom's average annual earnings are estimated to be $80,000. Of this amount, 50% ($40,000) will go for taxes and personal maintenance expenses, the remaining 50% ($40,000) will be available for the family. It is assumed that Tom will retire in 30 years and that 6 percent is the appropriate discount rate.

   To calculate the human life value, the present value of $40,000 per year for 30 years must be determined, assuming a 6 percent discount rate. Future cash flows must be discounted because dollars today are worth more than dollars in the future. Dollars today can be invested to earn a return, and we must take this fact into consideration in our calculation.

   The formula for the present value of an ordinary annuity is:

   Annuity Payment × Present Value Annuity Factor = Present Value of the Annuity

The formula for the Present Value Annuity Factor is:

$$\frac{1-(1+i)^{-n}}{i} = \text{Present Value Annuity Factor}$$

where "i" is the interest rate and "n" is the number of payments. It should be noted that the present value annuity factor can also be obtained from an interest rate factor table. Most introductory finance textbooks include tables that provide these factors.

Substituting 6 percent for i and 30 for n:

$$\frac{1-(1.06)^{-30}}{.06} = \text{Present Value Annuity Factor} = 13.7648$$

This factor is multiplied by the $40,000 net cash flow to arrive at the human life value:

$$\$40,000 \times 13.7648 = \$550,532$$

The problem could also be solved using a financial calculator. You would input $40,000 as the payment, 30 for "n," and 6 percent interest. Then you would compute the present value. Using formulas, tables, or a financial calculator, the result is the same.

2. The financial needs that Janine wishes to satisfy include:

Cost of Funeral/Final Illness	$15,000
Income Support—Daughter	$60,000
Income Support—Father	$70,000
Educational Fund—Daughter	$40,000
Total Financial Needs	$185,000

If Janine were to die today, her employer-provided life insurance, mutual fund, checking account, and Social Security survivor benefits would be available to meet some of the needs:

Checking Account	$6,000
Mutual Fund	$14,000
Employer-Provided Life Insurance	$90,000
Social Security Survivor Benefits	$25,000
Total Funds Available	$135,000

The difference between the financial needs and the funds available to meet the needs is the additional amount of life insurance that Janine should purchase:

Additional Life Insurance Needed $50,000

3. Toby's goal is to provide $20,000 per year to his family if he dies. Currently, the following cash flow would be available:

Real Estate Investment Income	$6,000
Preferred Stock Dividends	$2,500
CD Interest ($50,000 × .08)	$4,000
Total Income Currently Available	$12,500

So Toby must provide an additional $7,500 ($20,000 – $12,500) in pre-tax income through invested life insurance proceeds. Assuming that life insurance proceeds can be invested to provide a 5 percent return, we can determine how much life insurance is needed:

$$5\% \times \text{Life Insurance Proceeds} = \$7,500$$

Dividing both sides by 5 percent (.05), we obtain:

$$\text{Life Insurance Proceeds} = \$150,000$$

Therefore Toby should purchase $150,000 of life insurance. Again, recall that under the capital retention approach the capital is not liquidated.

Case Applications

Case 1

The two methods the agents used to determine how much life insurance to purchase are based on different sets of assumptions. The human life value calculates the present value of the net contribution the breadwinner would have made available to his or her family. The specific needs of the family are ignored—the focus is on the future net cash flows that the individual could earn. A successful, young investment banker could look forward to many years of high earnings, so the $350,000 human life value is not surprising.

The needs approach looks at an individual's current needs and objectives, rather than projected future earnings. We know that Kelly is an investment banker, that she is single, and that she has no dependents. Given that she is single and has no dependents, there is no one who will experience economic hardship if Kelly dies. She may have some employer-provided life insurance and some private savings to address most of her needs. So, according to the needs approach, little additional life insurance is required.

Case 2

The first schedule the agent gave Ron was obviously a yearly renewable term schedule. Given that Ron is 24 years old, there would only be a slight increase in premiums each year during the early coverage years. When Ron mentioned that he needed lifetime protection, the agent switched to a level-premium schedule. Through level premiums, lifetime protection can be made affordable. Ron is bothered by the fact that the level premiums exceeded the yearly renewable term premiums. Ron, however, did not see the complete yearly renewable term schedule. In later years, the term premium would be far greater that the level premium. Yearly renewable term premiums increase at an increasing rate, rendering this method inappropriate if the goal is lifetime protection.

Chapter 12
Life Insurance Contractual Provisions

Overview

Given the nature of the risk insured, the possible lengthy duration of the contract, the breadth of coverage provided, and the investment nature of some life insurance products; life insurance contracts are remarkable documents. To protect the interests of insurers, policyowners, insureds, and third-party beneficiaries, numerous contractual provisions have been developed and incorporated into life insurance contracts over the years. This chapter examines these important contractual provisions. Life insurance contracts also offer optional methods of using dividends (dividend options), using the cash value if the policy is surrendered (nonforfeiture options), and receiving policy proceeds upon the death of the insured (settlement options). A thorough understanding of life insurance contractual provisions is necessary for policyowners, insureds, and beneficiaries to maximize the benefits offered by these contracts.

Learning Objectives

After studying this chapter, you should be able to:

Describe the following contractual provisions that appear in life insurance policies: incontestable clause, suicide clause, and grace period provisions.

Identify the dividend options that typically appear in participating life insurance policies.

Explain the cash-surrender (nonforfeiture) options that appear in cash-value policies.

Describe the various settlement options for the payment of life insurance death benefits.

Describe the following riders that can be added to a life insurance policy: waiver of premium, guaranteed purchase option, accidental death benefit rider, cost-of-living rider, and accelerated death benefits rider.

Define the following:

Absolute assignment	Fixed-amount option
Accelerated death benefits rider	Fixed-period option
Accidental death benefits rider (double indemnity)	Grace period
	Guaranteed purchase option
Automatic premium loan provision	Incontestable clause
Aviation exclusion	Interest option
Change-of-plan provision	Irrevocable beneficiary
Class beneficiary	Life income options
Collateral assignment	Life settlement
Contingent beneficiary	Misstatement of age or sex clause
Cost-of-living rider	Nonforfeiture laws
Dividend accumulations option	Nonforfeiture options
Entire-contract clause	Nonparticipating policy
Extended term insurance	Ownership clause

Paid-up additions option
Participating policy
Policy loan provision
Primary beneficiary
Reduced paid-up insurance
Reinstatement provision
Revocable beneficiary

Settlement options
Specific beneficiary
Suicide clause
Viatical settlement
Waiver-of-premium provision
War clause

■ Outline

I.   Life Insurance Contractual Provisions

    A.   Ownership Clause

    B.   Entire-Contract Clause

    C.   Incontestable Clause

    D.   Suicide Clause

    E.   Grace Period

    F.   Reinstatement Clause

    G.   Misstatement of Age or Sex Clause

    H.   Beneficiary Designation

    I.   Change-of-Plan Provision

    J.   Exclusions and Restrictions

    K.   Payment of Premiums

    L.   Assignment Clause

    M.   Policy Loan Provision

    N.   Automatic Premium Loan

II.   Dividend Options

    A.   Cash

    B.   Reduction of Premiums

    C.   Dividend Accumulations

    D.   Paid-up Additions

    E.   Term Insurance (Fifth Dividend Option)

III.   Nonforfeiture Options

    A.   Cash Value

    B.   Reduced Paid-up Insurance

    C.   Extended Term Insurance

7. **Settlement Options**

   A. Cash

   B. Interest Option

   C. Fixed-Period Option

   D. Fixed-Amount Option

   E. Life Income Options

Additional Life Insurance Benefits

   A. Waiver-of-Premium Provision

   B. Guaranteed Purchase Option

   C. Accidental Death Benefit Rider

   D. Cost-of-Living Rider

   E. Accelerated Death Benefits Rider

Short Answer Questions

1. How does the entire contract clause protect beneficiaries?

2. How does the incontestable clause balance the interests of the insurer and the beneficiary?

3. What requirements must be fulfilled to reinstate a lapsed life insurance policy?

4. What is the difference between a primary beneficiary and a contingent beneficiary? What is the difference between a revocable beneficiary and an irrevocable beneficiary?

5. April lied about her age when she purchased a life insurance policy. She said she was 32 on the application, when she was really 35. Upon her death, the insurer discovered April's correct age. How will this situation be resolved?

6. Since Kent purchased a whole life policy, some questions have arisen with regard to his coverage. Name the policy provision that Kent should review to clarify each of the following questions.

    (a) When Kent purchased the policy, he lied about his family's health history. Kent wonders if his lie will prevent his beneficiary from collecting the face amount of the coverage when he dies.

    (b) Kent became distraught when his marriage and business failed simultaneously. He is considering killing himself, but wonders if his beneficiary will be permitted to collect the face amount of the policy if he takes his own life.

    (c) Kent is facing a liquidity crunch. He needs some cash, but he does not want to exercise a nonforfeiture option. He wonders whether his life insurance policy can help.

    (d) Kent would like to start a business. A friend is willing to loan him money, but the friend requires security for the loan. Kent wonders if the life insurance policy can be used to secure the loan.

    (e) Kent discovered the premium was due two weeks ago. He wonders if the coverage is still in force.

7. List the dividend options.

8. List the nonforfeiture options.

9. List the settlement options.

10. How does a guaranteed purchase option protect an insured who may need additional life insurance protection in the future?

1. When she purchased her whole life policy, Beth added a double indemnity rider. She was surprised to learn that adding the rider did not double the premium. She believes that she "slipped one past" the insurance company. Is Beth overlooking something? Explain.

2. Harold developed the AIDS virus after sharing a needle with another drug addict. His doctor's prognosis is that Harold will die in the next six to twelve months. Harold has exhausted all of his financial resources on treatment. His life insurance contract includes an accelerated death benefits rider. How can this rider help Harold?

Multiple Choice Questions

Circle the letter that corresponds to the BEST answer.

1. All of the following are dividend options EXCEPT:
   (a) dividend accumulations.
   (b) fixed-period option.
   (c) paid-up additions.
   (d) reduction of premiums.

2. Ned purchased a life insurance policy on his own life. He was concerned that he might not be able to pay premiums if he became disabled. He added a provision to his policy that relieved him from paying premiums if he becomes totally disabled before a specified age. This provisions is called a(n):

    (a) guaranteed purchase option.
    (b) waiver-of-premium provision.
    (c) automatic premium loan provision.
    (d) reinstatement provision.

3. Which statement is true with regard to the options available in life insurance contracts?

    I.   All life insurance policies provide dividend options.
    II. All life insurance policies provide nonforfeiture options.

    (a) I only
    (b) II only
    (c) both I and II
    (d) neither I nor II

4. Barb purchased a whole life policy on her son, Tom, twelve years ago. She named herself the beneficiary. Tom, now age 19, would like to take out a policy loan to help fund the purchase of a sports car. Barb does not believe that Tom has the right to take out a policy loan. Which contractual provision supports Barb's position?

    (a) the assignment clause
    (b) the incontestable clause
    (c) the reinstatement clause
    (d) the ownership clause

5. All of the following are settlement options EXCEPT:

    (a) fixed period.
    (b) interest option.
    (c) extended term insurance.
    (d) life income.

6. Which statement is true with regard to the incontestable clause?

    I.   It protects the beneficiary if the insurer attempts to deny payment of the death claim more than two years after the policy was purchased.
    II. It allows the insurer to deny a death claim during the first two years of coverage on the basis of concealment or misrepresentation by the applicant.

    (a) I only
    (b) II only
    (c) both I and II
    (d) neither I nor II

7. Rod committed suicide four months after purchasing a $100,000 life insurance policy. His insurer must pay the beneficiary:

    (a) $100,000.
    (b) $100,000 less the premiums paid for the coverage.
    (c) a refund of the premiums paid.
    (d) nothing.

8. Christine has a paid-up $50,000 whole life policy. She would like to transfer all ownership rights in the policy to her favorite charity. Christine can accomplish the transfer through a(n):
   (a) change of plan provision.
   (b) guaranteed purchase option.
   (c) reinstatement provision.
   (d) absolute assignment.

9. Tom was just diagnosed with an inoperable brain tumor. According to his doctor, Tom has less than three months to live. A life insurance premium notice just arrived. Tom purchased this whole life policy over 40 years ago. Tom does not want to pay the premium. Which nonforfeiture option should Tom exercise?
   (a) reduced paid-up insurance
   (b) extended term insurance
   (c) cash value
   (d) life income

10. Mary is concerned that inflation will reduce the purchasing power of her life insurance proceeds when she dies. To provide protection against this risk, she added a rider to her policy that allows her to purchase one-year term insurance equal to the cumulative change in the consumer price index from the issue date of the policy. This provision is called a:
    (a) cost-of-living rider.
    (b) guaranteed purchase option.
    (c) waiver-of-premium provision.
    (d) change of plan provision.

■ True/False

Circle the T if the statement is true, the F if the statement is false. Explain to yourself why a statement is false.

T   F   1. A change-of-plan provision permits the policyowner to exchange their present policy for a different life insurance contract.

T   F   2. Interest is not required on life insurance policy loans.

T   F   3. Reduced paid-up insurance is a dividend option.

T   F   4. Settlement options are available on all life insurance contracts.

T   F   5. The purpose of the suicide clause is to reduce adverse selection against the insurer.

T   F   6. Failure to pay a life insurance premium by the due date automatically results in a policy lapse.

T   F   7. All ownership rights in a policy are transferred through a collateral assignment.

T   F   8. Under a waiver-of-premium provision, if the insured becomes totally disabled before a stated age, all premiums coming due during the period of disability are waived.

T F   9. Evidence of insurability must be demonstrated to purchase additional life insurance under a guaranteed purchase option.

T F 10. If a policy loan has not been repaid by the time the insured dies, the amount paid to the beneficiary is reduced by the amount of the debt.

T F 11. Cash value life insurance contracts include nonforfeiture options.

■ Case Applications

Case 1

While sorting through their deceased grandmother's personal belongings, James and Tameka Williams found a life insurance contract. A cursory review showed that it was a $50,000 whole life insurance policy purchased by their grandmother on her own life in 1970. The last premium was paid in 2004, shortly before their grandmother had a stroke and lost some of her mental faculties. Why is there a good chance that this policy is still of value?

Case 2

Cal suffered from heart disease and was under the care of a physician for this problem. He lied on his life insurance application, stating that he had not seen a physician in the past two years and that he had never suffered from heart disease. Cal believes that regardless of when he dies, the insurer will not be able to use this lie to prevent payment to the beneficiary, his nephew Brian. Cal's reasoning is that he lied on the application, and the application is separate from the contract.

(a) Explain the error is Cal's thinking, citing the appropriate policy provision.

(b)   Cal thinks he has come up with another way of outsmarting his life insurer. This time he is thinking about the incontestable clause. Cal has instructed his beneficiary that if Cal dies during the first two years that the policy is in force, to not report his death to the insurer until two years have passed since the inception of the contract. Is Cal a shrewd planner or does his scheme represent a lack of understanding of the incontestable clause? Explain.

■ Solutions to Chapter 12

Short Answer Questions

1.   The entire contract clause specifies what constitutes the formal agreement between the insurer and the policyowner. The entire agreement consists of the completed application and the policy issued by the company. This clause prevents the insurer from attempting to bring in additional information in an effort to defeat a death claim. Claims are usually contested after the death of the insured. In that case, the insured cannot refute the claims of the insurer.

2.   Insurers are entitled to an honest disclosure of all material information when the contract is formed. The incontestable clause allows a two-year discovery period during which the insurer can contest death claims because of material concealment or misrepresentation. On the other hand, the interests of innocent beneficiaries must also be protected. The incontestable clause protects their interests by allowing the insurer only to contest claims during the first two years the policy is in force.

3.   Several requirements must be fulfilled to reinstate a lapsed policy. The requirements include:
   - provide evidence of insurability
   - payment of overdue premiums plus interest
   - repayment of all policy loans
   - the policy must not have been surrendered for the cash value
   - the reinstatement must be done within a certain time period, typically three or five years, of the date of the lapse

4.   The primary beneficiary is first in line to receive the policy proceeds when the insured dies. If the primary beneficiary dies before the insured, then the policy proceeds are paid to the contingent beneficiary when the insured dies. A policyowner is free to change a revocable beneficiary. An irrevocable beneficiary cannot be changed without his or her consent.

5.   Life insurers treat lies about age as "misstatements" rather than "misrepresentations." If someone misstates his or her age, the insurer will simply adjust the life insurance proceeds to the amount of coverage that the premiums paid would have purchased had the correct age been supplied.

6. (a) Kent should review the incontestable clause.
    (b) Kent should review the suicide clause.
    (c) Kent should review the policy loan provision.
    (d) Kent should review the collateral assignment provision.
    (e) Kent should review the grace period provision.

7. The dividend options include:
    - cash
    - reduction of premiums
    - dividend accumulations
    - paid-up additions
    - term insurance (not offered by all insurers)

8. The three nonforfeiture options are:
    - cash value
    - reduced paid-up insurance
    - extended term insurance

9. The settlement options are:
    - cash (lump sum payment)
    - interest option
    - fixed period option
    - fixed amount option
    - life income option

10. The guaranteed purchase option permits the insured to purchase additional life insurance coverage at specified times. The option protects insureds who have become uninsurable because evidence of insurability is not required to purchase the additional coverage.

11. Yes, Beth is overlooking several important facts. First, the face amount is doubled only if Beth dies as a result of an accident. If she dies because of heart disease, cancer, a stroke, or as a result of any other non-accidental cause, the insurer is liable for the face value only. In addition, there are other restrictions that apply to the rider (e.g., accidental death before a specified age, the death must occur within a specified number of days of the accident, etc.).

12. Under the accelerated death benefits rider, insureds can use the policy proceeds before they die. This rider will permit Harold to use some of the death benefit while he is still alive to help cover the cost of his treatment.

Multiple Choice Questions

1. (b) Fixed-period is a settlement option, not a dividend option.

2. (b) A waiver-of-premium provision relieves the insured from the payment of premiums if he or she becomes totally disabled before a specified date.

3. (d) Neither statement is true. Only participating (dividend-paying) life insurance policies have dividend options. Only cash value life insurance policies provide nonforfeiture options.

4. (d) The ownership clause vests the right to make decisions about the policy with the policyowner. The policyowner, not the insured, decides whether a policy loan will be made.

5. (c) Extended term insurance is a nonforfeiture option, not a settlement option.

6. (c) Both statements are true. The incontestable clause protects beneficiaries from nonpayment of the face value after the policy has been in force for two years. The clause also protects insurers against concealment and misrepresentation during the first two years.

7. (c) If the insured commits suicide during the suicide exclusion period, the insurer is only liable for a refund of premiums paid.

8. (d) Christine can accomplish this transfer through an absolute assignment of all rights under the policy to the charity.

9. (b) Given the scenario described, extended term insurance would be a logical nonforfeiture option. Under this option, the full-face amount of coverage remains in force. Given that the policy was purchased over 40 years ago, there will be enough accumulated cash value to provide term insurance coverage for far longer than Tom's three-month life expectancy.

10. (a) Mary is using a cost-of-living rider to index her life insurance proceeds. As purchasing power erodes because of inflation, an offsetting amount of term insurance is purchased.

True/False

1. T

2. F The funds you are borrowing legally belong to the insurer. When premium rates were determined, it was assumed the insurer would have these funds to invest. Thus interest is required on life insurance policy loans to compensate the insurer for lost investment income.

3. F Reduced paid-up insurance is a nonforfeiture option.

4. T

5. T

6. F Life insurance policies include a grace period provision that extends coverage beyond the premium due date if the premium has not been paid.

7. F A collateral assignment is a limited form of assignment designed to provide security for a loan. The assignee's rights are limited to the outstanding loan value.

8. T

9. F One of the beneficial aspects of this option is that additional insurance can be purchased without having to demonstrate insurability.

10. T

11. T

Case Applications

Case 1

According the facts presented, a whole life policy had been in force many years before the insured lost some of her mental faculties and died. If the 2005 premium notice was not answered, the grace period goes into effect. If the grace period expires and the company still has not heard from the policyowner, in most states the extended term nonforfeiture option will go into effect. Given that premiums had been paid for 34 years, there should have been adequate cash value to extend the coverage from 2004 until the date when the insured died. If this is the case, the beneficiary listed in the policy or the heirs of the estate should receive the policy proceeds.

Case 2

(a) Cal's actions represent a lack of understanding of life insurance contractual provisions. With regard to his view that the application is separate from the contract, under the entire contract clause the policy and the attached application form the entire contract between the policyowner and the insurer. Thus he cannot lie on the application and then assert that the application is not part of the contract.

(b) With regard to the strategy of delaying the report of his death if Cal dies during the contestable period, Cal should carefully review the incontestable clause. Insurers include the final portion of the definition provided in your text (". . . during the insured's lifetime") to handle the delayed death-reporting problem. Delay in reporting a death that occurred during the first two years will not prevent the insurer from contesting the claim; provided that death occurred during the first two years that the policy was in force.

Chapter 13
Buying Life Insurance

■ Overview

Would you purchase a major appliance, new home, or a new car without shopping around first? Many of the same consumers who would answer this question "of course not" purchase life insurance without considering the true cost of the coverage. Even though life insurers are pricing the same risk, there are significant variations in the cost of life insurance. In addition to cost, there are a number of other important considerations in purchasing life insurance. This chapter discusses the fundamentals of life insurance purchasing. Major topics covered include: methods of determining the cost of life insurance, methods of determining the rate of return on the cash value, taxation of life insurance, and suggestions to follow when purchasing life insurance. The appendix at the end of the chapter explains how life insurance premiums are calculated.

■ Learning Objectives

After studying this chapter, you should be able to:

Explain the defects in the traditional net cost method for determining the cost of life insurance.

● Explain the interest-adjusted surrender cost index and net payment cost index for determining the cost of life insurance.

● Explain the yearly rate-of-return method for determining the annual rate of return on the savings component in a life insurance policy.

● Describe the suggestions to follow when purchasing life insurance.

Understand how life insurance premiums are calculated (covered in the chapter appendix).

● Define the following:

Certified Financial Planner (CFP)
Chartered Financial Consultant (ChFC)
Chartered Life Underwriter (CLU)
Interest-adjusted cost method
Linton yield
Low-load life insurance
Net payment cost index
Surrender cost index
Traditional net cost method
Yearly rate-of-return method

■ Outline

I.   Determining the Cost of Life Insurance

    A.   Traditional Net Cost Method

    B.   Interest-Adjusted Cost Methods
        1.   Surrender Cost Index
        2.   Net Payment Cost Index

    C.   Substantial Cost Variation Among Insurers

    D.   Obtaining Cost Information

    E.   NAIC Policy Illustration Model Regulation

II.   Rate of Return on Saving Component

    A.   Linton Yield

    B.   Yearly Rate-of-Return Method

III. Taxation of Life Insurance

    A.   Federal Income Tax

    B.   Federal Estate Tax

IV. Shopping for Life Insurance

    A.   Determine Whether You Need Life Insurance

    B.   Estimate the Amount of Life Insurance You Need

    C.   Decide on the Best Type of Life Insurance for You

    D.   Decide Whether You Want a Policy that Pays Dividends

    E.   Shop Around for a Low-Cost Policy

    F.   Consider the Financial Strength of the Insurer

    G.   Deal with a Competent Agent

■ Short Answer Questions

1. Why is it incorrect to simply compare the premiums for cash value life insurance policies when comparing the cost of coverage?

2. What are the major defects of the traditional net cost method?

3. How do the surrender cost index and net payment cost index correct some of the defects inherent in the traditional net cost method?

4. In calculating the surrender cost and net payment cost, why is the future value annuity due factor used rather than the future value ordinary annuity factor?

5. Where can a consumer who is interested in comparing interest-adjusted cost data obtain the necessary information?

6. Is it enough to use interest-adjusted cost data in isolation to select a life insurance policy, or should additional factors be considered? If additional factors should be considered, identify the factors.

7. In addition to the financial strength of the present insurer, what other factors should be considered in determining whether to replace a life insurance policy?

8. What is the Linton yield?

9. How is the yearly rate of return calculated in the method developed by Professor Joseph Belth?

10. What income tax advantages are associated with life insurance?

11. To determine if federal estate taxes are payable upon death, the gross estate must first be calculated. How is the value of the gross estate determined?

12. What suggestions do consumer experts offer regarding shopping for life insurance?

■ Multiple Choice Questions

Circle the letter that corresponds to the BEST answer.

1. Which of the following provides the most meaningful cost index (dollars and cents per thousand per year) of cash value life insurance?
   (a) traditional net cost
   (b) Linton yield
   (c) surrender cost index
   (d) human life value

2. Which statement(s) is(are) true with respect to the traditional net cost method of calculating the cost of life insurance?
   I.   It ignores the time value of money.
   II. Life insurance is often shown to be free.

   (a) I only
   (b) II only
   (c) both I and II
   (d) neither I nor II

3. All of the following should be considered when determining whether to replace a life insurance policy EXCEPT:
   (a) the incontestable clause.
   (b) the cost of "getting out of" your present coverage.
   (c) the grace period.
   (d) tax considerations.

4. Karen is concerned about the rate of return she will earn on a cash value life insurance policy. To analyze the rate of return, she divided each premium into two components: cost of insurance coverage and savings. Then she calculated the average annual rate of return that would be needed to transform the annual savings contributions into the guaranteed cash value at a specified time. Karen calculated the:

    (a) net payment cost.
    (b) Linton yield.
    (c) yearly rate of return using the Belth method.
    (d) surrender cost.

5. Which statement is true with regard to the yearly rate of return method developed by Belth?

    (a) it ignores dividend payments
    (b) it calculates a cost per thousand per year
    (c) it ignores the increase in cash value from year to year
    (d) it uses an assumed price per thousand dollars of coverage

6. Which statement(s) is(are) true with regard to the surrender cost index?

    I.   It is based upon the assumption that the policy will be surrendered after a specified period.
    II. It ignores the time value of money.

    (a) I only
    (b) II only
    (c) both I and II
    (d) neither I nor II

7. Which of the following statements is true with regard to shopping for life insurance?

    (a) you can use the surrender cost index to determine how much coverage to purchase
    (b) the financial strength of the insurer writing the coverage is unimportant
    (c) the financial ratings assigned to life insurers are sometimes unreliable and confusing
    (d) you can use the needs approach to determine the cost of life insurance per thousand per year

8. Nathan is interested in analyzing the cost of life insurance. He wants to perform the analysis based on the assumption that the life insurance coverage will remain in force. Which of the following techniques would be most appropriate for Nathan to use?

    (a) net payment cost index
    (b) traditional net cost
    (c) Linton yield
    (d) surrender cost index

9. Which statement(s) is(are) true with regard to the Linton yield technique?

    I.   It determines a cost per thousand dollars of life insurance per year.
    II. It requires dividing the premium into two components: the cost of insurance protection and savings.

    (a) I only
    (b) II only
    (c) both I and II
    (d) neither I nor II

10. All of the following statements about the tax treatment of life insurance are true EXCEPT:
    (a) While a cash value policy is in force, the cash value accumulates tax-free.
    (b) Policyowners are required to pay taxes on policyowner dividends.
    (c) Lump-sum death benefits are received tax-free.
    (d) If life insurance proceeds are paid through an annuity, the portion of the payment that represent interest is taxable income.

11. The gross estate can be reduced by the value of property passed to a surviving spouse. This reductic is known as:
    (a) the unified tax credit.
    (b) the marital deduction.
    (c) the absolute assignment.
    (d) the homestead exemption.

12. The best life insurance for you to purchase is:
    (a) the policy with the highest surrender cost index.
    (b) the policy that pays the highest dividends.
    (c) the policy that has the highest Linton yield.
    (d) the policy that best fits your needs.

■ True/False

Circle T if the statement is true or F if the statement is false. Explain to yourself why the statement is false.

T F 1. When shopping for cash value life insurance, you can simply compare premiums to determir which policy is best.

T F 2. Because all life insurance companies are determining rates for the same risk, death, there is little variation in cost among similar life insurance contracts.

T F 3. The interest-adjusted methods ignore the timing and magnitude of dividend payments.

T F 4. The cost comparison techniques should be used to compare similar plans of insurance.

T F 5. A life insurance policy that pays dividends to the policyowner is known as a participating lif insurance policy.

T F 6. The future value ordinary annuity factor is used to calculate the future value of the premium when the interest-adjusted methods are employed.

T F 7. For a cash value life insurance policy in force long enough to have a cash value, the surrend cost per thousand per year will always be greater than the net payment cost per thousand per year.

T F 8. Belth's yearly rate-of-return method can only be used for participating life insurance policie

T F 9. If the insured has any incidents of ownership in a life insurance policy when he or she dies, the entire proceeds are included in his or her gross estate for federal estate tax purposes.

T F 10. It is wise to shop around when purchasing life insurance.

T   F   11. The financial strength of the company issuing the life insurance contract should be taken into consideration by a prospective purchaser.

T   F   12. Low load life insurance is characterized by low marketing expenses.

Problems

1. Andy is considering the purchase of a $20,000 whole life policy. The coverage will have an annual premium of $248.60. The coverage is participating, and based on the insurer's history with similar policies, it is estimated the company will pay a total of $814 in dividends over the first 20 years. If these dividends are invested at 5 percent interest, the dividends would accumulate to $1,163 after 20 years. The cash value after 20 years will be $4,314.20. For calculations involving the time value of money, 5 percent is the appropriate interest rate.

   (a) What is the traditional net cost per thousand per year?

   (b) What is the surrender cost per thousand per year?

   (c) What is the net payment cost per thousand per year?

2. The appendix at the end of Chapter 13 covers life insurance pricing. Using the mortality data provided in Exhibit A1 and the present value factors provided in Exhibit A2, determine the following premiums.

   (a) What is net single premium per thousand for a one-year term policy issued to man age 30, assuming a 5.5 percent interest rate?

(b) What is the net single premium per thousand for a three-year term policy issued to a man age 38 assuming a 5.5 percent interest rate?

■ Case Applications

Case 1

Jenny wants to purchase life insurance coverage. She calculated how much life insurance she needs and what type of policy to purchase, and she found a low-cost policy. Her final question to the agent was, "Tell me about the financial strength of your company." The agent replied, "I represent an A-rated company." What follow-up question should Jenny ask?

Case 2

John Johnson is president of Easy Pay Life Insurance Company. A life insurance rating service just published a list of surrender cost indexes for life insurance policies. Easy Pay's most popular product, The Easy Pay Wealth Accumulator Policy, ranked low on the list. John was bothered by the low rating, but he had an idea. He issued a press release noting that from now on, a "persistency bonus" in the form of an addition to the cash value, would be paid on each ten-year anniversary of the purchase of the Wealth Accumulator Policy. In announcing the persistency bonus, John said the bonus was "designed to recognize and reward our long-term policyowners." Is John just being generous, or might he have another motive? Explain.

Solutions to Chapter 13

Short Answer Questions

1. To properly consider the cost of coverage, you must also consider what you receive in exchange for the premium paid. A policy with a lower premium may also provide a lower cash value after a specified period and may not pay dividends. To obtain a clear picture, you should not only consider what you pay, but also what you receive in exchange for the premium.

2. The major defects of the traditional net cost method include: the time value of money is ignored, insurance is often shown to be free, the steepness of the dividend scale is ignored, the dividend scale is assumed to remain unchanged, and the traditional net cost method is based upon the assumption that the policy will be surrendered.

3. These interest-adjusted techniques take into consideration the time value of money and the steepness of the dividend scale. Rather than considering interest with respect to the cash value only, as does the traditional net cost method; the interest-adjusted techniques also time-value the premiums and the dividend payments. Rather than simply dividing the insurance cost by the number of years analyzed, the interest-adjusted techniques convert the total cost into equal annual cost outlays while considering interest.

4. This adjustment is necessary because insurance premiums are paid at the start of the year, rather than at the end of the year. The ordinary future value annuity formula calculates the future value if the payments occur at the end of each period, rather than at the beginning:

Ordinary Annuity		$X	$X	$X	$X	$X		
of $X a Period	+	+	+	+	+	+		
for Five Periods	0	1	2	3	4	5	FV = $Y	

Life insurance premiums, however, are paid at the start of each period. Life insurers will not cover you for a year, and then request the premium payment. Life insurance premiums are paid in advance, like rent payments:

Annuity Due	$X	$X	$X	$X	$X			
of $X a Period	+	+	+	+	+	+		
for Five Periods	0	1	2	3	4	5	FV = $Y	

Note how the premiums are paid at the beginning of each period rather than at the end. If each premium was invested when received, each annuity due payment would earn interest for one period more than each ordinary annuity payment. To adjust for this difference, the ordinary future value annuity formula can simply be multiplied by $(1 + i)$, where i is the interest rate, to obtain the future value annuity due factor. See the solution to the problem set immediately after the "True/False Questions solutions" for an illustration of how the future value annuity due factor is calculated and employed. How this factor can be obtained using a financial calculator is also explained.

5. Interest-adjusted cost data can be found in policy surveys published in *Best's Review*, Life/Health Edition. You can also ask your agent for this information. Certain states publish shoppers' guides and some personal finance magazines occasionally publish interest-adjusted cost data. Finally, a number of price-quote services are available online.

6. Using an interest-adjusted cost index in isolation is not enough. Other factors must be considered, such as the financial strength of the insurance company. Consumers are urged to shop for a policy and not an insurance company. The cost index must also be used to compare similar policies. Small differences in the cost indexes can be ignored as there may be other offsetting pros and cons associated with the policy or the insurer. The consumer should remember that the cost indexes apply to new policies and should not be used to determine whether a policy should be replaced. Finally, the type of policy you purchase should not be based solely on a cost index.

7. Other factors should be considered in addition to the strength of your present insurer. These factors include: your state of health and other factors affecting your ability to qualify for a new policy, the cost of getting out of your existing policy, the cost of getting into a new policy, tax implications should be reviewed, the incontestability and suicide clauses should be considered, and finally, remember that the individual recommending the change will probably receive some financial benefit if you replace the existing policy. This person may be placing his or her financial gain above your best interests.

8. The Linton yield is a method that can be used to determine the rate of return on the savings portion of a cash value life insurance policy. To calculate the Linton yield, each premium is divided into two parts: the cost of insurance and the savings component. The Linton yield is the average annual rate of return that must be earned on the savings component of each premium to make the savings component of the premiums grow to equal the guaranteed cash value at a specified time. Policies are compared based on the rates of return provided.

9. Belth's yearly rate of return is calculated through the following formula:

$$i = \frac{(CV + D) + (YPT)(DB - CV)(.001)}{(P + CVP)} - 1$$

The yearly rate of return, i, is equal to:

- in the numerator, the first term is the amount of funds available at the end of the year, the Cash Value (CV) at year-end plus Dividends (D). The second term in the numerator is the assumed price of the protection component. It is equal to the Yearly Price per Thousand (YPT) multiplied by the difference between the Death Benefit (DB) and the Cash Value at the end of the year. The product is multiplied by .001, a scale factor.

- the denominator is equal to the Annual Premium (P) plus the Cash Value at the end of the preceding policy year (CVP).

- the numerator is divided by the denominator and one is subtracted from this quotient to obtain the yearly rate of return.

10. Life insurance is provided a number of income tax benefits under the tax code. The cash value accumulates tax-free. If the policy is surrendered prior to a death claim, only the interest income (the difference in cost basis and cash value) is taxable. Life insurance policyowner dividends are received tax-free by the policyowner as these dividends are considered a refund of overpaid premium. The death benefit is received tax-free if taken as a lump sum. If the proceeds are paid through some type of annuity, then only the investment income is taxable. That portion of the periodic payment that represents a return of principal (death benefit) is received tax-free.

11. The gross estate includes the value of property you own when you die, plus one-half of the value of property owned jointly with a spouse, plus life insurance in which you have incidents of ownership, plus other property. This total can be reduced by funeral and administrative costs, estate settlement costs, probate costs, and charitable deductions.

2. Consumer experts typically make the following suggestions:

* determine if you need life insurance
* estimate the amount of life insurance you need
* decide on the best type of insurance for you
* decide whether you want a policy that pays dividends
* shop around for a low-cost policy
* consider the financial strength of the insurer
* deal with a competent agent

Multiple Choice Questions

1. (c) Of the methods listed, only the traditional net cost and the surrender cost provide a dollars and cents per thousand per year cost index. The traditional net cost method has numerous flaws, most notably the failure to consider the time value of money. The surrender cost is more meaningful.

2. (c) Both statements are true. Insurance is often shown to be free (to have a negative cost) because the time value of money is ignored.

3. (c) The grace period is not a consideration in the policy replacement decision as it is a standard provision in all life insurance contracts. The grace period does not influence whether a policy is a "good" policy or a "bad" policy. All of the other choices represent valid concerns when considering policy replacement.

4. (b) Karen calculated the Linton yield. The Linton yield is the average annual rate of return required to transform the savings portion of each premium payment into the guaranteed cash value at a specified time.

5. (d) An assumed price per thousand is used in the calculation. The cash value increase from one year to the next and dividends paid to the policyowner are considered. A rate of return, rather than a cost per thousand per year, is the result of the calculations.

6. (a) The surrender cost is based upon the assumption that the policy will be surrendered after a specified period and that the policyowner will receive the cash value at that time. The surrender cost index is an interest-adjusted technique because the time value of money is taken into consideration.

7. (c) The ratings assigned are sometimes unreliable and confusing. Some insurers that have become insolvent had favorable ratings from one or more of the rating services before the company became insolvent. Confusion may also develop because the ratings assigned are not standard among the rating services, and at least five different services assign ratings.

8. (a) Nathan should use the net payment cost index. Three of the choices listed provide a cost per thousand per year of life insurance. The traditional net cost method has many flaws, and the surrender cost index assumes the policy will be surrendered after a specified period. The Linton yield calculates a rate of return rather than a cost per thousand.

9. (b) The Linton yield does not determine a cost per thousand per year. Rather, an average annual rate of return is calculated. The premium must be divided into the cost of protection and savings to calculate the Linton yield.

10. (b) Policyowner dividends are received tax-free by the policyowner. Such dividends are considered to be a refund of overpaid premiums. If you are stockholder in a life insurance company, dividends you receive on your shares of stock are taxable. All of the other statements are true.

11. (b) The amount transferred to the surviving spouse is called the marital deduction.

12. (d) The best policy for you to purchase is the policy that best fits your needs.

True/False

1. **F** Comparing premiums will not tell you which policy is best. You must also consider what you receive in exchange for the premiums. For example, is the coverage participating and what is the guaranteed cash value after a specified period? There are factors besides cost that should also be considered, such as the financial strength of the insurer.

2. **F** There are wide variations in the cost of coverage. It is worthwhile to shop for a good policy because buying the wrong policy can cost you thousands of dollars over time, and it may be expensive to obtain coverage under a new policy.

3. **F** When an interest-adjusted method is used, the future value of each dividend payment is calculated assuming a specified interest rate. Thus the timing and magnitude of dividend payments are considered.

4. **T**

5. **T**

6. **F** The future value ordinary annuity factor assumes the premiums are paid at the end of the period. Life insurance premiums, like rent payments, are paid at the start of the period. The future value annuity due factor must be used to properly value the cash flows.

7. **F** The surrender cost index per thousand per year will always be less than the net payment cost per thousand per year for policies with a cash value. Under the surrender cost method, the cash value is subtracted from the net premiums and the resulting difference is converted to an annual cost. Under the net payment cost method, the net premiums are converted to an annual cost. Note that under the net payment cost method, the cash value is not subtracted from the net premiums.

8. **F** Belth's yearly rate-of-return method can be used for participating and nonparticipating policies. If nonparticipating policy is analyzed, a value of zero is assigned for the dividend term.

9. **T**

10. **T**

11. **T**

12. **T**

Problems

1. (a) The traditional net cost calculation:

Total premiums for 20 years (20 × 248.60)	$4,972.00
Less dividends for 20 years	− 814.00
Net premiums for 20 years	4,158.00
Less cash value after 20 years	− 4,314.20
Insurance cost for 20 years	−156.20
Net cost per year (−156.20/20)	− 7.81
Net cost per thousand per year (−7.81/20)	− 0.39

The traditional net cost is negative 39 cents per thousand dollars of coverage per year.

(b) Before the surrender cost can be calculated, the proper annuity factor must be determined. As shown in the solution to Short Answer question #4, the ordinary future value annuity factor must be adjusted to consider the fact that life insurance premiums are paid at the start of the year. To calculate the surrender cost and the net payment cost, the future value annuity due factor is required. This factor is the amount to which one dollar invested at the start of each year will become if credited with a specified interest rate.

The future value annuity due factor for 20 years, assuming 5 percent interest, is:

$$\left(\frac{(1.05)^{20} - 1}{.05} \right) \times 1.05 = 34.71925$$

Note that this factor, 34.719, is the same factor illustrated in Exhibits 13.2 and 13.3 in your text. The cost comparison in those illustrations also involves 20 years and 5 percent interest.

Many students, especially those who are business majors, use calculators with financial functions. The future value annuity due factor is easily obtained using a financial calculator. You can input: $1 as the Payment, 20 for N, and 5 Percent Interest, and then compute the Future Value.

If your calculator is in "ordinary annuity" mode, the resulting value you obtain is: 33.0660.

If you compound this value for one year at 5 percent (33.0660 × 1.05), you will get: 34.71925.

With this factor, we can calculate the surrender cost index:

Future value of the premiums (248.60 × 34.71925)	$8,631.21
Less future value of the dividends	− 1,163.00
Net premiums for 20 years	7,468.21
Less cash value after 20 years	− 4,314.20
Insurance cost for 20 years	3,154.01
Interest-adjusted cost per year: (3,154.01/34.71925)	90.84
Cost per thousand per year (90.84/20)	4.54

The surrender cost index is $4.54 per thousand per year.

(c) The net payment cost index calculation:

Future value of the premiums (248.60 × 34.71925)	$8,631.21
Less future value of the dividends	− 1,163.00
Net premiums for 20 years	7,468.21
Interest-adjusted cost per year: (7,468.21/34.71925)	215.10
Cost per thousand per year (215.10/20)	10.755

The net payment cost index is $10.755 per thousand per year.

2. (a) The probability of death at age 30, from the mortality table, is .00114. The expected value of the insurer's payment if the insured dies is $1.14 ($1,000 × .00114). The present value of this expected payment is $1.0806 ($1.14 × .9479). The NSP is $1.08 per thousand at age 30.

(b) A three-year term policy will require a single premium at the start of the coverage period. If death occurs during the period of coverage, the face value is paid at the end of the year in which death occurred. Death benefits can be paid at end of the first year, end of the second year, or end of the third year. The NSP is the sum of the discounted expected death payments. The NSP is $4.15 per thousand.

Age	Number Alive	Deaths	Probability of Death	Expected Payment	Discount Factor	PV of EV
38	9,707,516	13,979	.001440	1.440	.9479	1.3650
39		14,928	.001538	1.538	.8985	1.3819
40		15,970	.001645	1.645	.8516	1.4009
					NSP =	4.1478

Case Applications

Case 1

Jenny's follow-up question should be, "A-rated by whom?" At least four different organizations rate life insurance companies. As you can see in Exhibit 13.9 in your text, "A" is the third highest rating assigned by A.M. Best Company, the sixth highest rating assigned by Fitch, and the sixth highest rating assigned by Standard & Poor's. Simply knowing the rating without knowing who assigned the rating or the rating scale provides an incomplete picture. In addition, each of the rating services considers different aspects of an insurer's financial condition when assigning a rating. You should purchase a policy from an insurer that has received high ratings from several ratings services.

Case 2

John's sudden interest in rewarding long-term customers coincides with the publication of the unfavorable surrender cost index of his company's best-selling product. John's idea is to award a "persistency bonus" that will increase the cash value of the policy every 10 years. Consider what happens to the surrender cost index when the cash value is increased. If you review the calculation, you will see that as the cash value increases, the surrender cost index declines. John is only increasing the cash value at 10-year anniversaries. However, most cost comparisons are performed using 10-year multiples (10-year and 20-year surrender cost indexes are often quoted; 4-, 11-, and 17-year surrender cost indexes are not often quoted). While John is rewarding long-term policyowners, he is also making the surrender cost index appear more favorable in selected years.

Chapter 14
Annuities and Individual Retirement Accounts

Overview

Thus far we have examined life insurance in great detail. Life insurance companies market another product that addresses another important personal risk. That personal risk is the risk of outliving the income and assets that you have accumulated. The product that addresses this personal risk is called a life annuity. Life annuities provide periodic income to an individual for as long as he or she is living. These products help many retirees to achieve economic security. In addition to annuities, individuals have another retirement savings vehicle available to them. An individual may establish a tax-advantaged savings plan called an Individual Retirement Account (IRA). In this chapter we will examine the characteristics of individual annuities and IRAs (traditional and Roth). Group retirement plans and retirement plans for the self-employed are discussed in Chapter 17.

Learning Objectives

After studying this chapter, you should be able to:

Show how an annuity differs from life insurance.

Describe the basic characteristics of a fixed annuity and a variable annuity.

Explain the major characteristics of an equity-indexed annuity.

Describe the basic characteristics of a traditional tax-deductible individual retirement account (IRA).

Explain the basic characteristics of a Roth IRA.

Explain the income-tax treatment of a traditional IRA and a Roth IRA.

Define the following:

Accumulation period	Inflation indexed annuity option
Accumulation unit	Installment refund annuity
Annuitant	IRA rollover account
Annuity	Joint-and-survivor annuity option
Annuity settlement options	Life annuity (no refund)
Annuity unit	Life annuity with guaranteed payments
Cash refund annuity	Liquidation period
Deferred annuity	Nondeductible IRA
Equity-indexed annuity	Roth IRA
Exclusion ratio	Single-premium deferred annuity
Fixed annuity	Spousal IRA
Flexible-premium annuity	Traditional IRA
Immediate annuity	Variable annuity
Individual retirement account (IRA)	

■ Outline

I.   Individual Annuities

    A. Annuity Principle

II.   Types of Annuities

    A. Fixed Annuity

        1. Payment of Benefits

        2. Annuity Settlement Options

    B. Variable Annuity

        1. Basic Characteristics

        2. Guaranteed Death Benefit

        3. Fees and Expenses

    C. Equity-Indexed Annuity

        1. Participation Rate

        2. Cap on Maximum Percentage of Gain

        3. Indexing Method

        4. Guaranteed Minimum Value

III. Taxation of Individual Annuities

IV.   Individual Retirement Accounts

    A. Traditional IRA

        1. Eligibility Requirements

        2. Annual Contribution Limits

        3. Income Tax Deduction

        4. Spousal IRA

        5. Tax Penalty for Premature Distributions

        6. Taxation of Distributions

        7. Establishing a Traditional IRA

        8. IRA Investment

        9. IRA Rollover Account

    B. Roth IRA

        1. Income Limits

        2. Conversion to a Roth IRA

■ Short Answer Questions

1. Explain the annuity principle. Why is it said that annuities are the opposite of life insurance?

2. Explain the elements that comprise life annuity payments.

3. Differentiate between the accumulation period and the liquidation period of a fixed annuity.

4. Explain the life annuity (no refund), life annuity with guaranteed payments, and installment refund annuity settlement options.

5. Discuss the mechanics of a variable annuity.

6. Explain why an equity-indexed annuity is said to have characteristics of both a fixed annuity and a variable annuity.

7. Explain the tax treatment of the periodic annuity payments that a retiree receives from an individual annuity.

8. Are traditional IRA contributions fully income-tax deductible, partially deductible, or not deductible? Explain your answer.

9. Under what circumstances can withdrawals be made from a traditional IRA before age 59.5 without incurring the penalty tax?

0. How does a Roth IRA differ from a traditional IRA with respect to:

   (a) tax deductibility of contributions?

   (b) tax treatment of qualified distribution?

■ Multiple Choice Questions

Circle the letter that corresponds to the BEST *answer.*

1. Which of the following statements is (are) true with respect to annuities?
   I. Annuities pool the risk of premature death.
   II. Life annuities provide an income that the annuitant cannot outlive.

   (a) I only
   (b) II only
   (c) both I and II
   (d) neither I nor II

2. Income paid to an annuitant under a life annuity is comprised of all of the following EXCEPT:
   (a) interest earnings.
   (b) insurer expenses.
   (c) premiums paid.
   (d) unliquidated funds from those who die early.

3. Agnes, age 62, purchased an immediate annuity. The annuity will provide monthly payments to Agnes for as long as she lives. If Agnes dies before receiving payments for 10 years, the balance of these payments will go to a beneficiary. Agnes purchased a(n):
   (a) life annuity (no refund).
   (b) life annuity with guaranteed payments.
   (c) installment refund annuity.
   (d) joint-and-survivor annuity.

4. Which of the following statements is (are) true with respect to a joint and survivor annuity?
   I. Payments begin upon the death of the first annuitant.
   II. Payments end upon the death of the last annuitant.

   (a) I only
   (b) II only
   (c) both I and II
   (d) neither I nor II

5. Thomas wants to participate in the growth of the stock market through a deferred annuity; however, he wants downside protection against the loss of principal and prior investment earnings if the annuity is held to term. Thomas should purchase a(n):
   (a) equity-indexed annuity.
   (b) variable annuity.
   (c) fixed annuity.
   (d) life income (no refund) annuity.

6. Rochelle is preparing to do her taxes. To determine what percentage of her individual annuity income was taxable and not taxable, Rochelle divided her investment in the contract by the total of the expected payments that she will receive through the annuity. This quotient is called the:
   (a) percentage participation.
   (b) break-even point.
   (c) coinsurance percentage.
   (d) exclusion ratio.

7. All of the following statements about traditional IRAs are true EXCEPT:
   (a) No traditional IRA contributions are allowed for the tax year in which the participant attains age 70.5 (seventy and one-half) or for any later year.
   (b) If pretax contributions fund the IRA, the entire distribution is taxable.
   (c) Everyone is eligible to establish a traditional IRA and make fully tax-deductible contributions.
   (d) IRA funds can be invested in stocks, bonds, mutual funds, and certificates of deposit.

8. Which of the following statements is true regarding a traditional IRA?
   I. Contributions may be fully deductible, partially deductible, or not deductible.
   II. In certain circumstances, withdrawals are permitted before age 59.5 without triggering the penalty tax.
   (a) I only
   (b) II only
   (c) both I and II
   (d) neither I nor II

9. Kathy would like to save for retirement. She selected a plan through which she can make a limited contribution each year. Her contribution is not tax deductible, however the investment income accumulates income tax-free, and qualified distributions from the plan are not taxed. Kathy is funding a(n):
   (a) variable annuity.
   (b) Roth IRA.
   (c) traditional IRA.
   (d) equity-indexed annuity.

0. Some employers make a lump-sum distribution of pension assets to workers who are terminating employment. To avoid receiving the account assets directly and having to pay taxes on the money, the funds may be deposited tax-free into a special account. Such an account is called a(n):
   (a) spousal IRA account.
   (b) Roth IRA account.
   (c) Section 401-k account.
   (d) IRA rollover account.

True/False

ircle the T if the statement is true, the F if the statement is false. Explain to yourself why a statement false.

F   1. The fundamental purpose of a life annuity is to provide an income that cannot be outlived.

F   2. It is impossible for an insurer to make a profit by selling a refund annuity.

F   3. Annuities can be funded through a single premium or through multiple premiums.

F   4. During the funding period, a variable annuity purchaser is credited with annuity units.

F   5. A key advantage of variable annuities is that insurers marketing these products do not charge fees on these annuities.

F   6. Equity-indexed annuities provide downside protection against the loss of investment income if the annuity is held to term.

T   F   7.   Income from individual annuities is received tax-free by the annuitant at retirement.

T   F   8.   Roth IRA contributions are tax-deductible regardless of a person's income and whether or no he or she is covered by an employer-sponsored retirement account.

T   F   9.   Most spouses who do not work outside of the home can make a fully deductible contribution to a traditional IRA even through their spouse is covered under a retirement plan at work.

T   F   10.   Qualified distributions from traditional IRAs are received income tax-free after age 59.5.

T   F   11.   Qualified distributions from Roth IRAs are received income tax-free after age 59.5.

T   F   12.   In some cases, qualified distributions from Roth IRAs can be made before age 59.5.

■ Case Applications

Case 1

Andrea is considering the purchase of an annuity. She was surprised to learn about all of the annuity options that are available. She is also wondering how annuity income will be taxed upon her retirement.

(a)   Differentiate between:

   1.   Immediate and deferred annuities:

   2.   Single premium annuities and flexible premium annuities:

   3.   The life income no refund, life annuity with guaranteed payments, and installment refund annuit settlement options:

b) Assume that Andrea invests $120,000 in the annuity. At the time she begins to receive monthly distributions of $1,000, her life expectancy is 20 years. What is Andrea's exclusion ratio for this annuity?

Case 2

Which IRA (traditional or Roth) would you recommend in the two scenarios described below?

a) Charlene is single and will earn $36,000 this year. She is not eligible to participate in her employer's pension plan until next year.

b) Vern is concerned that all of his retirement distributions will be taxable once he starts to receive the money. Vern earns $90,000 per year and is covered under his employer's qualified retirement plan.

Solutions to Chapter 14

Short Answer Questions

1. Annuities pool the risk of excessive longevity in order to provide an income that cannot be outlived. By pooling the risk of excessive longevity, insurers offering annuities are able to continue payments to those who live far beyond life expectancy. Some individuals in the pool will die early, freeing up the unliquidated portion of their premiums to assist the insurer in continuing to make payments to those who live far beyond life expectancy.

Life insurance and life annuities can be viewed as opposites as one provides protection against the adverse financial consequences of premature death while the other provides protection against the adverse financial consequences of excessive longevity. Life insurance creates an immediate pool of funds while life annuities are a means through which a pool of funds is systematically liquidated.

2. Life annuity payments are comprised of three elements. First, there is a return of premiums that wer paid for the annuity. Second, there is interest income that was earned on the funds invested by the insurer. Finally, some life annuitants die before receiving back from the insurer what they paid for tl annuity. This third component is unliquidated principal of annuitants who die early.

3. The accumulation period of an annuity is the time when premiums are being paid and/or interest is being earned on the premiums paid to the insurer. This period is the time before the insurer begins t make payments to the annuitant. During the liquidation (payout) period, the insurer is making periodic payments back to the annuitant.

4. There are a number of settlement options for life annuities:

    *   The life annuity (no refund) provides the highest periodic income payment to the annuitant. This annuity provides no guarantees. Payments are made until the annuitant dies, and upon death of tl annuitant, payments end.

    *   The life annuity with guaranteed payments is a life annuity that promises that at least a specified number of payments will be made. For example, under a life income with 10 years for certain annuity, the insurer promises that payments will be made for at least 10 years. If the annuitant di before receiving the minimum number of guaranteed payments, a beneficiary will receive the balance of the guaranteed payments. After the guarantee period, the annuity is just like any othe life annuity—the insurer continues to make payments until the annuitant dies.

    *   The installment refund annuity is a life annuity that promises the insurer will pay out at least the total of the premiums paid for the annuity. Under this type of annuity, if the annuitant dies befor receiving from the insurer at least what was paid in premiums, annuity payments continue to a beneficiary until at least what was paid for the annuity has been paid out by the insurer. After the insurer has paid out an amount equal to the premiums, the annuity is just like any other life annuity.

5. Variable annuities can be funded through a lump sum contribution or through periodic installment premiums. During the funding period, the purchaser is credited with accumulation units. The value accumulation units fluctuates with the performance of the securities in the portfolio supporting the annuity. During the funding period, the purchaser continues to buy accumulation units. At retiremen the accumulation units are converted to annuity units. The purchaser will have a fixed number of annuity units throughout retirement, however the value of the units, and hence the periodic income distribution, will fluctuate with the value of the investment portfolio supporting the annuity.

6. An equity-indexed annuity provides the possibility of earning a higher, variable rate of return with downside risk protection as the return can never drop below a specified fixed interest rate. The annuity value is linked to the performance of a stock market index. If the stock market rises, the annuity is credited with a portion of the investment gain (e.g., 80 percent of the return, up to a specified cap). If the stock market declines, the annuity earns at least a minimum return, which typically is 3 percent on 90 percent of the principal invested. So while the annuity can profit from superior investment performance like a variable annuity, it also provides a minimum guaranteed interest rate, like a fixed annuity, when investment performance is unfavorable.

7. Premiums for individual annuities are not income-tax deductible and are paid with after-tax dollars. The investment income, however, is tax-deferred and accumulates free of taxes until the funds are distributed. The portion of an annuity distribution that is investment income is taxed as ordinary income. The portion of the payment that is a return of premiums is received tax-free. To determine the portion received tax-free and the taxable portion, it is necessary to calculate an exclusion ratio. The formula for the exclusion ratio is total annuity premiums paid divided by the expected payment to be received. This value is determined by multiplying the periodic income by life expectancy. If th exclusion ratio is multiplied by the periodic income payment, the resulting value is the nontaxable amount. The balance of the payment is taxable. Once the total investment in the annuity has been recouped, the entire annuity distribution is taxable.

8. Traditional IRA contributions may be fully taxdeductible, partially tax-deductible, or not tax-deductible:

   - to be fully tax-deductible, the worker must not be an active participant in an employer-sponsored retirement plan. Such a worker can make a fully deductible IRA contribution. Even if the worker is covered by an employer-sponsored plan, a deduction is permitted if the worker's modified adjusted gross income is below a specified amount.

   - if the modified adjusted gross income is within a threshold band, a partially tax-deductible IRA traditional IRA contribution can be made.

   - no deduction is permitted for taxpayers who have a modified adjusted gross income in excess of the phase-out deduction limit. Such taxpayers, however, should consider making a contribution to a Roth IRA if they are eligible.

9. The penalty tax doesn't apply if the distribution results from any of the following: death of the individual, disability of the individual, substantially equal payments paid over the life expectancy of the individual, portions of any distribution representing nondeductible contributions, distributions used to pay medical expenses that exceed 7.5 percent of adjusted gross income, distributions used to pay medical insurance premiums if the worker is separated from employment, distributions used to pay qualified higher-education expenses, and qualified acquisition costs for a first-time home buyer (maximum of $10,000).

0. (a) As discussed in question #8, traditional IRA contributions may be fully deductible, partially deductible, or not deductible. The contributions made to a Roth IRA are never tax-deductible.

   (b) Distributions from traditional IRAs are taxed as ordinary income except for any nondeductible IRA contributions, which are received income-tax free. Under a Roth IRA, after-tax contributions are made and investment income accumulates tax-free. If certain requirements are met, the entire distribution is received free of taxes.

Multiple Choice Questions

1. (b) Only the second statement is true. Annuities do not pool the risk of premature death. Annuities pool the risk of excessive longevity. Life annuities continue to make payments for as long as the annuitant is alive.

2. (b) Insurer expenses are not part of life annuity payments. Annuity payments are comprised of a return of premiums paid, interest, and unliquidated funds from annuitants who die early.

3. (b) Agnes purchased a life annuity with guaranteed payments. In this case, the insurer has promised to make at least 120 payments (10 years × 12 months).

4. (b) Only the second statement is true. Payments do not begin upon the death of the first annuitant. Payments are made jointly to the annuitants and continue until the last annuitant has died.

5. (a) An equity-indexed annuity will accomplish the goals that Thomas has set forth. He has the downside protection of a guaranteed minimum return, while he still has the potential of earning higher equity returns.

6. (d) Rochelle calculated the exclusion ratio. The ratio tells her what percentage of the individual annuity distribution she can exclude from taxation as it represents a return of premiums paid for the annuity. The balance (the amount not excluded) is fully taxable.

7. (c)   There are eligibility rules for establishing a traditional IRA. Contributions may be fully, partially, or not deductible, depending on an individual's income and whether he or she is covered under an employer's retirement plan.

8. (c)   Both statements are true. Depending on the eligibility status of the contributor and his or her income level, the contribution may be fully deductible, partially deductible, or not deductible. There are a number of situations in which distributions may be taken from traditional IRAs before age 59.5 without triggering the 10 percent penalty tax.

9. (b)   Kathy is funding a Roth IRA. After-tax contributions are used, but qualified distributions from Roth IRAs after age 59.5 are received tax-free.

10. (d)   Distributions made to an IRA rollover account do not result in current taxation.

True/False

1. **T**

2. **F** While it is true that the insurer will pay an amount that is at least equal to the premiums paid for the annuity, the issue is timing. The repayment of all of the money paid for the annuity may take many years. At the same time, however, the insurer will be investing the funds and earning investment income on the premiums.

3. **T**

4. **F** During the funding period, the variable annuity purchaser is credited with accumulation units, no annuity units.

5. **F** Insurers marketing variable annuities charge a variety of fees and expenses, including manageme fees, administrative fees, surrender charges, and expense charges.

6. **T**

7. **F** A portion of the distribution, the amount that is attributable to a return of premiums paid, is received tax-free. The balance, which is investment income, is fully taxable. After the basis in the annuity has been recovered, the entire distribution becomes taxable income.

8. **F** Roth IRA contributions are never tax-deductible. Roth IRA contributions are made with after-tax dollars, but the distributions at retirement are received tax-free.

9. **T**

10. **F** If pretax dollars are used to fund traditional IRAs, distributions from traditional IRAs at retireme are fully taxable. If any after-tax contributions were used to fund the traditional IRA, the portion of the distribution attributable to the after-tax contribution is received tax-free.

11. **T**

12. **T**

Case Applications

Case 1

(a) 1. Immediate annuities begin to make payments to the annuitant in the period after the annuity is purchased. For example, a retiree may give a life insurance company $50,000 in exchange for an annuity and begin to receive payments from the life insurer in the following month. A deferred annuity begins more than one period after the premium was paid. For example, an annuity purchaser age 30 may pay premiums over 20 years, then stop paying premiums, and begin to receive payments from the insurer at age 65.

2. Single premium annuities are funded through one, lump-sum premium. Flexible premium annuities are funded through premiums paid over a number of years. Often level installment premiums are used to fund an annuity.

3. A life income, no refund annuity has no special guarantees for the annuitant. Payments are made until the annuitant dies. If the annuitant dies after receiving only one or two payments, there are no refunds or guaranteed payments. A life annuity with guaranteed payments promises to make at least a specified number of payments. For example, life income with 10 years for certain promises to make at least 120 monthly payments. If the annuitant dies before receiving all 120 payments, the balance of the promised payments is paid to a beneficiary. An installment refund annuity promises that the amount paid by the insurer will be at least the sum of the premiums paid for the annuity. So if the annuitant has received payments totaling $100,000 when he or she dies, and $120,000 was paid for the annuity, payments will continue to a beneficiary until the additional $20,000 has been paid out by the insurer.

(b) Andrea's exclusion ratio is 50 percent as shown below:

$$\frac{\$120,000 \text{ in premiums}}{\$240,000 \text{ in expected payments}} = 50 \text{ percent exclusion ratio}$$

The $240,000 in the denominator was obtained by multiplying $1,000 per month by 12 months and 20 years ($1,000 \times 12 \times 20 = $240,000).

So Andrea can exclude 50 percent of the annual annuity income from taxation because it represents a return of premiums. Once the return of premiums equals $120,000, then the entire annual annuity distribution becomes fully taxable.

Case 2

(a) A traditional IRA makes sense for Charlene. Given that Charlene is not covered under her employer's retirement plan and her income does not exceed the limit, she can make a fully deductible traditional IRA contribution. The contribution will reduce her current taxable income and accumulate on a tax-deferred basis.

(b) Vern does not qualify for a tax-advantaged traditional IRA contribution—his income is too high and he is covered under a qualified retirement plan through his employer. Vern can, however, make a contribution to a Roth IRA using after-tax dollars. Although the contribution is made with after-tax dollars, the IRA accumulates on a tax-deferred basis. If certain rules are satisfied, Vern's entire distribution from the Roth IRA will be received tax-free when he retires.

Chapter 15
Individual Health Insurance Coverages

■ Overview

In this chapter we examine individual health insurance coverage. After a discussion of major problems with the present health care system, the various forms of individual health insurance are examined. The most important individual health coverages include: hospital-surgical insurance, major medical insurance, medical savings accounts, long-term care insurance, and disability income insurance. Next, important policy provisions found in individual health insurance coverage are examined. Finally, a number of important guidelines are discussed for purchasing individual health insurance coverage.

Learning Objectives

After studying this chapter, you should be able to:

• Explain the major health care problems in the United States.
• Explain the basic characteristics of individual major medical insurance.
  Describe the key characteristics of long-term care insurance.
• Identify the basic characteristics of health savings accounts.
• Describe the major characteristics of disability-income insurance contracts.
  Describe the guidelines to follow when purchasing individual health insurance.
• Define the following:

Accident-only policy	Limited policy
Activities of daily living (ADLs)	Long-term care insurance
Benefit period	Major medical insurance
Benefit trigger	Noncancellable policy
Calendar-year deductible	Nonrenewable for stated reasons only
Cancer policy	Optionally renewable policy
Coinsurance provision	Partial disability
Common-accident provision	Preexisting-conditions clause
Disability-income insurance	Preferred provider
Elimination (waiting) period	Reasonable and customary charges
Exclusionary rider	Reinstatement provision
Family deductible	Residual disability
Grace period	Schedule approach
Guaranteed renewable policy	Stop-loss limit
Health savings accounts	Time limit on certain defenses
Hospital indemnity policy	Total disability
Internal limits	Waiver of premium provision

■ Outline

I.   Health Care Problems in the United States

A. Rising Health Care Expenditures

B. Large Number of Uninsured People

C. Uneven Quality of Medical Care

D. Considerable Waste and Inefficiency

II.   Individual Health Insurance Coverages

A. Hospital-Surgical Insurance
   1. Hospital Expenses
   2. Surgical Expenses
   3. Outpatient Services
   4. Physicians' Visits

B. Major Medical Insurance
   1. Broad Coverage
   2. High Maximum Limits
   3. Benefit Period
   4. Deductible
   5. Coinsurance
   6. Exclusions

C. Health Savings Accounts
   1. Eligibility Requirements
   2. High Deductible Health Plan
   3. Contribution Limits
   4. Favorable Tax Treatment
   5. Rationale for HSAs

D. Long-Term Care Insurance
   1. Chance of Entering a Nursing Home
   2. Basic Characteristics

E. Disability-Income Insurance
   1. Meaning of Total Disability
   2. Benefit Period
   3. Elimination Period
   4. Waiver of Premium
   5. Rehabilitation Provision
   6. Accidental Death, Dismemberment, and Loss-of-Sight Benefits
   7. Optional Disability-Income Benefits

III. Individual Medical Expense Contractual Provisions

   A. Renewal Provisions

   B. Preexisting-Conditions Clause

   C. Notice of Ten-Day Right to Examine Policy

   D. Claims

   E. Grace Period

   F. Reinstatement

   G. Time Limit on Certain Defenses

IV. Shopping for Individual Health Insurance

   A. Insure for the Catastrophic Loss

   B. Consider Group Health Insurance First

   C. Purchase a Policy that has a Preferred Provider Network

   D. Don't Ignore Disability-Income Insurance

   E. Avoid Limited Policies

   F. Watch Out for Restrictive Provisions and Exclusions

   G. Use Deductibles and Elimination Periods to Reduce Premiums

■ Short Answer Questions

1. What are the major problems associated with the current health care system in the United States?

2. What are the most important types of individual health insurance coverage?

3. What are the two basic approaches for paying the daily room and board benefit under hospital expense insurance? What other benefit is provided under this coverage?

4. What are the typical characteristics of individual major medical insurance policies?

5. How does the coinsurance (percentage participation) provision operate in major medical insurance?

6. What is a health savings account (HSA)? Who is eligible to establish an HSA?

7. What are the basic characteristics of long-term care insurance?

8. Why do insurers marketing disability income coverage typically limit the amount of income replacement to no more than 60 to 80 percent of gross earnings? How is total disability defined in disability income insurance?

9. What is a renewal provision and why is the renewal provision important?

10. Carla purchased a basic health insurance policy. A number of questions have developed with regard to the coverage. Which policy provision should Carla review for clarification?

    (a) Her insurer denied a claim because Carla lied on the application. Carla does not believe the insurer has the right to deny the claim.

    (b) Carla was treated for high blood pressure three months before purchasing the coverage. Her insurer denied a claim for treatment of high blood pressure two months after Carla purchased the policy.

    (c) Carla received a notice from her health insurer that her premium would increase and that if she did not pay the higher premium, the coverage would not be renewed. Carla does not believe the insurer has the right to raise premiums or not renew her coverage.

    (d) Carla forgot to pay the premium that was due last week. She wonders if she can still pay the premium and have coverage in force.

1. What suggestions do consumer experts offer when shopping for individual health insurance?

■ Multiple Choice Questions

Circle the letter that corresponds to the BEST answer.

1. All of the following are methods of compensating surgeons under a surgical expense policy EXCEPT:
    (a) schedule approach.
    (b) surgeon's discretion.
    (c) reasonable and customary charges.
    (d) none of the above.

2. Which statement is true with regard to individual major medical insurance?
    I.   The coverage provided is broad in scope.
    II. Major medical insurance plans emphasize first-dollar coverage by the insurer.

    (a) I only
    (b) II only
    (c) both I and II
    (d) neither I nor II

3. Susan's health insurance coverage cannot be canceled, is guaranteed renewable to age 65, and under no circumstances can her premium rate be increased. What type of renewal provision is found in Susan's health insurance coverage?
    (a) renewable at the insurer's option
    (b) conditionally renewable
    (c) guaranteed renewable
    (d) noncancellable

4. All of the following are major problems with the health care system in the United States EXCEPT:
   (a) rising health care expenditures.
   (b) waste and inefficiency.
   (c) uneven quality of medical care.
   (d) too many people covered under the present system.

5. Ted's health insurance lapsed because he didn't pay the premium on time. Ted wants the coverage back in force. Which policy provision explains the requirements he must satisfy to place the coverag back in force?
   (a) time limit on certain defenses
   (b) renewal provision
   (c) reinstatement provision
   (d) claims provision

6. All of the following are characteristics of health savings accounts (HSAs) EXCEPT:
   (a) contributions to a qualified HSA are income tax-deductible.
   (b) there is no annual contribution limit to an HAS.
   (c) HSAs are used in conjunction with a high deductible health plan.
   (d) HSA investment income accumulates income tax-free and distributions are tax-free if used to pa qualified medical expenses.

7. Which statement is true with regard to long-term care insurance?
   I.   This coverage is not needed if you are covered under Medicare.
   II. Coverage is typically provided for skilled nursing care and custodial care.
   (a) I only
   (b) II only
   (c) both I and II
   (d) neither I nor II

8. Health insurance typically includes a two-year discovery period after which the insurer can't void coverage or deny a claim because of concealment or misrepresentation by the applicant. This provision is called:
   (a) the time limit on certain defenses provision.
   (b) the recurrent disability provision.
   (c) the renewal provision.
   (d) the reinstatement provision.

9. All of the following are characteristics of major medical insurance EXCEPT:
   (a) coinsurance (percentage participation).
   (b) deductibles.
   (c) high limits.
   (d) no exclusions.

0. All of the following are characteristics of long-term care insurance EXCEPT:
   (a) benefit triggers used to determine eligibility for benefits.
   (b) inflation protection.
   (c) elimination periods.
   (d) unlimited benefits.

1. Which statement is true with regard to disability-income insurance?
   I. An increase in the elimination period will decrease the premium.
   II. Disability can be defined in a number of ways.

   (a) I only
   (b) II only
   (c) both I and II
   (d) neither I nor II

2. Tina's health insurance coverage includes a provision that excludes from coverage physical or mental conditions that existed prior to issuance of the policy and were not disclosed on the application. This provision is the:
   (a) preexisting-conditions clause.
   (b) second injury clause.
   (c) recurrent disability clause.
   (d) renewal provision.

■ True/False

Circle the T if the statement is true, the F if the statement is false. Explain to yourself why a statement is false.

T F 1. Hospital expense insurance provides coverage for miscellaneous expenses, such as laboratory charges and X-rays.

T F 2. The economic loss from long-term total disability can be greater than the economic loss that results from premature death.

T F 3. The guaranteed renewable renewal provision provides the greatest security to a health insurance purchaser.

T F 4. Long-term care insurance is expensive.

T F 5. Although the United States spends a significant percentage of gross domestic product on health care, not everyone has health insurance coverage.

T F 6. Disability income insurance usually replaces all of a disabled person's lost income.

T F 7. Consumer experts agree that dread disease policies are a wise purchase.

T F 8. Under a common accident provision in major medical insurance, only one deductible must be paid if two family members are injured in the same accident.

T F 9. Residual disability refers to whether a second disability is considered a continuation of a prior disability or considered a new disability.

T   F   10.   Physicians' visits insurance pays for surgical and nonsurgical care provided by a physician.

T   F   11.   A single, uniform definition of disability is used in all disability income policies.

T   F   12.   High deductible health savings account plans limit annual out-of-pocket expenses.

■ Case Applications

Case 1

Sarah purchased a major medical insurance policy that included a $250 deductible and an 80-20 coinsurance (percentage participation) provision. She required medical care and the cost of the care provided was $40,750. How much of this amount must Sarah pay and how much will her insurer pay? How would your answer change if Sarah's policy included a $3,000 stop-loss limit that applied to coinsurance payments?

Case 2

Mark works for a company that does not provide any group health insurance benefits to its employees. Mark is the Treasurer and earns $160,000 per year. Although covered by workers compensation and Social Security, Mark is considering the purchase of a private disability income policy. A number of questions have arisen with respect to the purchase of the coverage. How would you respond to the following questions/concerns?

(a)   Mark wonders if the coverage is really necessary because he is covered by workers compensation and Social Security.

b) Mark asked an agent to quote the premium for complete replacement of his work earnings as soon as Mark is disabled. The premium was much higher than Mark anticipated. How can he reduce the premium?

c) Mark wonders how sick or badly injured he must be in order to collect benefits under a disability income policy. He is convinced that if he is sick or injured, regardless of the severity of the impairment, the insurer will say that he is not eligible to collect benefits.

■ Solutions to Chapter 15

Short Answer Questions

1. There are many problems with the present health care system in the United States. The major problems include: rising health care expenditures, large number of uninsured people, uneven quality of medical care, and considerable waste and inefficiency.

2. The most important types of individual health insurance are: hospital-surgical insurance, major medical insurance, health savings accounts, long-term care insurance, and disability income insurance.

3. The first method of paying the room and board benefit is an indemnity plan. Here the actual charges are paid up to a maximum daily limit. The second approach is the use of service benefits. Such plans provide a description of the service covered, such as the full cost of a semi-private room for a specified number of days.

   The second benefit provided under hospital expense coverage is miscellaneous hospital expenses. This coverage pays for X-rays, inpatient drugs, laboratory fees, and other benefits.

4. A typical individual major medical insurance policy has the following characteristics: broad coverage, high maximum limits, a benefit period during which benefits are paid after the deductible is satisfied, deductibles, coinsurance (percentage participation), and some exclusions.

5. The coinsurance provision in major medical insurance is simply the cost sharing percentages after the deductible has been met. If the major medical plan includes an 80-20 coinsurance provision, the insurer pays 80 percent of covered medical expenses after the deductible has been satisfied and the insured pays the other 20 percent. Case 1 illustrates a major medical coinsurance settlement.

6. A health savings account (HSA) is a tax-exempt or custodial account established exclusively for the purpose of paying qualified medical expenses of the account beneficiary who is covered under a high-deductible health insurance plan. Certain requirements must be met to be eligible to establish an HSA. First, you must be covered by a high deductible health plan and no other comprehensive plan that is not a high deductible plan. Second, you must not be eligible for Medicare benefits. Finally, you must not be claimed as a dependent on someone else's tax return.

7. The basic characteristics of long-term care insurance include: coverage for skilled nursing, intermediate nursing care, and custodial care; choice of benefits; an elimination period; a benefits trigger tied to activities of daily living and cognitive impairment, inflation protection, the coverage is guaranteed renewable, premiums are high, and long-term care insurance receives favorable income tax treatment.

8. Insurers limit the replacement of income under disability income policies to prevent overinsurance and to reduce moral hazard and malingering. In addition, some work-related expenses do not continue in the case of disability.

   Total disability can be defined in several ways. Common definitions include: inability to perform all duties of your job or occupation, inability to perform duties of any occupation for which you are reasonably suited by education and experience, inability to perform duties of gainful employment, and some insurers define total disability in term of the loss of income after the illness or injury.

9. A renewal provision specifies under what conditions the coverage can be renewed and if the insurer can raise the premium for the coverage. A number of different renewal provisions are found in individual health insurance plans. As this provision specifies the conditions for coverage continuation and the cost of coverage, it is a critical issue.

10. (a) Carla should review the time limit on the certain defenses provision. Under this provision, the insurer can deny claims based on concealment and misrepresentation during the first two years of coverage.
    (b) Carla should review the preexisting conditions clause in the policy. Through this clause, the insurer can avoid liability for conditions present when the coverage went into effect.
    (c) Carla should review the renewal provision included in her health insurance policy. Depending on the provision, the insurer may be well within its rights to increase the premium and to not renew her policy.
    (d) As the premium was due last week, Carla is protected through the grace period provision. This mandatory provision typically extends coverage for up to 31 days if the premium payment is late.

11. Consumer experts offer the following suggestions when shopping for individual health insurance coverage:
    - insure for the catastrophic loss
    - consider group health insurance first
    - purchase a policy that has a preferred provider network
    - don't ignore disability-income insurance
    - avoid limited policies
    - watch out for restrictive policy provisions and exclusions
    - use deductibles and elimination periods to reduce premiums

Multiple Choice Questions

1. (b)   Compensation for the surgeon is not left to the surgeon's discretion. Surgical schedules and reasonable and customary charges may be used to determine the compensation for surgical procedures.

2. (a)   Only the first statement is true. Major medical coverage is broad in scope. Major medical insurance does not emphasize first-dollar coverage. Indeed, there are several types of deductibles used in major medical plans.

3. (d)   Susan's health insurance policy contains the most favorable and most expensive renewal provision. This type of renewal provision is called "noncancellable."

4. (d)   Lack of coverage, rather than "too many people covered," is a major problem. Millions of Americans have no health insurance coverage.

5. (c)   An explanation of how to put lapsed coverage back in force is provided in the reinstatement provision.

6. (b)   There are annual contribution limits to HSAs. The limits apply to individuals and to family coverage plans. The limits are indexed each year for inflation.

7. (b)   Only the second statement is true. Medicare only covers skilled care for a limited time per benefit period and custodial care is excluded. Private long-term care plans typically cover skilled care, intermediate nursing care, and custodial care.

8. (a)   The time limit on certain defenses provision provides for a two-year discovery period. This provision is similar to the incontestable clause in life insurance.

9. (d)   Major medical insurance policies contain a number of common exclusions. Major medical plans typically have the other characteristics listed (coinsurance, deductibles, and high limits).

10. (d)   Benefits are limited under most long-term care policies. There are daily limits, such as $100 or $120 per day; and a limit placed on benefits paid over the insured's lifetime, such as $250,000 or $500,000.

11. (c)   Both statements are true. If you increase the elimination period, it increases the time period you must wait to receive benefits. This change is analogous to increasing the size of a deductible. There are several definitions of disability used in private disability insurance coverages.

12. (a)   Such a provision is called a preexisting conditions clause.

True/False

1. **T**

2. **T**

3. **F** Although the coverage is guaranteed renewable, the insurer can increase premiums for the entire underwriting class. The noncancellable renewal provision provides coverage that is guaranteed renewable until a specified age and also specifies that the premium cannot be increased.

4. **T**

5. **T**

6. **F** Disability-income insurance typically replaces less than all of the disabled person's lost income. Most insurers limit the amount of income replaced to no more than 60 to 80 percent of the person's gross earnings. Replacing less than the full amount of lost income reduces moral hazard and provide an incentive to recover and to return to work.

7. **F** Dread disease policies (e.g., cancer insurance) are not recommended by consumer experts. These policies are narrow, providing benefits only if you have the "correct" illness.

8. **T**

9. **F** Residual disability refers to a reduction in earnings because of the accident or sickness once the worker is able to return to the work force.

10. **F** A physicians' visits insurance provides coverage for nonsurgical care only.

11. **F** There are variations in the definition of disability. That is why it is important to review the definition of disability before you purchase coverage.

12. **T**

Case Applications

Case 1

With the deductible, Sarah is responsible for the first $250 of covered medical expenses. Then the remaining expenses are shared on an 80 percent/20 percent basis:

Eligible Medical Expenses	$40,750	
Deductible (Sarah Pays)	–250	
Expenses to be Shared	$40,500	
	The insurer pays 80% of this amount $32,400.	Sarah pay 20% of this amount, $8,100.

So Sarah would pay a total of $8,350 ($8,100 + $250), and the insurer would pay $32,400.

As $8,350 is a large out-of-pocket expense, many major medical insurance policies contain a stop-loss limit. This provision caps out-of-pocket expenses of the insured at a specified amount after the deductible is satisfied. If the policy included a $3,000 stop-loss limit that applies to coinsurance, Sarah would pay only $3,250 ($3,000 plus the deductible), and the insurer would pay the balance.

Case 2

(a) Private disability income insurance is a necessary coverage. It provides benefits in case of nonoccupational disability. Workers compensation will pay for work-related illness and injury only. Social Security uses a harsh definition of disability and requires serving a 5-month waiting period before benefits are paid. An individual disability income policy would be a wise purchase for Mark.

b)   Mark can get a lower premium by reducing the level of income replaced, for example, 75 percent or 80 percent income replacement. He can also include an elimination (waiting) period in the contract. The elimination period is a period of time after the disability occurs during which no benefits are paid. The longer the elimination period, the lower the premium.

c)   Whether Mark will be able to collect benefits under the disability policy will be determined by his condition and the definition of disability stated in the policy. If Mark satisfies the definition of disability stated in the policy, he should be able to collect disability income benefits. Several different definitions of disability are used. For example, disability may be defined in terms of your current job, any job you could perform based on your training and experience, etc.

Chapter 16
Employee Benefits: Group Life and Health Insurance

Overview

This chapter and the next chapter are devoted to employee benefits. Employee benefits are often taken for granted and you may be surprised by the magnitude of these plans. Each year the U.S. Chamber of Commerce surveys employers about their employee benefit plans. The Chamber uses a broad definition of employee benefits, including social insurance (social security, workers compensation, and unemployment insurance), payment for time not worked, private insurance (life, health, and disability), retirement plans, and other benefits. Using the broad definition, the average employer spends about an additional 40 percent of payroll on employee benefits. Employee benefits are an important part of total compensation and are important in assisting employees, their dependents, and retirees in achieving financial security.

In this chapter, we examine group life and health insurance coverages. As an introduction, group insurance underwriting principles and eligibility requirements are discussed. Next, group life and health insurance coverages are examined, as well as group health insurance providers, managed care plans, and group health insurance policy provisions. The chapter closes with a discussion of cafeteria plans.

Learning Objectives

After studying this chapter, you should be able to:

Explain the underwriting principles followed in group insurance.

Describe the basic characteristics of group term life insurance.

Explain the major characteristics of the following group medical expense plans: group basic medical expense insurance, major medical insurance, and dental insurance.

Show how short-term group disability income plans differ from group long-term disability plans.

Describe the basic characteristics of the following managed care plans: health maintenance organizations (HMOs), preferred provider organizations (PPOs), and point-of-service plans (POS).

Describe the major characteristics of cafeteria plans.

Define the following:

Basic medical expense insurance

Blue Cross and Blue Shield plans

Cafeteria plans

Calendar-year deductible

Capitation fee

COBRA law

Coinsurance provision

Comprehensive major medical insurance

Consumer-driven health plans (CDHP)

Contributory plan

Coordination-of-benefits provision

Corridor deductible

Defined contribution health plan

Eligibility period

Experience rating

Family deductible provision

Flexible spending account

Gatekeeper physician

Group accidental death and dismemberment insurance (AD&D)

Group dental insurance

Group disability-income insurance

Group medical expense insurance

Group term life insurance

Group universal life insurance

Health Insurance Portability and
  Accountability Act (HIPAA)

Health maintenance organization (HMO)

Health savings account (HSA)

High deductible health plan

Hospital expense insurance

Individual practice association (IPA) plan

Major medical insurance

Managed care

Master contract

Noncontributory plan

Nonoccupational disability

Nonscheduled dental insurance plan
  (comprehensive dental insurance)

Point-of-service (POS) plan

Portability

Preexisting condition

Preferred provider organization (PPO)

Probationary period

Reasonable and customary charges

Scheduled dental insurance plan

Self-insurance (self-funding)

Service benefits

Stop-loss limit

Supplemental major medical insurance

Surgical expense insurance

Traditional indemnity plan (fee-for-serice)

Voluntary accidental death and dismemberment
  insurance

■ Outline

I. Group Insurance

A. Basic Underwriting Principles

1. Insurance Incidental to the Group
2. Flow of Persons through the Group
3. Automatic Determination of Benefits
4. Minimum Participation Requirements
5. Third-party Sharing of Cost
6. Simple and Efficient Administration

B. Eligibility Requirements in Group Insurance

1. Eligible Groups
2. Eligibility Requirements of Employees

II. Group Life Insurance Plans

A. Group Term Life Insurance

B. Group Accidental Death and Dismemberment Insurance (AD&D)

C. Group Universal Life Insurance

III. Medical Expense Insurance Providers

A. Commercial Insurers

B. Blue Cross and Blue Shield Plans

C. Health Maintenance Organizations (HMOs)

D. Self-insured Plans by Employers

V. Traditional Indemnity Plans

   A. Basic Medical Expense Insurance
      1. Hospital Expense Insurance
      2. Surgical Expense Insurance
      3. Physicians' Visits
      4. Miscellaneous Benefits

   B. Major Medical Insurance
      1. Supplemental Major Medical Insurance
      2. Comprehensive Major Medical Insurance

. Managed Care Plans

   A. Health Maintenance Organizations

   B. Preferred Provider Organizations (PPOs)

   C. Point-of-Service (POS) Plans

   D. Advantages of Managed Care Plans

   E. Disadvantages of Managed Care Plans

   F. Current Developments in Managed Care Plans

I. Consumer-Driven Health Plans

   A. Defined Contribution Health Plans

   B. High Deductible Health Plans

II. Patients' Bill of Rights

III. Group Medical Expense Contractual Provisions

   A. Preexisting Conditions

   B. Coordination of Benefits

   C. Continuation of Group Health Insurance

X. Group Dental Insurance

   A. Benefits

   B. Cost Controls

. Group Disability-Income Insurance

   A. Short-term Plans

   B. Long-term Plans

I. Cafeteria Plans

■ Short Answer Questions

1. List the basic underwriting principles used in group insurance.

2. What groups are typically eligible for group insurance? What are the eligibility requirements for individuals who are members of these groups?

3. What are the major types of group life insurance plans? Describe the typical provisions of group term life insurance.

4. From what sources are group medical expense insurance plans available?

5. What coverages are typically provided through group basic medical expense plans?

6. How does supplemental major medical insurance differ from comprehensive major medical insurance?

7. What is "managed care" and how do managed care plans differ from traditional group health insurance plans?

8. What is a preferred provider organization (PPO)?

9. Why are preexisting conditions provisions and coordination of benefits provisions often used in group health expense insurance plans?

10. What cost control measures are typically included in group dental insurance plans?

1. How do group short-term disability income insurance plans differ from group long-term disability income insurance plans?

2. What are the common characteristics of cafeteria plans?

Multiple Choice Questions

Circle the letter that corresponds to the BEST *answer.*

1. Which statement(s) is(are) true with regard to group insurance underwriting principles?
    I.   A flow of people through the group is undesirable.
    II. Benefits should be automatically determined.
    (a) I only
    (b) II only
    (c) both I and II
    (d) neither I nor II

2. Group basic medical expense plans usually provide all of the following benefits EXCEPT:
    (a) hospital expense insurance.
    (b) supplemental major medical insurance.
    (c) surgical expense insurance.
    (d) physicians' visits.

3. Swanson Enterprises gives each employee covered under the employee benefit plan 250 credits. Wi‍ the credits, the employees can select which employee benefits they desire, and the magnitude of the benefits (up to certain limits). This type of plan is called a:

    (a) managed care plan.

    (b) universal coverage plan.

    (c) preferred provider plan.

    (d) cafeteria plan.

4. Under one cost control measure used in dental insurance, if the estimated cost of dental treatment exceeds a specified value, a plan of treatment is submitted to the insurer. The insurer calculates the amount that will be covered under the plan. This information is then shared with the employee who makes the decision whether to have the procedure performed. Such a provision is called a:

    (a) predetermination of benefits provision.

    (b) coordination of benefits provision.

    (c) flexible spending account.

    (d) relative value schedule provision.

5. Union Atlantic Railroad entered into an agreement with St. Joseph's Hospital. Under the agreement St. Joseph's Hospital discounts services provided to Union Atlantic employees, and Union Atlantic provides a financial incentive for their employees to receive their care from St. Joseph's. In this relationship, St. Joseph's Hospital is a(n):

    (a) private health insurance company.

    (b) Blue Cross/Blue Shield organization.

    (c) preferred provider organization.

    (d) health maintenance organization.

6. Which statements is(are) true with regard to health maintenance organizations (HMOs)?

    I.   Health maintenance organizations emphasize cost containment.

    II. Health maintenance organization members receive comprehensive health services in exchange for a fixed, prepaid fee.

    (a) I only

    (b) II only

    (c) both I and II

    (d) neither I nor II

7. A group of cardiac rehabilitation patients exercise together at the local fitness club. All of these patients have had at least two heart attacks or coronary bypass surgery; and none have been able to purchase health insurance because of preexisting conditions. If these patients form a group to obtaiℓ group health insurance coverage, which group insurance underwriting principle would be violated?

    (a) automatic determination of benefits

    (b) minimum participation requirements

    (c) insurance incidental to the group

    (d) flow of persons through the group

8. Tyndall Manufacturing covers employees under a basic medical expense plan supplemented with major medical insurance. Before the major medical insurance will begin to pay, the employee is required to pay a portion of covered medical expenses in excess of the limits of the basic coverage. This type of deductible is called a(n):

(a) aggregate deductible.
(b) franchise deductible.
(c) corridor deductible.
(d) straight deductible.

9. All of the following are characteristics of group major medical insurance EXCEPT:

(a) first-dollar coverage.
(b) high maximum limits.
(c) broad coverage.
(d) coinsurance (percentage participation).

0. Which statement(s) is(are) true with regard to short-term disability income plans?

I.   The maximum duration of benefits is usually three years.
II. Most of these plans cover non-occupational disability.

(a) I only
(b) II only
(c) both I and II
(d) neither I nor II

1. All of the following are major characteristics of group universal life insurance EXCEPT:

(a) coverage issued on a guaranteed basis up to certain limits with no evidence of insurability.
(b) the policyowner chooses where the cash value is invested.
(c) minimum guaranteed rate of return, but a higher rate may be credited.
(d) policy loans and withdrawals are available.

2. One provision of the Health Insurance Portability and Accountability Act requires that when employees change jobs, the new employer must give credit for previous and continuous health insurance coverage. This provision is called:

(a) convertibility.
(b) renewability.
(c) portability.
(d) renewal provision.

■ True/False

Circle the T if the statement is true, the F if the statement is false. Explain to yourself why a statement is false.

T   F   1. Most group life insurance in force is term insurance.

T   F   2. Employer-sponsored group insurance plans typically cover part-time workers.

T   F   3. Without a flow of younger workers into the group and older workers out of the group, group insurance premiums will increase.

T F 4. Group accidental death and dismemberment insurance will pay the principal sum regardless of the cause of death.

T F 5. Group disability income insurance is not needed if the employer provides workers compensation coverage.

T F 6. In a noncontributory group term insurance plan, the employer pays the entire cost of life insurance coverage.

T F 7. Group major medical insurance is characterized by high limits, deductibles, and coinsurance (percentage participation).

T F 8. Evidence of insurability is usually not required in group insurance plans.

T F 9. Blue Cross and Blue Shield plans typically reimburse their members for medical services after their members have reimbursed the care provider.

T F 10. Under a defined contribution health plan, the employer makes a fixed contribution towards an employee's health coverage, but the employee selects the plan to which the premiums apply.

T F 11. Under an individual practice association (IPA) health maintenance organization (HMO), physicians treat both HMO members and patients who are not members of the HMO.

T F 12. Flexible spending accounts provide no tax advantages to cafeteria plan participants.

T F 13. Employees are required to use the employer's preferred provider organization (PPO).

T F 14. High deductible health plans are used in conjunction with health savings accounts.

■ Case Applications

Case 1

Ned just attended an orientation session for new employees. The employee benefits director spoke for an hour about the various employee benefits the company offered and the provisions of these benefits. In the course of the presentation, the employee benefits director discussed (1) probationary periods, (2) eligibility periods, and (3) elimination (waiting) periods. Ned is confused about these terms and has asked you to explain the meaning and importance of each "period." How would you explain these "periods" to Ned?

ase 2

he employee benefit plan at Taylor Brothers Stores provides the following group insurance coverages:

Life Insurance: Accidental death and dismemberment insurance, with a principal sum of $50,000.

Health Insurance: Basic medical expense plan, overall limit of $25,000.

Disability Income Insurance: Short-term plan, no waiting period, 100 percent income replacement, six months duration.

ll of these benefits are funded on a noncontributory basis.

ritique Taylor Brothers Stores' group insurance offerings.

Solutions to Chapter 16

hort Answer Questions

1. These principles include: insurance incidental to the group, flow of persons through the group, automatic determination of benefits, minimum participation requirements, third-party sharing of cost, and simple and efficient administration

2. Eligible groups include individual employer groups, multiple-employer groups, labor union groups, debtor-creditor groups, and some other miscellaneous groups. Group insurers also require that the group satisfy a minimum size requirement.

    Employees must meet certain eligibility standards including: be a full-time employee, satisfy a probationary period, apply for insurance during the eligibility period, and be actively at work when the coverage becomes effective.

3. The major types of group life insurance are group term life insurance, group accidental death and dismemberment insurance (AD&D), and group universal life insurance.

    The amount of group term provided is typically a salary multiple such as one- to five-times salary. The coverage remains in force as long as the employee is a member of the group. If the employee leaves the group, the term insurance is usually convertible to individual cash value coverage without having to provide evidence of insurability. Small amounts of coverage may be available for dependents and retired workers.

4. Group medical expense insurance is available from commercial insurers, Blue Cross and Blue Shield plans, health maintenance organizations (HMOs), and through self-insured employer plans.

5. Group basic medical expense plans typically provide the following benefits: hospital expense insurance, surgical expense insurance, physicians' visits coverage, and miscellaneous benefits.

6. Supplemental major medical insurance is written to supplement the benefits provided under a basic medical expense plan. Medical expenses not covered under the basic plan may be eligible for reimbursement under the supplemental major medical plan. Comprehensive major medical combines basic plan benefits and major medical insurance in one policy.

7. Managed care is a generic term for medical expense plans that attempt to provide covered medical services to members in a cost-effective manner.

    These plans differ from traditional group health insurance plans in that the employee's choice of physicians and hospitals may be limited to certain providers, utilization review is conducted at all levels, preventive care and wellness are emphasized, providers share in financial results through risk-sharing techniques, and prevention and wellness are stressed.

8. A preferred provider organization (PPO) is a plan that contracts with health care providers to obtain medical services for members at reduced fees. PPOs benefit employers because the care is provided to their employees at a discount over the provider's normal charge. PPOs benefit care providers because they receive prompt payment and increased patient volume for their services. PPOs permit members to receive health services outside the network of health care providers, however, the reimbursement rate for members may be lower.

9. A preexisting conditions provision excludes from coverage medical conditions diagnosed or treated prior to coverage commencing. The purpose of the provision is to reduce adverse selection against the insurer. The Health Insurance Portability and Accountability Act of 1996 limits the right of insurers and employers to restrict coverage for preexisting conditions in group health plans.

    A coordination of benefits provision specifies the order of payment when medical services are covered under two or more group health insurance plans. The purpose of a coordination of benefits provision is to prevent overinsurance and the duplication of benefits.

10. Cost control measures typically found in group dental insurance plans include: deductibles and coinsurance, maximum limit on benefits, waiting periods, exclusions, and a predetermination-of-benefits provision.

11. Group short-term disability income plans typically pay benefits for 13 weeks to 2 years, with 26 weeks the most common duration of benefits. Group long-term plans pay benefits ranging from 2 years to age 65. Waiting periods in short-term plans are typically one to seven days, while long-term plans typically have waiting periods ranging from three to six months. Most short-term plans cover nonoccupational disability only, while long-term plans typically cover both occupational and nonoccupational disability. Short-terms plans define disability in terms of your own occupation while long-term plans typically use a dual definition of disability. For the first two years, the employee's own occupation is considered. After two years, the definition changes to any job for which you are reasonably fitted by education, training, and experience.

2. Cafeteria plans have a number of common characteristics. First, employees are given a number of dollars or credits that can be spent on benefits or taken as cash. The employee decides which benefits will be purchased with the dollars or credits. Second, many cafeteria plans are also premium conversion plans that allow employees to make their premium contributions with pretax dollars. Third, most cafeteria plans make available an optional flexible spending account (FSA). Finally, if the plan meets certain criteria required under the Internal Revenue Code, the employer's credits are not considered currently taxable income to the employee.

Multiple Choice Questions

1. (b)   Only the second statement is true. Automatic determination of benefits prevents individual selection of benefits and adverse selection. A flow of people through the group is desirable. As older employees leave the group, younger employees enter. Without such a flow through the group, the average age of members in the group would increase, and the premium charged for group insurance would also have to increase.

2. (b)   Supplemental major medical is used to supplement basic medical expense plans. Medical expenses not covered under the basic plan may be eligible for reimbursement under the supplemental major medical plan.

3. (d)   A cafeteria plan is described. These plans allow employees to choose the benefits they desire, within limits.

4. (a)   This provision is known as a predetermination of benefits provision.

5. (c)   St. Joseph's Hospital is a preferred provider for Union Atlantic. In exchange for the guaranteed demand for health care services, St. Joseph's Hospital provides care to Union Atlantic employees on a discounted basis.

6. (c)   Both statements are true. HMOs deliver comprehensive benefits to members in exchange for a fixed, prepaid fee. These organizations emphasize prevention and cost containment.

7. (c)   As the group would be formed for the purpose of obtaining group health insurance, clearly insurance would not be incidental to the group's existence.

8. (c)   The provision described is a corridor deductible. Such a deductible is used between basic medical expense plans and supplemental major medical insurance.

9. (a)   Group major medical insurance does not provide first-dollar coverage. A variety of deductibles are used in major medical insurance plans.

0. (b)   Only the second statement is true. Short-term plans typically cover nonoccupational disability only. While some short-term plans may pay benefits for as long as 2 years, the majority pay benefits for a maximum period of only 26 weeks.

1. (b)   As with individual universal life insurance, policyowners do not select where the cash value is invested.

2. (c)   Portability means that when an employee changes jobs, the new employer must give credit for previous and continuous health insurance coverage.

True/False

1. **T**

2. **F** Group insurance plans normally restrict eligibility to full-time workers.

3. **T**

4. **F** The death benefit will only be paid if the cause of death is an accident.

5. **F** Workers compensation provides benefits for work-related illnesses and injuries only. Disability income insurance is needed for nonoccupational illness and injuries.

6. **T**

7. **T**

8. **T**

9. **F** Blue Cross and Blue Shield plans are prepayment plans. The plan directly reimburses the care provider.

10. **T**

11. **T**

12. **F** Because flexible spending accounts are funded through before-tax reductions in workers' pay, taxes paid are reduced, and spendable income is increased.

13. **F** Employees are not required to use the preferred provider. However, employees are given a financial incentive to do so, often through reduced deductibles or greater employer cost-sharing if the preferred provider is used.

14. **T**

Case Applications

Case 1

A probationary period usually begins when employment starts. It is a period of time a new employee must satisfy before he or she can participate in the employee benefit plan. Some workers may be with the firm for only a short period of time. A probationary period at the start of employment reduces the cost of adding workers who will only be with the company for a short period of time.

An eligibility period is used in contributory plans. Under a contributory plan, the employee funds part or all of the cost of an employee benefit. An eligibility period is a short period of time—typically 31 days—during which an employee can sign up for a benefit without demonstrating evidence of insurability. The purpose of limiting the opportunity to select an optional benefit is to avoid adverse selection. For example, an employee benefit plan might allow employees to purchase additional life insurance. Without an eligibility period, a worker just diagnosed with a terminal illness might try to purchase more coverage. The eligibility period restricts the time during which a contributory benefit may be elected.

Waiting (elimination) periods are used in disability income insurance. The waiting period is a period of time after an illness or injury during which no benefits are paid. The waiting period is similar to a deductible because the insured must absorb a portion of the loss before the insurer begins payment.

Case 2

The group insurance coverages offered in this employee benefit plan are quite limited and/or not wisely designed. Accidental death and dismemberment insurance pays death benefits if the cause of death is an accident. There's no coverage for death from cancer, heart disease, or other nonaccidental means. The health insurance is a basic plan with a $25,000 limit. This limit will not go far if an employee has a serious medical condition. The disability income plan is subject to abuse as employees can receive 100 percent of lost income without having to serve a waiting period. Also, there's no coverage for long-term disabilities.

The risk management adage "insure for the large loss" also applies to group insurance. By modifying the benefits (e.g., dropping AD&D and replacing it with group term insurance, purchasing supplemental major medical insurance, etc.), additional security for the employees and their dependents can be achieved. If more funds are needed to pay for these benefits, some or all of the benefits could be made contributory.

Chapter 17
Employee Benefits: Retirement Plans

Overview

Americans, on average, are spending a longer period of their lives in retirement. The early retirement trend combined with increasing life expectancy makes income during retirement a critical concern. There are three primary sources of retirement income: Social Security old-age benefits, income generated from personal investments and savings, and private retirement plans. To encourage employers to provide retirement plans, certain tax benefits have been made available. To qualify for these tax benefits, the employer is required to satisfy certain coverage and nondiscrimination requirements, as well as other rules. This chapter examines the basic features of private retirement plans, the distinctions between defined benefit plans and defined contribution plans, the funding instruments used to finance retirement plans, and the features of several types of retirement plans.

Learning Objectives

After studying this chapter, you should be able to:

Explain the basic features of private retirement plans, including: minimum age and service requirements, retirement ages, and vesting rules.

Distinguish between defined-contribution and defined-benefit retirement plans.

▪ Describe the basic characteristics of Section 401(k) plans.

Explain the major features of profit-sharing plans.

Describe the basic characteristics of Keogh plans for the self-employed.

▪ Identify the major features of SIMPLE retirement plans for small employers.

▪ Define the following:

Actual deferral percentage (ADP) test	Funding agency
Advance funding	Funding instrument
Average benefit test	Guaranteed investment contract (GIC)
Career-average earnings	Highly compensated employees
Cash-balance plan	Investment guarantee contract
Deferred retirement age	Keogh plans
Defined-benefit plan	Minimum age and service requirement
Defined-contribution formula	Minimum coverage requirements
Defined-contribution plan	Minimum vesting standards
Early retirement age	Money purchase plan
Economic Growth and Tax Relief Reconciliation Act of 2001	Normal retirement age
	Past-service credits
Employee Retirement Income Security Act of 1974 (ERISA)	Pension Benefit Guaranty Corporation (PBGC)
	Profit-sharing plan
Final average pay	Qualified plan

Roth 401(k) plan
Roth 403(b) plan
Section 401(k) plan
Section 403(b) plan
Self-employed 401(k) plan
Separate investment account

SEP-IRA
SIMPLE retirement plan
Simplified employee pension (SEP)
Top-heavy plan
Trust-fund plan
Vesting

■ Outline

I.   Fundamentals of Private Retirement Plans

    A.   Favorable Income Tax Treatment

    B.   Minimum Coverage Requirements

    C.   Minimum Age and Service Requirements

    D.   Retirement Ages

    E.   Benefit Formulas
       1. Defined-Contribution Formulas
       2. Defined-Benefit Formulas

    F.   Vesting Provisions

    G.   Limits on Contributions and Benefits

    H.   Early Distribution Penalty

    I.   Minimum Distribution Requirements

    J.   Funding of Pension Benefits

    K.   Integration with Social Security

    L.   Top-Heavy Plans

II.   Types of Qualified Retirement Plans

III. Defined-Contribution Plans

IV. Defined-Benefit Plans

    A.   Traditional Defined-Benefit Plans

    B.   Cash Balance Plans

V.   Section 401(k) Plans

    A.   Annual Limit on Elective Deferrals

    B.   Actual Deferral Percentage Test

    C.   Limitations on Distributions

VI. Section 403(b) Plans

VII. Profit-Sharing Plans

VIII. Retirement Plans for the Self-Employed

A. Limits on Contributions and Benefits

B. Other Requirements

IX. Simplified Employee Pension (SEP)

X. SIMPLE Retirement Plans

A. Eligible Employees

B. Employee Contributions

C. Employer Contributions

XI. Funding Agency and Funding Instruments

A. Trust-Fund Plan

B. Separate Investment Account

C. Guaranteed Investment Contract (GIC)

D. Investment Guarantee Contract

■ Short Answer Questions

1. What tax benefits are available to qualified retirement plans?

2. Explain the minimum coverage tests for qualified retirement plans.

3. What is the difference between a defined benefit plan and a defined contribution plan?

4. What formulas can be used to determine retirement income under a defined-benefit plan?

5. What is vesting? Explain the two minimum vesting standards for qualified defined-benefit retirement plans.

6. What is the early distribution penalty? What distributions are exempt from the early distribution penalty?

7. What is a top-heavy pension plan? What additional restrictions are imposed on top-heavy plans?

8. What is a 401(k) plan? What is the actual deferral percentage (ADP) test for 401(k) plans?

9. What are the major characteristics of Keogh (HR-10) plans?

10. What are the major characteristics of Simplified Employee Pension plans (SEPs)?

11. What employers are eligible to establish SIMPLE (Savings Incentive Match Plan for Employees) plans? What special incentive exists for these employers to establish SIMPLE plans?

12. What are the major types of funding instruments for private pension plans?

Multiple Choice Questions

Circle the letter that corresponds to the BEST *answer.*

1. Which of the following benefit formulas is used in defined contribution plans?
   (a) flat dollar amount for each year of service
   (b) unit-benefit formula
   (c) flat dollar amount for all employees
   (d) fixed percentage of salary

2. Which statement(s) is (are) true with regard to qualified retirement plans?
   I. Distributions from qualified plans are not taxable.
   II. Investment income accumulates tax-deferred in qualified plans.

   (a) I only
   (b) II only
   (c) both I and II
   (d) neither I nor II

3. Jennings Inc. just started a pension plan. The company has many long-term employees who are within 10 years of retirement. Which of the following will help Jennings provide more adequate retirement benefits to these workers?
   (a) early distribution penalties
   (b) advance funding
   (c) past service credits
   (d) minimum vesting standards

4. Bailey Company just started a qualified plan for their employees. Under the plan, Bailey provides an additional 5 percent of each employee's salary as a bonus, and each employee is given the option of receiving the bonus in cash or putting some or all of the bonus funds aside for retirement. What type of plan did Bailey initiate?
   (a) Keogh (HR-10) plan
   (b) Simplified Employee Pension (SEP)
   (c) SIMPLE plan
   (d) 401(k) plan

5. The present value of the cumulative accrued pension benefits of highly compensated employees at JL Drug Company is 70 percent of the total of all accrued benefits. JL's plan therefore is described as:
   (a) defined contribution.
   (b) top-heavy.
   (c) overfunded.
   (d) qualified.

6. All of the following statements about profit-sharing plans are true EXCEPT:
   (a) profit-sharing plans are a type of defined-contribution plan.
   (b) profit-sharing plans provide an incentive for employees to work more efficiently.
   (c) profit-sharing plans are exempt from the 10 percent penalty tax on early distributions.
   (d) profit-sharing contributions are more flexible than defined-benefit plan contribution.

7. Which statement(s) is(are) true with regard to minimum vesting for qualified defined benefit plans?
    I.   Under cliff vesting, workers must be fully vested after three years.
    II. Under the graded vesting rule, the worker must be 60 percent vested after three years, and then vested an additional 10 percent for each of the next four years.

    (a) I only
    (b) II only
    (c) both I and II
    (d) neither I nor II

8. Mom and Pop's Grocery is a sole proprietorship. Mom and Pop would like to establish a qualified plan to take advantage of the same tax advantages to which corporations are entitled. Mom and Pop should establish a(n):

    (a) 401(k) plan.
    (b) Simplified Employee Pension (SEP).
    (c) Individual Retirement Account (IRA).
    (d) Keogh (HR-10) plan.

9. A funding arrangement in which an insurer guarantees the interest for a number of years on a lump-sum deposit is called a(n):

    (a) guaranteed investment contract (GIC).
    (b) separate investment account.
    (c) unit benefit formula.
    (d) trust fund plan.

10. Lewis Company adjusts retirement benefits to consider Social Security retirement benefits. As Social Security slants benefits in favor of the less highly compensated workers, this adjustment reduces benefits for lower-paid employees and increases benefits for the highly compensated employees. Because the Lewis Company plan makes this adjustment, it can be described as:

    (a) indexed.
    (b) discriminatory.
    (c) top-heavy.
    (d) integrated.

11. One type of retirement plan is designed for the employees of public schools and tax-exempt organizations such as hospitals, non-profit groups, and churches. These plans are called:

    (a) 401(k) plans.
    (b) 403(b) plans.
    (c) Keogh plans.
    (d) SIMPLE plans.

■ True/False

Circle the T if the statement is true, the F if the statement is false. Explain to yourself why a statement is false.

T   F   1. Profit-sharing plans provide greater funding flexibility than other types of qualified plans provide.

T   F   2. For most workers, a pension benefit based on career average earnings is more beneficial than a pension benefit based on final pay.

F   3. Although the normal retirement age in most plans is 65, many workers retire before the normal retirement age.

F   4. Under present law, all employees eligible for coverage who are at least age 21 and who have completed one year of service must be allowed to participate in a qualified retirement plan.

F   5. Employees must pay taxes on the amount they elect to defer in a 401(k) plan in the year the deferral is elected.

F   6. A self-employed 401(k) plan combines a profit-sharing plan with an individual 401(k) plan.

F   7. A top-heavy plan is one that is overfunded.

F   8. The amount that can be contributed each year to a defined-contribution plan is limited.

F   9. Under a unit-credit formula, both earnings and years of service are considered.

F   10. An employee has a better idea what his or her retirement benefit will be prior to retirement under a defined-contribution plan than under a defined-benefit plan.

F   11. Early distributions from qualified plans are subject to a 10 percent penalty tax.

■ Case Applications

Case 1

Stained Panes (SP) is a small company specializing in stained-glass windows, primarily for churches. The company was just purchased and the new owner was amazed to learn that there was no retirement plan for SP workers. The new owner would like to provide adequate retirement benefits for workers and reward long-time service. The work force consists of 14 skilled artisans, each of whom is over age 50 and has been with the company for over 25 years; two salespeople ages 40 and 55; three packing and delivery workers ages 35, 27, and 38; and a bookkeeper age 54. Based on this situation, should this company adopt a defined-benefit or a defined-contribution plan? Explain your answer.

Case 2

Midsouth Diesel specializes in the repair and overhaul of diesel engines. The company has 10 employees who are "highly compensated," and 8 of these employees are covered by the company's 401(k) plan. There are 40 "nonhighly compensated" employees, and 24 of these workers are covered under the 401(k) plan. Is Midsouth Diesel satisfying the minimum coverage requirement for qualified plans?

■ Solutions to Chapter 17

Short Answer Questions

1. If a private retirement plan meets certain standards, favorable income tax treatment is afforded the plan. These tax benefits include: the employer's contributions are tax-deductible up to specified limit as an ordinary cost of doing business, the employer's contributions are not considered currently taxable income to the employee, the investment income accumulates on a tax-deferred basis, and benefits attributable to employer contributions are not taxed until the employee retires or receives the funds.

2. There are three minimum coverage tests. To qualify, the plan must satisfy one of the tests:

    Percentage test: The plan must cover at least 70 percent of all nonhighly compensated employees.

    Ratio test: The plan must cover a percentage of nonhighly compensated employees that is at least 70 percent of the percentage of highly compensated employees covered. So if 90 percent of the highly compensated are covered, at least 63 percent (.70 × .90 = .63) of the nonhighly compensated employees must be covered.

    Average benefits test: Under this test, two requirements must be satisfied: (1) the plan must benefit reasonable classification of employees and must not discriminate in favor of highly compensated employees, and (2) the average benefit for the nonhighly compensated employees must be at least 70 percent of the average benefit provided to the highly compensated employees.

3. With a defined-benefit plan, the retirement benefit is known in advance, but the contributions needed to fund the benefit vary. For example, the benefit may be defined as 50 percent of career average earnings. With a defined-contribution plan, the contribution is known in advance, but the benefit is variable. For example, an employer may agree to contribute 5 percent of a covered employee's salary to the retirement plan. The benefit that these contributions plus investment income will provide at retirement is unknown—all the employer defines is the contribution to the plan.

4. A number of formulas can be used to determine retirement income under defined-benefit plans. They include: flat dollar amount for all employees, flat percentage of annual earnings, flat dollar amount for each year of service, and a unit-benefit formula that considers both earnings and service.

5. Vesting refers to the employee's right to the benefits attributable to the employer's contributions or benefits promised by the employer if employment terminates prior to retirement. A qualified defined benefit retirement plan must meet one of the two minimum vesting standards. Under the first standard, the employee must be 100 percent vested after five years of service. This rule is sometime called "cliff vesting," because up until five years, nothing is vested. The second rule, the graded vesting rule, provides for gradual vesting over a longer period of time. Under this standard, an employee must be 20 percent vested after three years, and then vested an additional 20 percent for each of the next four years so that after seven years the employee is fully vested. These two standards are minimums—the employer is free to vest benefits more rapidly.

6. Under the law, there is a 10 percent early distribution tax penalty if funds are withdrawn from a qualified retirement plan before age 59.5. In addition to the penalty, ordinary income taxes must be paid on part or all of the amounts withdrawn. The early distribution tax penalty does not apply to any of the following distributions: distributions after age 59.5, distributions made after death or total and permanent disability of the employee, termination of employment after age 55, substantially equal payments over the worker's life expectancy or over the joint life expectancy of the worker and beneficiary after termination of employment, payments to an alternate payee as a result of a qualified domestic relations order, and payments in connection with certain employee stock ownership plans. Additional exceptions apply to certain IRA, SIMPLE plan, and SEP distributions.

7. A pension plan that primarily benefits highly compensated employees is considered top-heavy. If the present value of the cumulative accrued benefits for highly compensated exceeds 60 percent of the present value of the all accrued benefits, the plan is top-heavy. If a plan is top-heavy, additional restrictions apply. A rapid vesting schedule must be used for nonhighly compensated employees and certain minimum benefits or contributions must be provided for nonhighly compensated employees.

8. A 401(k) plan is a qualified cash or deferred arrangement (CODA) that allows eligible employees the option of deferring income by making a contribution to the plan or receiving the funds in cash. The 401(k) plan can use employer contributions only, employee contributions only, or a mixture of employer and employee funding.

   To prevent discrimination in favor of highly compensated employees, an actual deferral percentage (ADP) test must be met. Covered employees are divided into two groups, the highly compensated and the nonhighly compensated. The percentage of salary deferred is calculated for each employee and averaged for the members in each group. Then the average ADP of the two groups is compared. There are rules that specify by how much the ADP of the highly compensated employees can exceed the ADP of the nonhighly compensated employees. Employers often provide generous matching contributions to encourage less-highly compensated employees to participate in the plan.

9. Keogh (HR-10) plans are qualified retirement plans for sole proprietorships and partnerships. These plans allow owners of unincorporated businesses to enjoy the same tax advantages that qualified corporate plans enjoy. Contributions to the plan are tax-deductible up to certain limits, investment income accumulates on a tax-deferred basis, and the funds are not taxed until distributed.

10. Simplified Employee Pension plans (SEPs) are essentially employer-sponsored IRAs that meet certain requirements. Each employee establishes and owns an individual IRA with fully vested rights. The employer makes annual tax-deductible contributions to the account. Contribution limits are substantially higher than for individual IRAs.

11. SIMPLE retirement plans are limited to employers with 100 or fewer eligible employees and who do not maintain another qualified retirement plan. Because SIMPLE plans are exempt from most nondiscrimination and administrative rules that apply to qualified plans, employers have an incentive to establish these plans.

12. The major types of funding instruments for private pension plans include: trust-fund plans, separate investment accounts, guaranteed investment contracts, and investment guarantee contracts.

Multiple Choice Questions

1. (d)   A fixed percentage of salary formula is used in defined-contribution plans. The other choices are all defined-benefit formulas.

2. (b)   Only the second statement is true. As pretax dollars are usually used to fund benefits, and the investment income accumulates tax-deferred, taxes must be paid on part or all of retirement plan distributions.

3. (c)   If Jennings Inc. allows credit for past service to the company, additional benefits can be credited for long-term employees. Jennings can fund the past service benefits over time.

4. (d)   Bailey Company established a 401(k) plan. These plans give employees the option of taking the benefit in cash or deferring some or all of the benefit for retirement. If a deferral is elected, the income is not currently taxable.

5. (b) JL's plan is top-heavy because more than 60 percent of the present value of the accrued benefit is for the highly compensated employees.

6. (c) Profit-share plans are subject to the 10 percent penalty tax for distributions prior to age 59.5.

7. (d) Neither statement is correct. Cliff vesting uses a five-year cut-off rather than three years. Under the graded vesting standard, employees must be 20 percent vested after three years, with an additional 20 percent vested per year for the next four years.

8. (d) A Keogh (HR-10) plan is a qualified plan for proprietorships and partnerships.

9. (a) The funding alternative described is called a guaranteed investment contract (GIC).

10. (d) Private pension plans can be integrated with Social Security. Low-income workers have their benefits reduced through integration, while high-income workers benefit from integration.

11. (b) The plans designed for employees of public schools and tax-exempt organizations such as hospitals, nonprofit groups, and churches are called Section 403(b) plans.

True/False

1. T

2. F As an employee's salary tends to increase over his or her working years, an average that considers final pay only is more beneficial than an average based on career earnings. A benefit based on career earnings would average in early years when compensation was lower.

3. T

4. T

5. F One of the advantages of 401(k) plans is that employees do not pay taxes on the amount they defer until the funds are distributed.

6. T

7. F A top heavy plan is a plan in which over 60 percent of the present value of the accrued benefits are for the highly compensated employees. Additional restrictions apply to top-heavy plans.

8. T

9. T

10. F If the retirement benefit is defined (e.g., $300 per month or 40 percent of final pay), the employee has a better idea of what his or her retirement benefit will be than if the contribution is defined (e.g., the employer contributes $250 per month to a retirement plan).

11. T

Case Applications

Case 1

Stained Panes should adopt a defined-benefit plan for several reasons. Of the company's 20 employees, 6 are over age 50. Adopting a defined-contribution plan would not allow enough time to accumulate adequate funds for retirement. If a defined-benefit plan was adopted, however, the plan could base benefits on career earnings or final pay. The company could also give credit for past service under a defined-benefit plan, and fund these past service credits over time. This strategy will permit Stained Panes to enjoy the tax advantages of qualified plans while rewarding the long-term service the employees have provided to the company.

Case 2

Under the percentage test, the plan must cover at least 70 percent of the nonhighly compensated employees. As only 24 out of 40 nonhighly compensated workers are covered (60%), this test is not met. Under the ratio test, the plan must benefit at least 70 percent of the percentage of the highly compensated who are covered. As 80 percent of the highly compensated are covered (8 of 10), at least 56 percent of the nonhighly compensated ($.70 \times .80 = .56$) must be covered. As 60 percent (24 of 40) of the nonhighly compensated employees are covered, this minimum coverage test is satisfied.

Chapter 18
Social Insurance

Overview

A multitude of errors in thinking surround our social insurance programs."—George E. Rejda*

These "errors in thinking" are unfortunate, given the importance of social insurance programs. These programs, which are enacted to solve complex social problems, provide a base of economic security to the population. In this chapter we examine social insurance programs. As an introduction, we examine why social insurance programs are needed and basic characteristics of social insurance programs. Next, we examine the provisions and issues relating to three important social insurance programs: OASDI and Medicare (Social Security), unemployment insurance, and workers compensation.

Social Insurance and Economic Security, 5th Edition. Prentice Hall, 1994, Englewood Cliffs, NJ, pg 21.

Learning Objectives

After studying this chapter, you should be able to:

Explain the reasons why social insurance programs are established.

Describe the basic characteristics of social insurance programs.

Identify the major benefits provided by the Old-Age, Survivors, and Disability Insurance (OASDI) program.

Identify the major benefits under the Medicare program.

Describe the basic objectives and important provisions of state unemployment insurance programs.

Explain the basic objectives and major provisions of workers compensation programs.

Define the following:

Assumption-of-risk doctrine	Full retirement age
Average indexed monthly earnings (AIME)	Fully funded program
Competitive state fund	Fully insured
Contributory negligence doctrine	Hospital Insurance (Part A)
Credit (quarter of coverage)	Individual equity
Currently insured	Liability without fault
Diagnosis-related groups (DRGs)	Means (needs) test
Disability insured	Medical Insurance (Part B)
Earnings test (retirement test)	Medicare Advantage plans
Exclusive remedy doctrine	Medicare Prescription Drug Coverage
Experience rating	Medigap policy
Extended-benefits program	Monopoly state fund
Fellow-servant doctrine	Primary insurance amount (PIA)

Short-term involuntary
  unemployment
Social adequacy

Social Security (OASDI)
Unemployment insurance
Workers compensation

■ Outline

I.   Social Insurance

  A.   Reasons for Social Insurance

  B.   Basic Characteristics of Social Insurance
    1. Compulsory Programs
    2. Floor of Income
    3. Emphasis on Social Adequacy Rather than Individual Equity
    4. Benefits Loosely Related to Earnings
    5. Benefits Prescribed by Law
    6. No Means Test
    7. Full Funding Unnecessary
    8. Financially Self-Supporting

II.   Old-Age, Survivors, and Disability Insurance (OASDI)

  A.   Covered Occupations

  B.   Determination of Insured Status
    1. Fully Insured
    2. Currently Insured
    3. Disability Insured

III.   Types of Benefits

  A.   Retirement Benefits

  B.   Survivor Benefits

  C.   Disability Benefits

  D.   Taxation of OASDI Benefits

  E.   Financing Social Security Benefits

IV.   Medicare

  A.   The Original Medicare Plan
    1. Part A—Hospital Insurance
    2. Part B—Medical Insurance

  B.   Medical Advantage Plans

  C.   Other Medicare Health Plans

  D.   Medicare Prescription Drug Plans

  E.   Medigap Insurance

. **Unemployment Insurance**

   A.   Coverage

   B.   Eligibility Requirements

   C.   Benefits

   D.   Financing

   E.   Problems and Issues

I.   **Workers Compensation**

   A.   Development of Workers Compensation

   B.   Objectives of Workers Compensation

   C.   Complying with the Law

   D.   Covered Occupations

   E.   Eligibility Requirements

   F.   Workers Compensation Benefits

   G.   Problems and Issues

Short Answer Questions

1. Given the availability of private insurance, why are social insurance programs needed?

2. List the basic characteristics of social insurance programs.

3. While social insurance benefits are based largely on social adequacy, benefits are also related to earnings. Explain how both of these seemingly contradictory characteristics can apply to social insurance programs.

4. Why is an insured status important under the OASDI program? How is an insured status obtained?

5. What are the three principal benefits payable under the OASDI program?

5. How are retirement, survivor, and disability insurance benefits funded under the OASDI program?

7. What benefits are provided through Part A and Part B of the original Medicare program?

8. What is Medigap insurance and why is there a market for Medigap insurance?

9. What are the basic objectives of unemployment insurance?

10. What are the usual eligibility requirements that an unemployed worker must satisfy to collect unemployment benefits?

11. Explain the common law defenses that employers could invoke to avoid liability for work-related injuries prior to the passage of workers compensation statutes.

12. What are the objectives of workers compensation laws?

13. What are the four principal benefits payable under workers compensation?

Multiple Choice Questions

Circle the letter that corresponds to the BEST answer.

1. Survivor benefits under the OASDI program most closely resemble which of the following private insurance coverages?

   (a) life insurance

   (b) life annuities

   (c) health insurance

   (d) liability insurance

2. Prior to passage of the workers compensation laws, employers could avoid liability to employees injured on the job by invoking common law defenses. Under one such defense, the employer asserted that because the employee helped to bring about the injury, the employer was not responsible. This common law defense is:

   (a) assumption of the risk.

   (b) liability without fault.

   (c) the fellow servant doctrine.

   (d) contributory negligence.

3. Which statement is true with regard to social insurance programs?

   I.   Adverse selection is reduced because the programs are compulsory.

   II. A means (needs) test must be satisfied in order to receive social insurance benefits.

   (a) I only

   (b) II only

   (c) both I and II

   (d) neither I nor II

4. All of the following are basic objectives of unemployment insurance plans EXCEPT:

   (a) to reduce incentives for the unemployed to return to work.

   (b) to encourage employers to stabilize employment.

   (c) to help unemployed workers find jobs.

   (d) to provide cash income during involuntary unemployment.

5. Under Part A of Medicare, hospitals are reimbursed for inpatient services according to:

   (a) a relative-value scale.

   (b) whatever the hospital charges for the care rendered.

   (c) the diagnosis-related group (DRG) reimbursement.

   (d) the usual, reasonable, and customary charges.

6. All of the following benefits are available through workers compensation EXCEPT:

   (a) disability income.

   (b) medical benefits.

   (c) rehabilitation.

   (d) retirement income.

7. One insured status under OASDI requires at least 6 quarters of coverage out of the last 13 quarters ending with the quarter of death, disability, or entitlement to old-age benefits. This insured status i
    (a) disability insured.
    (b) currently insured.
    (c) Medicare insured.
    (d) fully insured.

8. To be eligible for unemployment benefits, an unemployed worker must meet all of the following eligibility requirements EXCEPT:
    (a) have qualifying wages and employment during the base year.
    (b) actively seek work.
    (c) be unemployed because of voluntary termination.
    (d) be able to work and available for work.

9. Part B of the original Medicare program covers:
    (a) survivor benefits.
    (b) disability income payments.
    (c) physician's fees and related medical services.
    (d) inpatient hospital care.

10. All of the following are characteristics of social insurance programs EXCEPT:
    (a) compulsory programs.
    (b) benefits emphasize individual equity rather than social adequacy.
    (c) benefits are loosely related to earnings.
    (d) benefits are prescribed by law.

■ True/False

Circle the T if the statement is true, the F if the statement is false. Explain to yourself why a statement is false.

T   F   1. Unemployment insurance programs are designed to provide benefits in the case of long-te▶ voluntary unemployment.

T   F   2. For those born today, the full retirement age under Social Security is 67 and the early retirement age is 62.

T   F   3. Although workers compensation covers work-related injuries, occupational diseases are excluded from coverage.

T   F   4. Most states require a qualified unemployed worker to serve a one-week waiting period bef collecting unemployment benefits.

T   F   5. OASDI benefits are susceptible to loss of purchasing power because they are not adjusted inflation.

T   F   6. Social insurance benefits are means-tested.

T   F   7. Under the Medicare Prescription Drug Plan, beneficiaries pay a monthly premium in exchange for first-dollar, comprehensive coverage of prescription drugs.

T   F   8. Unemployment benefits are uniform from state to state.

F   9. A liberal definition of disability is used in determining whether an individual is eligible for Social Security disability-income benefits.

F   10. Although it is a mandated social insurance coverage, most states permit employers to privately insure or self-insure their workers compensation exposure.

F   11. Monthly payments under the OASDI program are based upon an individual's primary insurance amount (PIA), which in turn is based upon the individual's average indexed monthly earnings (AIME).

F   12. If you are covered under the OASDI program and under workers compensation, there is no need to purchase private disability income insurance.

F   13. The OASDI program faces a long-range actuarial deficit.

F   14. There is no limit on the duration of monthly benefits payable through state unemployment insurance programs.

Case Applications

Case 1

Stephanie Lewis is a Certified Public Accountant (CPA) who retired from a large accounting firm last year after providing 30 years of service. During her employment, her average salary was $70,000 per year. Walt Adams retired from the same CPA firm last year after providing 30 years of service. Walt worked as a custodian and averaged $28,000 per year.

a)   Which individual will receive higher monthly retirement benefits through the OASDI program? Explain your answer.

b)   Which individual will have a higher percentage of his or her pre-retirement income replaced by OASDI retirement benefits? Explain your answer.

Case 2

Water Wheel Company manufactures irrigation systems. Each year, Water Wheel has a company picnic for employees and their families. The highlight of the picnic is a softball game between "management" and "labor." At this year's game, Fred from Accounting tried to stretch a double into a triple. Pete, a welder, made a perfect throw and Fred slid to avoid the tag. Not only was Fred "out" on the play, but he also broke his ankle and suffered ligament damage in his knee. It is unclear whether Fred's injury is covered under workers compensation as the injury occurred at a company picnic. What are the positives and negatives for Fred of having his injuries covered under workers compensation?

■ Solutions to Chapter 18

Short Answer Questions

1. Social insurance programs are necessary for at least three reasons. First, social insurance programs are enacted to solve complex social problems. Second, social insurance programs are necessary because certain risks are difficult to insure privately. Finally, social insurance programs are necessa to provide a base of economic security to the population.

2. The basic characteristics of social insurance programs include:

    *   compulsory programs
    *   floor of income
    *   emphasis on social adequacy rather than individual equity
    *   benefits loosely related to earnings
    *   benefit prescribed by law
    *   no means (needs) test
    *   full funding unnecessary
    *   financially self-supporting

3. Social insurance benefits are largely based on social adequacy. One of the goals of social insurance programs is to provide a certain standard of living to all contributors. To accomplish this goal, benefits are slanted in favor of certain groups, such as low-income workers and large families. At th same time, however, benefits are loosely (not proportionately) related to earnings. So if you earn higher wages than another worker, you will receive higher OASDI benefits. However, the benefits you receive will not be proportionately higher than the benefits received by a worker who earned lower wages.

. An insured status is important under the OASDI program because to be eligible for the various benefits, a certain insured status is necessary. An insured status is obtained by working in covered employment and receiving credits (quarters of coverage) for OASDI taxes paid. In 2004, for example, one quarter of coverage is earned for each $900 of covered work earnings. No more than four quarters of coverage can be earned in a calendar year. Insured status is based upon the number of quarters of coverage earned, and in some cases, how recently the quarters of coverage were earned.

. The three benefits payable under the OASDI program are: retirement benefits, survivor benefits, and disability benefits. The initials "OASDI" spell out the benefits: "OA" is for old-age (retirement) benefits, "S" is for survivor benefits, and "D" is for disability income benefits.

. OASDI benefits are funded through a payroll tax paid by employers, employees, and the self-employed; interest income on the trust fund investments; and revenues derived from the taxation of part of the monthly cash benefits. Social Security payroll taxes are levied up to a maximum taxable wage base.

. Part A of Medicare, Hospital Insurance, provides coverage for hospital care and other benefits. Part A benefits include: inpatient hospital care, skilled nursing facility care, home health care services, hospice care, and blood transfusions. Part B, Medical Insurance, covers physicians' services, outpatient hospital services, home health services, and some other health care services.

. The Medicare program is characterized by deductibles, co-pays, limitations, and exclusions. Because of these "holes" in Medicare, a market developed for private health care policies designed to supplement Medicare. As these plans were designed to fill the gaps in Medicare coverage, they became known as Medigap insurance.

. The basic objectives of unemployment insurance are: to provide cash income during periods of involuntary unemployment, to help unemployed workers to find jobs, to encourage employers to stabilize employment, and to help stabilize the economy.

. To be eligible to receive unemployment benefits, the unemployed worker must satisfy a number of eligibility requirements. First, he or she must have qualifying wages and employment during the base year. Second, he or she must be able to work and be available to work. The worker must also seek work and be free from disqualification. Finally, the unemployed worker must serve a one-week waiting period.

. Prior to the passage of workers compensation laws, employers could use three common law defenses to defeat claims from their employees for work-related illnesses and injuries. First, they could assert that the employee assumed the risk when he or she took the job. Second, the employer could assert the fellow servant doctrine, arguing that it was a coworker's fault that the employee was injured rather the employer's fault. Finally, employers could use the doctrine of contributory negligence to defeat claims. Under this doctrine, if an employee contributes in any way to the illness or injury, he or she is barred from recovering from the employer.

. Workers compensation statutes have several objectives. First, they are designed to provide broad coverage for occupation injury and disease. Second, they provide protection against the loss of income. Third, they provide medical care and rehabilitation benefits. Fourth, they encourage safety at the workplace. Finally, workers compensation statutes are intended to reduce litigation over work-related injuries.

. The four benefits payable under workers compensation include: unlimited medical care, disability income, death benefits, and rehabilitation services.

Multiple Choice Questions

1. (a) Survivor benefits are payable upon the death of the covered worker, just like life insurance dea
benefits. OASDI survivor benefits should be taken into consideration in life insurance plannin

2. (d) Under contributory negligence, if the worker in any way contributed to his or her injury,
recovery was barred.

3. (a) Only the first statement is true. Because coverage is compulsory, individuals cannot choose
whether they wish to be covered. In addition, there is no individual selection of benefits. Soci
insurance benefits are not means (needs) tested to determine eligibility.

4. (a) Unemployment benefits are not intended to reduce incentives to return to work. The benefits a
payable during short periods of involuntary unemployment while the unemployed worker is
looking for another job.

5. (c) Reimbursement under Part A of Medicare is determined by the diagnosis-related group (DRG
prospective reimbursement amount. Treatment is preclassified into a number of DRGs, and th
reimbursement level for each DRG is determined in advance.

6. (d) Workers compensation coverage does not provide retirement income benefits.

7. (b) The status described is "currently insured."

8. (c) Voluntary unemployment will disqualify a worker from receiving unemployment insurance
benefits.

9. (c) Part B of Medicare is the voluntary component, Medical Insurance. Part B covers physician's
fees and related medical services.

10. (b) Social insurance programs emphasize social adequacy rather than individual equity.

True/False

1. **F** Unemployment insurance programs are designed to provide benefits in case of short-term
involuntary unemployment.

2. **T**

3. **F** Workers compensation covers both work-related illnesses and work-related injuries.

4. **T**

5. **F** OASDI benefits are indexed to prevent the erosion of purchasing power. Benefits are increased
the percentage change in the Consumer Price Index (CPI) from the third quarter of the previous ye
to the third quarter of the present year.

6. **F** Social insurance benefits are not means-tested.

7. **F** While beneficiaries pay a monthly premium for prescription drug coverage, the benefits are neith
"first dollar" nor "comprehensive." There is an annual deductible the insured must satisfy. After th
deductible, the insured must pay 25 percent of costs between $250 and $2,250. Then the beneficia
pays 100 percent of the next $2,850 in drug costs, and 5 percent of the costs after the beneficiary h
spent $3,600 out-of-pocket (these figures are for 2006).

8. **F** Each state has its own formula for determining unemployment benefit levels. Some states are ve
strict with regard to benefit payments, while other states provide significantly higher benefits.

9. **F** Social Security uses a harsh definition of disability. To be eligible, the worker must have "a physical or mental condition that prevents him or her from doing any substantial gainful work and is expected to last (or has lasted) at least 12 months or is expected to result in death."

0. **T**

1. **T**

2. **F** Coverage under workers compensation and the OASDI program should not discourage you from purchasing private disability income insurance. To collect under workers compensation, the illness or injury must be work-related. Nonoccupational illness and injury are not covered. Coverage under the OASDI program is problematic because you must have a "disability insured" status, satisfy the harsh definition of disability, and serve a five-month waiting period in order to receive benefits.

3. **T**

4. **F** In almost all jurisdictions, the maximum duration of regular benefits is limited to 26 weeks. During periods of high unemployment, many workers exhaust their regular benefits. A permanent federal-state program of extended benefits is available providing benefits for up to 13 additional weeks. So there is an overall limit of 39 weeks of benefits (regular plus extended).

Case Applications

Case 1

a) Stephanie will receive higher Social Security retirement benefits than Walt will receive. Based on Stephanie's average salary, we can assume that she earned an amount greater than the maximum taxable wage base each year she was employed. Based on Walt's average earnings, we can assume that he earned far less than the maximum taxable amount each year. Therefore Stephanie will receive a higher monthly retirement benefit than Walt will receive, although the benefits will not be proportionately higher.

b) Although Stephanie's dollar benefits will be higher than Walt's, Walt will have a higher percentage of his preretirement income replaced by his retirement benefit. OASDI benefits are slanted in favor of certain groups, including lower-income participants. Lower-income participants have higher wage replacement ratios than higher-income participants, even though the higher-income participants receive higher dollar benefits.

Case 2

Workers compensation provides the certainty of unlimited medical benefits, rehabilitation, and disability income. The negative, however, is that if Fred's injury is covered under workers compensation, then Fred may not be able to bring a successful tort action against the employer.

If this injury is not covered under workers compensation, Fred gives up the certainty of generous medical benefits, disability income benefits, and rehabilitation through workers compensation. However, he would have the right to bring a legal action against the employer. Fred could allege, for example, that the playing conditions were unsafe or that the game was not adequately supervised.

The determination of whether workers compensation applies to work-related injuries is sometimes difficult. A similar case involved a cervical spine injury suffered in a touch football game at a company picnic. Ultimately, that case was decided by the Supreme Court of the state of Nebraska.

Chapter 19
The Liability Risk

▌ Overview

The chapter begins a block of material on property and liability risks, and the personal and business insurance coverages designed to address these risks. In this first chapter, we consider the liability risk. The number of lawsuits and the magnitude of settlements have increased significantly in recent years. In this chapter we examine the basis for most of these suits, negligence. The elements of a negligent act are discussed as well as legal defenses in cases where negligence is alleged. Next, applications of the law of negligence are presented; and special problems associated with several problem areas are discussed. Finally, defects in the present civil justice system and tort reform ideas are discussed.

Learning Objectives

After studying this chapter, you should be able to:

Define negligence and explain the elements of a negligent act.

Explain the following legal defenses that can be used in a lawsuit: contributory negligence, comparative negligence, assumption of the risk, and the last clear chance rule.

Apply the law of negligence to specific liability situations.

Explain the defects in the current tort liability system and the proposals for tort reform.

Explain the following tort liability problems: medical malpractice crisis, corporate fraud and lax corporate governance, and an increase in asbestos lawsuits.

Define the following:

Alternative dispute resolution techniques	Last clear chance rule
Arbitration	Legal wrong
Assumption of risk	Licensee
Attractive nuisance	Mediation
Collateral source rule	Negligence
Combined ratio	Plaintiff
Comparative negligence law	Proprietary function
Compensatory damages	Proximate cause
Contributory negligence law	Punitive damages
Dram shop law	*Res ipsa loquitur*
Elements of negligence	*Respondeat superior*
Family purpose doctrine	Sovereign immunity
General damages	Special damages
Governmental function	Strict (absolute) liability
Imputed negligence	Tort
Invitee	Tortfeasor
Joint and several liability rule	Trespasser
Joint underwriting association (JUA)	Vicarious liability law

■ Outline

I. Basis of Legal Liability

    A. Intentional Torts

    B. Strict (Absolute) Liability

    C. Negligence

II. Law of Negligence

    A. Elements of Negligence

        1. Existence of a Legal Duty

        2. Failure to Perform that Duty

        3. Damage or Injury to the Claimant

        4. Proximate Cause Relationship between the Negligent Act and the Infliction of Damages

    B. Defenses Against Negligence

        1. Contributory Negligence

        2. Comparative Negligence

        3. Last Clear Chance Rule

        4. Assumption of Risk

III. Imputed Negligence

IV. *Res Ipsa Loquitur*

V. Specific Applications of the Law of Negligence

    A. Property Owners

    B. Attractive Nuisance Doctrine

    C. Owners and Operators of Automobiles

    D. Governmental Liability

    E. Charitable Institutions

    F. Employer and Employee Relationships

    G. Parents and Children

    H. Animals

VI. Current Tort Liability Problems

    A. Defective Tort Liability System

    B. Medical Malpractice Crisis

    C. Corporate Fraud and Lax Corporate Governance

    D. Increase in Asbestos Lawsuits

Short Answer Questions

1. What are the three categories of torts?

2. A claimant (plaintiff) alleging negligence on the part of a defendant (tortfeasor) must establish that the tortfeasor was negligent. What are the four essential elements of a negligent act?

3. What types of damages may be awarded in negligence cases?

4. What defenses could a defendant use to defeat the plaintiff's claim that the defendant was negligent?

5. In what situations may the negligence of one person be attributed (transferred) to another person?

6. What requirements must be satisfied in order for the doctrine of *res ipsa loquitur* to be applied?

7. What duty of care does a property owner owe to a trespasser, to a licensee, and to an invitee?

8. Critics of the present tort liability system in the U.S. cite a number of defects with the system. What are these major defects?

9. Most states have enacted or are considering enacting some tort reform measures. What are some important tort reforms?

10. What factors contribute to the medical malpractice problem in the United States?

11. What health problems can exposure to asbestos cause? One of the complicating factors in asbestos liability is the long "latency period." What does "latency period" refer to in the context of asbestos liability?

■ Multiple Choice Questions

Circle the letter that corresponds to the BEST *answer.*

1. All of the following are elements of a negligent act EXCEPT:
   (a) existence of a legal duty.
   (b) failure to perform that duty.
   (c) damages or injury to the claimant.
   (d) inability of the tortfeasor to pay the damages.

2. One tort reform proposal calls for modifying a rule under which a defendant cannot introduce evidence that shows the injured party has received other forms of compensation for the injury. This rule is called the:
   (a) attractive nuisance rule.
   (b) collateral source rule.
   (c) joint and several liability rule.
   (d) last clear chance rule.

3. Which statement(s) is(are) true with regard to defenses against liability claims?

I.   Under contributory negligence, if you contribute to your injury, you cannot recover damages.

II. Under comparative negligence, if you contribute to your injury, you cannot recover damages.

(a) I only

(b) II only

(c) both I and II

(d) neither I nor II

4. Jenny needed surgery on her right knee. When the anesthesia wore off, she noticed surgical wrapping around both knees. When she asked the nurse why both knees were wrapped, the nurse replied that the surgeon made an incision on her left knee, discovered the mistake, and proceeded with the operation on the right knee. What modification of the law of negligence will Jenny be able to invoke to recover damages from the surgeon?

(a) contributory negligence

(b) privity of contract

(c) *res ipsa loquitur*

(d) absolute liability

5. All of the following are legal defenses to liability claims EXCEPT:

(a) contributory negligence.

(b) assumption of the risk.

(c) vicarious liability.

(d) comparative negligence.

6. An insurance company was found guilty of illegal sales and claims practices and ordered to pay compensatory damages to a group of plaintiffs. To "make an example" of the insurer, the court also ordered the insurer to pay an additional $10 million to deter other insurers from engaging in the same wrongful acts. The $10 million award is an example of:

(a) punitive damages.

(b) special damages.

(c) collateral source payments.

(d) general damages.

7. In the past, federal, state, and local governments could not be sued unless they agreed to the suit. Upon what doctrine was this freedom from litigation based?

(a) philosophy of entitlement

(b) joint and several liability rule

(c) assumption of the risk doctrine

(d) sovereign immunity

8. Because of potential harm to individuals or society, some persons may be held liable for harm or injury to others even though negligence cannot be proven. These types of torts are called:

(a) intentional torts.

(b) negligence.

(c) strict (absolute) liability.

(d) breach of contract.

9. All of the following are torts EXCEPT:
   (a) In a case of mistaken identity, Diane locked a customer she suspected was a shoplifter in a dressing room until the police arrived. The customer was innocent.
   (b) Bob punched another bar patron who made disparaging comments about Bob's wife.
   (c) Nicole called the high school principal "an ignorant moron" at the PTA meeting.
   (d) While robbing a bank, Art shot and killed a bank employee.

10. All of the following are conditions under which negligence can be imputed to another party EXCEPT:
    (a) family purpose doctrine.
    (b) collateral source rule.
    (c) employer-employee relationships.
    (d) vicarious liability.

11. A property owner owes the highest degree of care to a(n):
    (a) trespasser.
    (b) invitee.
    (c) licensee.
    (d) an equal degree of care is owed to all of these.

12. John was involved in an accident in a state that uses a pure comparative negligence rule. John was found to be 75 percent responsible for the accident and his actual damages were $20,000. How much will John be able to recover?
    (a) $5,000
    (b) $10,000
    (c) $15,000
    (d) $20,000

■ True/False

Circle the T if the statement is true, the F if the statement is false. Explain to yourself why a statement is false.

T F 1. Alternative dispute resolution involves formal jury trials.

T F 2. The person who was injured as a result of a negligent act is called the tortfeasor.

T F 3. Corporate officers and board members are immune from liability claims under provisions of the Sarbanes-Oxley Act.

T F 4. A property owner owes a higher degree of care to children than to adults.

T F 5. A government unit can be held liable if it is negligent in the performance of a proprietary function.

T F 6. Under the joint and several liability rule, a defendant who is only slightly responsible may be required to pay the full amount of damages.

T F 7. General damages are awarded for losses that can be determined and documented, such as loss of work earnings and the cost of medical care.

T F 8. Many medical malpractice suits are due to medical errors by health care providers.

F   9.   The last clear chance rule bars recovery by the plaintiff.

F   10.   A licensee is someone who is invited onto the premises for the benefit of the occupant.

F   11.   Under the doctrine of *respondeat superior*, an employer may be held liable for negligent acts of employees who are acting on the employer's behalf.

F   12.   One current problem with the tort liability system in the U.S. is long delays.

Case Applications

Case 1

Brendan was late for an important meeting. He was driving 75 miles an hour on a narrow highway. He caught up to the car ahead of him and attempted to pass the car while driving up a steep hill. About that time, a delivery truck heading in the opposite direction came over the top of the hill. Brendan swerved to miss the truck. He hit the car he was passing and the driver lost control of the car and hit a tree. Brendan was not injured and his car sustained only slight damage. The other car was a total loss and the driver was severely injured. A lawsuit alleging that Brendan was negligent has been filed by the other driver. Was Brendan negligent?

Case 2

Last Saturday Janet and her daughter had lunch at the local franchise of a national fast-food chain. As they were returning to their car, a driver who had just picked up his order at the drive-through window sped round the corner of the restaurant and hit Janet and her daughter. Janet received multiple lacerations and five broken bones. Her child was not physically injured, but since witnessing the accident she has been traumatized. In filing her lawsuit, why did Janet name the car driver, the franchise owner, and the national fast-food chain as defendants? What types of damages may be awarded to Janet and her daughter as a result of this incident?

■ Solutions to Chapter 19

Short Answer Questions

1. The three categories of torts are intentional torts, strict (absolute) liability, and the tort of negligence.

2. There is a four-part test to determine if an act is negligent. First, there must be a legal duty to use reasonable care. Second, there must be a failure to perform that duty. Third, damages or injury must be suffered by the plaintiff. Finally, there must be a proximate cause relationship between the negligent act and the infliction of injury.

3. Three types of damages may be awarded in negligence cases. Special damages are paid for losses that can be determined and documented, such as lost earnings and medical bills. General damages are paid for losses that cannot be specifically measured or itemized, such as pain and suffering or disfigurement. Punitive damages are awarded to punish the negligent party and to deter others from committing similar acts.

4. The defendant could claim that the injured party contributed to his or her injury. Under contributory negligence, any fault of the plaintiff will prevent recovery of damages. Under a comparative negligence law, any fault of the plaintiff will reduce the damage award. The last clear chance rule could be used, as well as the assumption of risk doctrine.

5. Several situations give rise to the transfer of liability from one person to another person. One example is the employer-employee relationship. When acting on behalf of the employer, the negligent acts of the employee may be imputed to the employer. Another situation in which liability can be imputed from one person to another involves use of an automobile by someone other than the owner. Through vicarious liability laws and the family purpose doctrine, liability for negligent acts may be imputed to the owner of the auto. In a joint business venture, one partner may be responsible for another partner's acts. Finally, under dramshop laws a business that sells alcoholic beverages may be responsible if an impaired customer injures someone.

6. To apply the doctrine of *res ipsa loquitur*, a number of requirements must be met. The loss-causing event must not normally occur unless there is negligence. The defendant must have superior knowledge of the cause of the accident, and the injured party cannot prove negligence. The defendant must have control over the instrumentality causing the accident. Finally, the injured party must not have contributed to the loss/event.

7. The degree of care owed varies with the classification of the person who comes onto the owner's property. Trespassers are owed the least care. The property owner is under no obligation to keep the land safe and the trespasser accepts the land "as is." This duty is called "slight care." Greater care is owed a licensee. Licensees enter or remain on the property with the occupant's permission. The property owner is required to warn the licensee of unsafe conditions or activities on the premises. The last class of individuals who can come onto property is invitees. Invitees are asked onto the property to benefit the occupant. A higher degree of care is required. The owner has the obligation to inspect the premises and correct any dangerous conditions.

8. The alleged defects include: rising tort liability costs, inefficiency in compensating injured victims, uncertainty of legal outcomes, higher liability awards, and long delays in settling lawsuits.

9. Some important tort reforms measures include: capping noneconomic damages, reinstating the state-of-the-art defense in product liability cases, restricting punitive damages awards, modifying the collateral source rule, modifying the joint and several liability rule, and making greater use of alternative dispute resolution (ADR) techniques.

). A number of factors contribute to the medical malpractice problem. These factors include: medical errors by health care providers, underwriting losses by insurers, people being more litigious than in the past, increasing awareness of the vulnerability of physicians to malpractice claims, deterioration of the doctor-patient relationship, willingness of medical professionals to testify against each other, attorneys' willingness to file medical malpractice claims because of high fees they can collect if they are successful, the reluctance of state medical boards to discipline members, and growing resentment of for-profit providers and managed care plans.

1. Exposure to asbestos has been shown to cause lung cancer and other respiratory disorders. One of the problems in asbestos liability is the period of time between when an individual is exposed to asbestos and the time at which a respiratory disease manifests itself. This period of time, the latency period, may make it difficult to determine liability.

Multiple Choice Questions

1. (d) The ability of the tortfeasor to pay damage awards is independent of whether the act is negligent. The first three choices are elements of a negligent act. The fourth element is proximate cause between the failure to perform the legal duty and the injury to the claimant.

2. (b) Under the collateral source rule, evidence of other sources of recovery cannot be introduced in court.

3. (a) Under contributory negligence, even slight guilt on the part of the claimant will prevent the claimant from recovering damages. Under comparative negligence, any fault on the part of the claimant will simply reduce the damages awarded.

4. (c) The fact that an incision was made on her "good knee" is grounds for recovery under *res ipsa loquitur*. The operation was performed by a skilled surgeon who had exclusive control over the surgical procedure. Jenny did not contribute to the negligent act, and such an act normally does not occur unless negligence is involved.

5. (c) Vicarious liability is not a defense against a claim of liability. Vicarious liability shifts liability from one party to another party.

6. (a) Punitive damages are awarded to punish the tortfeasor for negligent acts and to deter others from committing the same act.

7. (d) This freedom from litigation was based on sovereign immunity. This doctrine has been modified over the years.

8. (c) Such torts involve strict (absolute) liability. Employers are held absolutely liable for injuries to their employees under workers compensation statutes. This doctrine is also applied in situations involving activities where great harm may result if there is negligence (e.g., blasting operations, crop dusting, owning dangerous animals, etc.).

). (d) The first three choices involve legal wrongs for which the law allows a remedy through money damages. Armed robbery and murder are crimes. Crimes are punishable by fines, imprisonment, and in some jurisdictions, death if the offense is severe.

). (b) The collateral source rule has nothing to do with imputing the negligent acts of one person to another person. Under the collateral source rule, the defendant cannot introduce evidence that shows the injured party has received compensation from other sources.

11. (b) The highest degree of care is owned an invitee. In addition to warning the invitee of dangerous conditions, the owner is also required to inspect the premises and eliminate any unsafe conditions.

12. (a) Under a pure comparative negligence law, the liability award is reduced proportionately. So if John is 75 percent responsible, his recovery will be reduced by 75 percent. He will only collect $5,000.

True/False

1. **F** Alternative dispute resolution attempts to avoid costly legal proceedings, such as jury trials. Parties to the action may agree to arbitration or mediation of the conflict.

2. **F** The tortfeasor is the person who caused the harm. In a legal proceeding, a plaintiff (also called the claimant) would bring legal action against the tortfeasor (also called the defendant).

3. **F** The Sabanes-Oxley Act was passed in response to corrupt business practices. Corporate officers and directors can be held responsible for fraud and other illegal business practices under the act.

4. **T**

5. **T**

6. **T**

7. **F** Special damages are awarded for losses that can be determined and documented, such as lost work earnings and the cost of medical care. General damages are awarded for losses that cannot be itemized, such as pain and disfigurement.

8. **T**

9. **F** Under the last clear chance rule, a plaintiff who is endangered by his or her own negligence can still recover damages if the defendant had a last clear chance to avoid the accident and failed to do so.

10. **F** A licensee is someone who enters or remains on the premises with the occupant's expressed or implied permission. An invitee is someone invited to come onto the premises for the benefit of the occupant.

11. **T**

12. **T**

Case Applications

Case 1

To determine if Brendan was negligent, the four-part test of negligence must be examined in relation to the facts of the case. First, there is a legal duty to obey the speed limit and not to pass other vehicles in an unsafe manner. Second, there must be a failure to meet the duty. Brendan clearly failed to perform this duty because he was speeding and he tried to pass another vehicle while going up a steep hill. The third requirement is injury. The party bringing the lawsuit against Brendan clearly suffered damages—his property was destroyed and he suffered severe bodily injuries. Finally, there is proximate cause in this scenario. In the absence of Brendan's violation of his legal duty, no accident would have occurred. There is an unbroken chain of events between Brendan's speeding and unsafe passing, the motorist's collision with the tree, and the resulting injuries.

Case 2

Janet named all three parties because each party may bear some responsibility. Also, she wants to make sure all of the damages are paid and/or that she collects the largest award possible. If her state permits joint and several liability, any plaintiff that is responsible may have to pay a disproportionate share of the damages. The driver of the vehicle that hit Janet and her child was directly involved in the accident. As an individual, however, the driver might not have enough financial resources to pay the damages. The local restaurant franchise might be responsible from a safety and design perspective. The exit from the drive-through window may not be easily visible to patrons leaving the restaurant. Perhaps a speed bump in this lane would force drivers to reduce their speed. The franchise owner may be in a better financial position to pay for the damages than the driver of the car. Naming the national restaurant chain as a defendant brings the "deepest pockets" of all to the claim. If local franchises are required to use a specific building design, the national chain may bear some responsibility for the accident.

Janet and her child may be awarded special damages for losses that can be determined and documented; general damages for pain, suffering, and mental anguish; and punitive damages to punish the tortfeasor and deter similar negligent acts.

Chapter 20
Homeowners Insurance, Section I

Overview

With this chapter we begin our study of property and liability insurance contracts. The first coverage we will examine is a popular personal lines coverage, homeowners insurance. Homeowners insurance is called a "package policy" because it combines more than one line of coverage in a single contract. A variety of homeowners forms are available, providing coverage for homeowners, renters, and condominium owners. Because of its widespread use, we will examine the Insurance Services Office (ISO) Homeowners 3 contract in greater detail. Section I of the homeowners policy provides coverage for damage to the dwelling, damage to other structures, losses to personal property, and loss of use coverage if an insured peril makes the property unusable. Section II of the homeowners policy (covered in Chapter 21) provides personal liability insurance and medical payments to others coverage.

Learning Objectives

After studying this chapter, you should be able to:

Identify the major homeowners policies for homeowners, condominium owners, and renters.

Explain the major provisions in the Homeowners 3 policy, including:
- —Section I property coverages
- —Section I perils insured against
- —Section I exclusions.

Given a specific loss situation, explain whether the Homeowners 3 policy would cover the loss.

Explain the insured's duties after a loss occurs.

Explain and give an illustration of the loss settlement provision in the Homeowners 3 policy.

Define the following:

Additional living expense	Homeowners 6 (unit owners form)
Appraisal clause	Homeowners 8 (modified coverage form)
Extended replacement cost endorsement	Liberalization clause
Fair rental value	Loss to a pair or set
Guaranteed replacement cost	Mortgage clause
Homeowners 2 (broad form)	Proximate cause
Homeowners 3 (special form)	Replacement cost
Homeowners 4 (contents broad form)	Schedule
Homeowners 5 (comprehensive form)	

■ Outline

I.   Homeowners Insurance

    A. Eligible Dwellings

    B. Overview of Homeowners Policies
       1. HO-2 (Broad Form)
       2. HO-3 (Special Form)
       3. HO-4 (Contents Broad Form)
       4. HO-5 (Comprehensive Form)
       5. HO-6 (Unit-Owners Form)
       6. HO-8 (Modified Coverage Form)

II.   Analysis of Homeowners 3 Policy (Special Form)

    A. Persons Insured

    B. Section I—Coverages
       1. Coverage A: Dwelling
       2. Coverage B: Other Structures
       3. Coverage C: Personal Property
       4. Coverage D: Loss of Use
       5. Additional Coverages

    C. Section I—Perils Insured Against
       1. Dwelling and Other Structures
       2. Personal Property

    D. Section I—Exclusions

    E. Section I—Conditions

    F. Section I and II Conditions

■ Short Answer Questions

1. Homeowners insurance is a multiple-line policy. What three types of coverage are provided through homeowners policy?

2. Besides the living units insured, what are the major differences between the current homeowners forms?

3. What persons are insured under Section I of the Homeowners 3 policy?

4. What four coverages are provided under Section I of the Homeowners 3 contract?

5. Is the property damage coverage under Section I of the Homeowners 3 policy written on a "direct physical loss not excluded" basis, a named-perils basis, or both? Explain.

6. What additional coverages are provided under Section I of the Homeowners 3 contract?

7. Personal property is covered on a named-perils basis under Coverage C of Section I of the Homeowners 3 policy. What are the insured perils?

8. In addition to the specific exclusions that apply to individual coverages under Section I, what general exclusions appear in the HO-3 policy?

9. Are property losses under Section I of the HO-3 policy settled on a replacement cost basis, actual cash value basis, or both? Explain your answer.

0. What is the purpose of the mortgage clause in a homeowners policy and how does the mortgage clause achieve this purpose?

11. Explain the purpose of the appraisal clause and the loss to a pair or set clause.

■ Multiple Choice Questions

Circle the letter that corresponds to the BEST *answer.*

1. Which statement(s) is(are) true with regard to Section I of an unendorsed Homeowners 3 policy?

    I.   Damage to the dwelling and other structures by an insured peril is usually settled based on actual cash value.

    II. Damage to personal property by an insured peril is settled based on replacement cost.

    (a) I only

    (b) II only

    (c) both I and II

    (d) neither I nor II

2. Coverage D under Section I of the Homeowners 3 policy provides coverage for:

    (a) personal property.

    (b) loss of use.

    (c) the dwelling.

    (d) other structures.

3. Under the Homeowners 3 policy, personal property is insured against damage from all of the following perils EXCEPT:

    (a) fire.

    (b) earthquake.

    (c) windstorm.

    (d) explosion.

4. To determine if a covered peril is the cause of loss, insurers check to see if there is an unbroken chain of events between the occurrence of a covered peril and the damage to property. This unbroken chain of events is called:

    (a) prohibited use.

    (b) the pair or set clause.

    (c) proximate cause.

    (d) subrogation.

5. Which statement(s) is(are) true with regard to homeowners insurance?
   I.   The homeowners policy can be assigned validly with the insurer's written consent.
   II. The insurer has the right to repair or replace damaged property with like property instead of making a cash settlement.
   (a) I only
   (b) II only
   (c) both I and II
   (d) neither I nor II

6. The Homeowners 4 (HO-4) policy is specifically designed for:
   (a) owners of private dwellings.
   (b) renters.
   (c) condominium unit owners.
   (d) homes that have a replacement cost exceeding the market value.

7. The mortgagee has an insurable interest in a home because:
   (a) the mortgagee loaned money for the purchase of the home and the home is collateral for the loan.
   (b) the mortgagee is the insurer writing coverage on the home.
   (c) the mortgagee purchased the home and resides in the home.
   (d) none of the above.

8. A rapidly spreading fire endangered Tom and Claire MacKenzie's home. They wanted to stay to protect the home, but a fire marshal ordered them to leave. Which statement is true regarding Tom and Claire's lodging expenses?
   (a) Lodging expenses are not covered unless their home is actually damaged.
   (b) Lodging expenses are covered under Coverage D's "additional living expenses."
   (c) Lodging expenses are covered under Coverage D's "fair rental value."
   (d) Lodging expenses are covered under Coverage D's "prohibited use."

9. Which statement(s) is(are) true with regard to an unendorsed Homeowners 3 policy?
   I.   The dwelling and other structures are covered on a direct physical loss not excluded basis.
   II. Personal property is covered on a direct physical loss not excluded basis.
   (a) I only
   (b) II only
   (c) both I and II
   (d) neither I nor II

10. All of the following are additional coverages provided under Section I of the Homeowners 3 policy EXCEPT:
    (a) debris removal.
    (b) reasonable repairs.
    (c) medical payments to others.
    (d) property removal.

11. The Homeowners 6 (HO-6) policy is specifically designed for:
    (a) general homeowners use.
    (b) renters.
    (c) condominium unit owners.
    (d) homes that have a replacement cost exceeding the market value.

■ True/False

Circle the T if the statement is true, the F if the statement is false. Explain to yourself why a statement is false.

T   F   1. Theft of personal property by an insured is excluded from coverage under the Homeowners ? policy.

T   F   2. In the event of loss to one piece of a pair or set, the insurer must pay the replacement cost of complete pair or set.

T   F   3. If more than one homeowners policy covers a loss, liability is determined on a pro-rata basis

T   F   4. The homeowners policy provides coverage for damage to property, personal liability, and medical payments to others.

T   F   5. The appraisal clause explains how a settlement is determined if the insurer and insured cannc agree on the value of a covered loss.

T   F   6. Family pets are covered under Section I of the homeowners policy.

T   F   7. If a homeowner rents a room above the garage to a tenant, and the room cannot be used after fire damages the garage, lost rent is covered under Coverage D—Loss of Use.

T   F   8. Property removed from the premises because it is endangered by an insured peril is covered on a named-perils basis.

T   F   9. Ordinary wear and tear and gradual deterioration of building materials are excluded under Coverage A.

T   F   10. A detached garage is covered under Coverage A—Dwelling.

T   F   11. Deductibles are not used in homeowners insurance.

■ Problems

1. Tom and Wendy Williams purchased an HO-3 policy with $150,000 in coverage on the dwelling. Ignoring "additional coverages," what is the most their insurer will be required to pay as a result of a single property loss occurrence? Remember to consider other structures, personal property, and additional living expenses.

2. Gail Thomas purchased an unendorsed HO-4 policy to cover her personal property. A fire damaged her apartment. Her only major loss was a stereo system that was purchased two years ago for $500. The system was 20 percent depreciated when the loss occurred, and a comparable replacement system will cost $600. How much will Gail receive from her insurer?

3. Roberto and Elena Martinez have a home that has a replacement cost of $200,000. They insured the home under an HO-3 policy for $140,000. When a fire destroyed the attached garage, it was 25 percent depreciated. It will cost $16,000 to replace the garage. Ignoring any deductible, how much will Roberto and Elena receive from their insurer?

■ Case Applications

Case 1

Last Friday was a bad day for Dave and Gwen Forester. A fire destroyed the garage attached to their home and the apartment above the garage. They rented the apartment to a tenant for $800 a month. A thief entered the home through an unlocked door and took a coin collection and sterling silverware. When Gwen backed the car out of the garage, she ran over Dave's 10-speed racing bike. To top off this miserable day, a plate shift along a previously unknown fault line caused an earthquake that damaged the foundation of their home. Dave and Gwen have an unendorsed HO-3 policy covering their home. Are these losses covered?

Case 2

Rachel and Ted Miller own a home insured by an HO-3 policy. Last Saturday, a spark from the fireplace in the family room ignited the carpet. Before the fire was extinguished, the home was approximately 40 percent destroyed. Rachel and Ted phoned their agent, gave the agent an address where the insurer could send the check, and then left town for an extended European vacation. In what ways are the Millers endangering their right to recover from their insurer by not following policy conditions?

■ Solutions to Chapter 20

Short Answer Questions

1. The three types of coverage provided through a homeowners policy are: property coverage (dwelling, other structures, personal property, and loss of use), personal liability insurance, and medical payments to others. The latter two coverages are discussed in Chapter 21.

2. The HO-2 (Broad Form) insures the dwelling, other structures, and personal property against losses from a list of specified perils.

    The HO-3 (Special Form) insures the dwelling and other structures against risk of direct loss to property. All physical damage losses are covered unless specifically excluded. Personal property is covered against loss from the same perils listed in the HO-2 policy.

    The HO-4 (Contents Broad Form) is designed for renters. This policy covers a tenant's personal property against loss or damage from the same perils listed in the HO-2 policy.

    The HO-5 (Comprehensive Form) provides open-perils ("all-risks") coverage on the dwelling and other structures, and on the personal property.

    The HO-6 (Unit-Owners Form) is designed for the owners of condominium units and cooperative apartments. The condominium association carries insurance on the building and other property owned in common by the owners of different units. The HO-6 covers the personal property of the insured for the same perils as the HO-2.

    The HO-8 (Modified Coverage Form) covers losses to the dwelling and other structures based on the amount required to repair or replace property using common construction materials and methods. It is designed for older homes having a replacement cost exceeding market value. The perils insured against are more limited than under the HO-2 form.

    The Section II coverages, Personal Liability and Medical Payments to Others, are identical under the various homeowners forms.

3. The persons insured under Section I of the HO-3 coverage include: the named insured and spouse (if a resident of the named insured's household), relatives residing in the named insured's household, children attending college full-time and temporarily away from home, and other persons under age 21 in the care of the insured (e.g., foster children and foreign exchange students).

4. Section I of the HO-3 policy provides four coverages. Coverage A insures against damage to the dwelling. Coverage B insures against damage to other structures, such as a detached garage, tool shed, or stable. Coverage C is protection against damage to personal property. Coverage D provides loss of use coverage in case the property cannot be used because of a loss caused by a covered peril.

5. The coverage is written under both an all-risk (direct physical loss not excluded) basis and a named-perils basis. The dwelling and other structures are insured against the risk of direct physical damage to property except for losses that are specifically excluded. The personal property coverage is written on a named-perils basis.

6. Additional coverage is provided for debris removal, reasonable repairs, trees/shrubs and other plants, fire department service charges, property removal, credit card forgery and counterfeit money, loss assessments, certain collapse losses, glass or safety glazing material, landlord's furnishings, ordinance or law, and grave markers.

7. The insured perils under Coverage C include: fire or lightning, windstorm or hail, explosion, riot, civil commotion, aircraft, vehicles, smoke, malicious mischief, theft, falling objects, weight of ice or sleet or snow, accidental discharge or overflow of water or steam; sudden and accidental tearing apart, cracking, burning, or bulging of a steam, hot water, air conditioning, or automatic fire protective sprinkler system, or from within a household appliance; freezing of a plumbing, heating, air conditioning, or automatic fire sprinkler system, or of a household appliance; sudden and accidental damage from artificially generated electrical current, and volcanic eruption.

8. In addition to the specific exclusions, the general exclusions are: ordinance or law, earth movement, water damage, power failure, neglect, war, nuclear hazard, intentional loss, governmental action, weather conditions, acts or decisions, and faulty or inadequate planning and design.

9. Personal property losses are settled based on actual cash value. The insured can add an endorsement to change the coverage to replacement cost if desired. Losses to the dwelling and other structures usually are paid on the basis of replacement cost. If the insured carries coverage equal to at least 80 percent of the dwelling's replacement cost at the time of the loss, the full replacement cost is paid with no deduction for depreciation up to the limits of the policy. If coverage that is less than 80 percent of the replacement cost is in force at the time of the loss, the insured receives the greater of the actual cash value of the loss or the ratio of the amount of insurance carried to 80 percent of replacement cost, multiplied by the amount of the loss.

10. The mortgage clause is designed to protect the mortgagee's insurable interest. The mortgagee is usually a lending institution that made a loan to the mortgagor so the property can be purchased. As the property is collateral for the loan, the mortgagee is harmed if the property is damaged. Under the mortgage clause, the mortgagee is entitled to receive a loss payment from the insurer to the extent of the mortgagee's insurable interest, regardless of policy violations. So if a mortgagor violates the provisions of the policy, the insurer must still pay the mortgagee to the extent of the mortgagee's insurable interest.

11. Although the insurer and insured may agree that a covered loss has occurred, they may disagree about the value of the covered loss. The appraisal clause is designed to predetermine how such disputes will be settled. Each party names an appraiser and the appraisers select an umpire. If the appraisers cannot settle the dispute, differences are submitted to the umpire who renders a decision.

If the loss is damage to a portion of a pair or set of items, the insurer can elect either to repair or replace that portion of the pair or set, or to pay the difference between the actual cash value of the property before and after the loss occurred. Through this clause, the insurer limits its liability and not responsible for replacing the entire pair or set because one portion was damaged or destroyed.

Multiple Choice Questions

1. (d) Neither statement is correct. Losses to the dwelling and other structures usually are settled on replacement cost basis. Losses to personal property are settled based on actual cash value.

2. (b) Coverage D is for loss of use. If an insured peril makes the property unusable, Coverage D responds.

3. (b) Earthquake is excluded under Section I of the homeowners policy.

4. (c) This unbroken chain of events is called proximate cause. There must be proximate cause betwe the covered peril and the loss to property for the policy to respond.

5. (c) Both statements are true. The insurer must approve an assignment for it to be valid. The insure has the right to repair or replace the property rather than to make a cash settlement.

6. (b) The HO-4 policy is also called the "contents form," as renters do not insure the structure, only their personal property.

7. (a) The mortgagee loaned money for the purchase of the home. The mortgagee has an insurable interest because the home is usually pledged as collateral for the loan. If the home is damaged the collateral is impaired.

8. (d) The lodging expenses are covered under Coverage D's "prohibited use" coverage. In this case, insured peril threatened the home, and the residents evacuated because a civil authority ordere them to leave.

9. (a) Only the first statement is true. The all-risk coverage applies to the dwelling and other structu only. Personal property is covered on a named-perils basis.

10. (c) Medical payments to others coverage is provided under Coverage F in Section II of the policy All of the other choices are additional coverages under Section I.

11. (c) The Homeowners 6 (HO-6) policy addresses the specific needs of condominium owners.

True/False

1. T

2. F The insurer can elect either to repair or replace any part of the pair or set, or pay the difference between the actual cash value of the property before and after the loss.

3. T

4. T

5. T

6. F Pets are specifically excluded from coverage under Section I.

7. **T**

8. **F** Property removed because of an insured peril is covered on an all-risk basis.

9. **T**

0. **F** A detached garage would be covered under Coverage B—Other Structures. If the garage is connected to the home, it is covered under the dwelling coverage.

1. **F** Deductibles are used with the dwelling, other structures, and personal property coverages. The type of deductible used is a straight deductible.

roblems

1. There may be more coverage available under the homeowners policy than you realize. Under the worst case scenario, there would be a complete loss of property (dwelling, other structures, and personal property), and the maximum additional living expenses would be required. The insurer would pay up to:

Coverage A—Dwelling	$150,000
Coverage B—Other Structures (10% of A)	$15,000
Coverage C—Personal Property (50% of A)	$75,000
Coverage D—Loss of Use (30% of A)	$45,000
Total	$285,000

2. As Gail's policy does not include a personal property replacement cost endorsement, this personal property loss is settled according to actual cash value (ACV):

ACV = Replacement Cost – Depreciation
ACV = $600 – ($600 × 20%)
ACV = $480

Gail will collect $480 from her insurer, assuming no deductible.

3. Under the Homeowners 3 policy, if less than 80 percent of the replacement cost of the dwelling is carried, the insured receives the larger of the following two amounts:
1) Actual Cash Value, or

2) $$\frac{\text{Amount of Insurance Carried}}{80\% \times \text{Replacement Cost}} \times \text{Loss}$$

The actual cash value of the loss is:
ACV = $16,000 – ($16,000 × 25%)
ACV = $12,000
Under the alternative settlement method:

$$\frac{\$140,000}{80\% \times \$200,000} \times \$16,000 = \$14,000$$

Roberto and Elena will receive $14,000 from their insurer as the replacement cost settlement exceeds the actual cash value settlement.

Case Applications

Case 1

As fire is not excluded under the Homeowners 3 (HO-3) dwelling coverage, the damage to the attached garage is covered. The lost rent is also covered under Coverage D—Loss of Use. The stolen property is covered, however there are dollar limits of liability that apply. The damage to the racing bike is covered under the personal property coverage as "vehicles" is a named peril. Unfortunately for the Foresters, damage to the foundation of their home caused by an earthquake would not be covered. Earth movement excluded under Section I of the HO-3. Earthquake coverage can be added through an endorsement.

Case 2

As we learned in Chapter 9, insurance contracts are conditional. The insurer's promise to indemnify is conditional upon the insured abiding by the terms of the contract. After a loss occurs, certain duties are required. Although the Millers gave notice of the loss, their assistance with loss settlement ended there. They are also required to protect the property from further harm, to prepare an inventory of the property to exhibit the property, and to file proof of loss. In addition, their "send us the check" attitude is presumptuous. Losses are settled at the insurer's option. If the claim is covered, the insurer decides whether to make a cash settlement or to repair or replace damaged property with like property.

Chapter 21
Homeowners Insurance, Section II

❚ Overview

This chapter examines Section II of the ISO Homeowners 3 insurance contract. Section I was examined in the previous chapter. Section II provides personal liability insurance that will respond to liability claims. Section II also includes medical payments to others coverage. As both of these coverages are provided on an all-risk basis, the exclusions applicable to these coverages are examined. Some additional coverages provided under Section II are discussed, as well as some endorsements that can be added to your homeowners policy to broaden the coverage. The chapter closes with some important suggestions to follow when shopping for homeowners insurance. The Appendix to Chapter 21 provides some tips on how to save money when buying homeowners insurance.

Learning Objectives

After studying this chapter, you should be able to:

Explain the personal liability coverage found in Section II of the homeowners policy.

Explain the medical payments to others coverage found in Section II of the homeowners policy.

Identify the major exclusions that apply to the Section II coverages in the homeowners policy.

Explain the following endorsements that can be added to a homeowners policy: inflation guard endorsement and personal property replacement cost endorsement.

Explain the suggestions that consumers should follow when shopping for a homeowners policy.

Define the following:

Claim expenses	Occurrence
Contractual liability	Personal injury endorsement
Damage to the property of others	Personal liability
Earthquake endorsement	Personal property replacement cost loss
First-aid expenses	settlement endorsement
Home business insurance coverage endorsement	Personal umbrella policy
Inflation guard endorsement	Scheduled personal property endorsement (with
Insurance score	agreed value loss settlement)
Medical payments to others	Watercraft endorsement

■ Outline

I.   Personal Liability Insurance

A.   Insuring Agreements

1.   Coverage E: Personal Liability

2.   Coverage F: Medical Payments to Others

II.   Section II Exclusions

A.   Exclusions that Apply to Both Coverage E and Coverage F

B.   Exclusions that Apply Only to Coverage E

C.   Exclusions that Apply Only to Coverage F

III.   Section II Additional Coverages

A.   Claim Expenses

B.   First-Aid Expenses

C.   Damage to Property of Others

D.   Loss Assessment

IV.   Endorsements to a Homeowners Policy

A.   Inflation Guard Endorsement

B.   Earthquake Endorsement

C.   Personal Property Replacement Cost Loss Settlement Endorsement

D.   Scheduled Personal Property Endorsement (with Agreed Value Loss Settlement)

E.   Personal Injury Endorsement

F.   Watercraft Endorsement

G.   Home Business Insurance Coverage Endorsement

V.   Shopping for Homeowners Insurance

A.   Cost of Homeowners Insurance

B.   Suggestions for Buying a Homeowners Policy

Short Answer Questions

1. What two coverages are provided under Section II of the homeowners policy?

2. Is the limit of liability under Coverage E an aggregate limit or a per-occurrence limit? What is an "occurrence"?

3. How do the two coverages provided under Section II of the homeowners policy differ with regard to who is covered and whether liability must be established for the coverage to respond?

4. What exclusions are common to both Coverage E and Coverage F?

5. What additional exclusions apply to Coverage E?

6. What additional exclusions apply to Coverage F?

7. What additional coverages are provided under Section II of the homeowners policy?

8. What endorsements can be added to the homeowners contract to make the coverage more complete?

9. What factors determine the cost of homeowners insurance?

10. What factors should you consider when shopping for homeowners insurance coverage?

■ Multiple Choice Questions

Circle the letter that corresponds to the BEST *answer.*

1. All of the following are excluded under Section II of the homeowners policy EXCEPT:
   (a) bodily injury to others.
   (b) business activities.
   (c) motor vehicles.
   (d) personal injury.

2. All of the following are additional coverages automatically provided under Section II of the homeowners policy EXCEPT:
   (a) first-aid expenses.
   (b) inflation protection.
   (c) damage to property of others.
   (d) claim expenses.

3. Which statement(s) is(are) true with regard to Section II of the homeowners policy?
   I. It provides coverage for damage to the dwelling, other structures, and personal property.
   II. It provides personal liability insurance and medical payments to others coverage.

   (a) I only
   (b) II only
   (c) both I and II
   (d) neither I nor II

4. Dr. Mary Chang is a dentist. She misread a patient's X-ray and extracted the wrong tooth. The patient has filed a lawsuit against Dr. Chang, alleging malpractice. This claim will not be covered under the homeowners policy because:
   (a) it involves personal injury, not bodily injury.
   (b) intentional injury is excluded.
   (c) liability resulting from professional services is excluded.
   (d) the act was an occurrence, not an accident.

5. Gilda does not want depreciation taken into consideration if her personal property sustains a loss. Which of the following endorsements should Gilda consider adding to her Homeowners 3 policy?

    (a) personal property replacement cost endorsement

    (b) scheduled personal property coverage

    (c) personal injury endorsement

    (d) inflation guard endorsement

6. Which statement is true with regard to Section II of the homeowners policy?

    I. Before the insurer will pay a personal liability insurance claim, an insured must be legally liable.

    II. Before the insurer will cover medical payments to others, an insured must be legally liable for the injury.

    (a) I only

    (b) II only

    (c) both I and II

    (d) neither I nor II

7. All of the following are endorsements that can be added to the homeowners policy EXCEPT:

    (a) home business insurance coverage endorsement.

    (b) bodily injury liability endorsement.

    (c) earthquake endorsement.

    (d) watercraft endorsement.

8. Which statement(s) is(are) true with regard to Coverage E—Personal Liability?

    I. In addition to liability coverage, the insurer will cover legal defense costs.

    II. The coverage will only respond to accidents, not occurrences.

    (a) I only

    (b) II only

    (c) both I and II

    (d) neither I nor II

9. Which statement is true with regard to shopping for homeowners insurance?

    (a) Selecting a lower deductible will lower your premium.

    (b) There is no cost variation among homeowners policies.

    (c) It may be necessary to use a scheduled personal property endorsement to provide coverage for some personal property.

    (d) Although the actual cash value coverage on personal property is limited, replacement cost coverage is not available.

10. All of the following statements regarding the cost of homeowners insurance are true EXCEPT:

    (a) Insurers charge less to insure newer homes than to insure older homes.

    (b) Wooden homes cost more to insure than do brick homes.

    (c) The HO-3 policy is less expensive than the HO-2 policy.

    (d) If a higher deductible is selected, the premium will be lower.

■ True/False

Circle the T if the statement is true, the F if the statement is false. Explain to yourself why a statement is false.

T   F   1. Personal injury is covered under Section II of an unendorsed homeowners policy.

T   F   2. Intentional injury is excluded from coverage under Section II of the homeowners policy.

T   F   3. Medical expense coverage applies to resident employees injured on the premises.

T   F   4. All watercraft are explicitly excluded from coverage under Section II of the homeowners policy.

T   F   5. Section II of the homeowners policy applies to accidents only. Gradual damage that occurs over time is not covered.

T   F   6. In addition to providing personal liability protection under Coverage E, the insurer also provides for the cost of a legal defense even if the claim is groundless.

T   F   7. The age, construction, fire protection class, and location of your home will affect the premium you pay for homeowners insurance.

T   F   8. Damage to personal property owned by the insured is covered under Section II of the homeowners policy.

T   F   9. Legal liability of an insured must be established before the medical payments to others coverage will apply.

T   F   10. Your credit history may have an influence upon an insurer's willingness to sell you a homeowners insurance policy.

■ Case Applications

Case 1

Last Friday was a horrible day for Dr. Brian and Lynn Green. A patient filed a medical malpractice claim against Dr. Green. While playing golf, Lynn sliced a shot and hit another golfer. The normally docile family dog bit their next-door neighbor. Dr. Green was charged with defamation of character by another physician. The other doctor claims Dr. Green slandered her at an American Medical Association meeting. The maid, who lives with the Greens, received a severe laceration when a glass she was washing shattered. Will Section II of the HO-3 policy cover these claims?

ase 2

enny Franklin insured her home with an unendorsed Homeowners 3 policy. Penny taught kindergarten nd first grade up until her son was born last year. Penny misses the classroom and needs to earn some money. However, she would like to spend time with her baby. She is considering opening a "pre-preschool" her home. Parents will leave their children in the morning before they go to work, and in addition to ormal day-care services, Penny will prepare the children for kindergarten. What advice would you offer enny with regard to her homeowners insurance and this proposed child care operation?

Solutions to Chapter 21

hort Answer Questions

1. Section II of the Homeowners 3 policy provides two coverages. Coverage E is personal liability insurance. This coverage is provided with a $100,000 per occurrence limit. The insurer also provides coverage for legal defense costs, with the cost of the legal defense not counted against the limit of liability. Coverage F is medical payments to others coverage. Up to $1,000 per person is provided.

2. The limit of liability under Coverage E is a per-occurrence limit. Several occurrences could happen during the year, and the full limit of liability is available to respond to each separate occurrence. While accidents are sudden events, an "occurrence" may take place over time. The homeowners policy defines occurrence to include accidental losses as well as losses that happen over a period of time.

3. Personal liability coverage protects the named insured, spouse, family members residing at home, and some other miscellaneous persons. The medical payments coverage, in contrast, does not apply to the homeowner or regular residents of the home, except resident employees. The words "to others" are added to the medical payments coverage—"medical payments to others." The liability coverage is based upon establishing legal liability. The medical payments coverage is not based on legal liability.

4. Several exclusions apply both to personal liability (Coverage E) and medical payments to others (Coverage F). These common exclusions are: motor vehicle liability, liability arising from use of certain watercraft, aircraft and hovercraft liability, expected or intentional injury, business activities, professional services, uninsured locations, war, communicable disease, sexual molestation/abuse and corporal punishment, and controlled substances.

5. Additional exclusions that apply to personal liability (Coverage E) include: contractual liability, property owned by the insured, property in the care of the insured, workers compensation, nuclear energy, and bodily injury to an insured.

6. The final set of exclusions applies to medical payments to others (Coverage F). These exclusions are injury to a resident employee off an insured location, workers compensation, nuclear energy, and persons regularly residing at the insured location.

7. Several additional coverages are provided under Section II of the homeowners policy. The additional coverages are claim expenses, first-aid expenses, coverage for damage to the property of others, and certain loss assessment charges.

8. A number of endorsements can be added to the homeowners contract to broaden the coverage. These endorsements include: an inflation guard endorsement, an earthquake endorsement, a personal property replacement cost endorsement, a scheduled personal property endorsement, a personal injury endorsement, an endorsement covering certain watercraft and recreational vehicles, and a home business insurance coverage endorsement.

9. A number of factors determine the cost of homeowners insurance. Major rating and underwriting factors include: construction, location, fire-protection class, construction costs, age of the home, type of policy purchased, deductible level, insurance score, and CLUE report.

10. Some guidelines when shopping for homeowners insurance include: purchase an adequate amount of insurance, add necessary endorsements, shop around for a policy, consider a higher deductible, take advantage of discounts, don't ignore disaster perils, consider purchasing a personal umbrella policy, and improve your credit rating.

Multiple Choice Questions

1. (a) Bodily injury to others is not excluded—it is covered. Personal injury and the other listed choice are excluded under Section II of the homeowners policy.

2. (b) Inflation protection is not provided automatically. The insured must periodically adjust the amount of coverage in force or purchase an inflation-guard endorsement to have this protection.

3. (b) Damage to the dwelling, other structures, and personal property of the insured are provided under Section I of the homeowners policy. Section II provides personal liability and medical payments to others coverage.

4. (c) Liability arising out of professional services is excluded under Section II of the homeowners policy.

5. (a) The personal property coverage in a Homeowners 3 policy is written on an actual cash value basis. Should a loss occur, depreciation will be considered when determining the loss settlement. A personal property replacement cost endorsement changes the basis of recovery to replacement cost.

6. (a) Coverage E, Personal Liability, is based on establishing legal liability. Medical Payments to Others (Coverage F) is paid regardless of legal liability.

7. (b) There is no need to add a bodily injury liability endorsement as this coverage is already provided under the policy. The other endorsements listed may be added by the insured.

3. (a) Only the first statement is true. As the insurer will pay the claim if you are legally liable, the insurer has an incentive to make sure that you have competent legal representation. The coverage is written to insure "occurrences," not accidents. Occurrence coverage is broader, insuring accidents as well as damage that happens gradually over time.

9. (c) Certain property, such as furs, silverware, and collectibles, is subject to limits under the homeowners policy. To overcome these internal policy limits, a scheduled personal property endorsement can be added to the homeowners policy.

0. (c) The HO-3 policy is more expensive than the HO-2 policy. The HO-3 provides broader coverage, and insurers charge accordingly.

rue/False

1. **F** While bodily injury and property damage liability are covered under Section II, personal injury is excluded. This coverage can be added through an endorsement. Personal injury is also covered by some personal umbrella liability policies.

2. **T**

3. **T**

4. **F** Although there is a watercraft exclusion, only certain watercraft are excluded. Excluded watercraft are mainly those above certain length and horsepower limits.

5. **F** Section II of the homeowners policy is written on an occurrence basis. Occurrence coverage protects against accidents and also damage that occurs gradually over time.

6. **T**

7. **T**

8. **F** Coverage for damage to personal property owned by the insured is covered under Coverage C of Section I of the homeowners policy. It is excluded under Section II.

9. **F** The medical payments to others coverage under Section II does not require establishing legal liability.

0. **T**

ase Applications

ase 1

he first claim is a medical malpractice claim against Dr. Green. Professional liability is excluded under ction II, so this claim is not covered. The coverage would respond to the golfer injured by the misguided olf shot Lynn Green hit. A claim brought by the next-door neighbor as a result of the dog bite would be overed. As defamation and slander are considered personal injury, Section II would not respond unless e coverage was added by endorsement. The maid's medical expenses would be eligible for coverage. 'hile the medical expense coverage applies "to others," an exception is made for resident employees who e injured at the insured's home.

Case 2

Before Penny starts this business in her home, her homeowners coverage must be modified. There is a general business activity exclusion in Section II that makes it clear that liability resulting from business activities is not covered. She must endorse her policy to have coverage for day-care–related liability claims or purchase a separate policy to have the necessary coverage.

Chapter 22
Auto Insurance

Overview

If you hit a pedestrian, another car, a large animal or bird, or another object while driving your car, damage is likely to result. You could injure someone and damage his or her property. You could also injure yourself and your passengers and damage your own vehicle. Fortunately, automobile insurance is available to cover these losses. Like homeowners insurance, automobile insurance is a package policy designed to provide coverage for several types of losses. In this chapter we examine the provisions of the Personal Auto Policy (PAP). The PAP provides coverage for bodily injury and property damage liability, physical damage protection, medical payments coverage, uninsured motorists protection, and a number of other coverages.

Learning Objectives

After studying this chapter, you should be able to:

Identify the parties that are insured for liability coverage under the personal auto policy (PAP).

Describe the liability coverage in the PAP.

Explain the medical payments coverage in the PAP.

Describe the uninsured motorists coverage in the PAP.

Explain the coverage for damage to your auto in the PAP.

Explain the duties imposed on the insured after an accident or loss.

Define the following:

Appraisal provision	Nonowned auto
Betterment	Nonrenewal
Cancellation	Other-than-collision loss
Collision	Personal Auto Policy (PAP)
Coverage for damage to your auto	Single limit
Diminution of value	Split limits
Extended nonowned coverage endorsement	Supplementary payments
Gap insurance	Temporary substitute auto
Liability coverage	Underinsured motorist coverage
Medical payments coverage	Uninsured motorists coverage
Miscellaneous-type vehicle endorsement	Your covered auto

■ Outline

I. **Overview of 2005 Personal Auto Policy**
   A. Eligible Vehicles
   B. Your Covered Auto
   C. Summary of PAP Coverages

II. **Part A: Liability Coverage**
   A. Insuring Agreement
   B. Insured Persons
   C. Supplementary Payments
   D. Exclusions
   E. Limit of Liability
   F. Out-of-State Coverage
   G. Other Insurance

III. **Part B: Medical Payments Coverage**
   A. Insuring Agreement
   B. Insured Persons
   C. Exclusions
   D. Other Insurance

IV. **Part C: Uninsured Motorists Coverage**
   A. Insuring Agreement
   B. Insured Persons
   C. Uninsured Vehicles
   D. Exclusions
   E. Other Insurance
   F. Underinsured Motorists Coverage

V. **Part D: Coverage for Damage to Your Auto**
   A. Insuring Agreement
   B. Transportation Expenses
   C. Exclusions
   D. Limit of Liability
   E. Payment of Loss
   F. Other Sources of Recovery
   G. Appraisal Provision

I.   Part E: Duties after an Accident or Loss

II. Part F: General Provisions

   A.   Policy Period and Territory

   B.   Termination

III. Insuring Motorcycles and Other Vehicles

Short Answer Questions

1. What four classes of autos are considered "covered autos" under the PAP?

2. In addition to a declarations page and a definitions page, what are the six parts of the Personal Auto Policy (PAP)?

3. Who is insured under the liability coverage of the PAP?

4. What exclusions apply to the liability coverage under the PAP?

5. What persons are insured for medical payments under the PAP?

6. What important points must be recognized with respect to the insuring agreement of Part C of the PAP, Uninsured Motorists Coverage?

7. What vehicles are considered uninsured under the PAP?

8. What is the difference between a collision loss and an other-than-collision loss under the PAP?

9. What duties are required of an insured under the PAP after an accident or loss has occurred?

10. What is the difference between cancellation of the PAP, nonrenewal of the PAP, and automatic termination of the PAP?

11. What is the purpose of the miscellaneous-type vehicle endorsement that can be added to the PAP?

■ Multiple Choice Questions

Circle the letter that corresponds to the BEST *answer.*

1. All of the following are covered vehicles under the liability coverage of an unendorsed PAP EXCEPT:
    (a) newly acquired vehicles.
    (b) a trailer owned by the insured.
    (c) a motorcycle owned by the insured.
    (d) all vehicles listed in the declarations.

2. Bruce carries automobile liability limits of 25/50/10. He was just involved in an accident in which he was negligent. The two occupants of the other vehicle incurred $7,500 and $32,000, respectively, in bodily injury expenses. The damage to the other car, a Mercedes, was $16,000. How much will Bruce's insurer pay under the liability coverage?
    (a) $42,500
    (b) $60,000
    (c) $39,500
    (d) $55,500

3. Which statement(s) is(are) true with regard to Part D of the PAP, coverage for damage to your auto?

   I. If you hit a tree with your car, the resulting damage is a collision loss.

   II. If you hit a deer with your car, the resulting damage is an other-than-collision loss.

   (a) I only

   (b) II only

   (c) both I and II

   (d) neither I nor II

4. If there is a dispute between the insurer and the policyowner over the value of a physical damage loss, which policy provision explains how the dispute will be settled?

   (a) stated amount endorsement

   (b) supplementary payments

   (c) miscellaneous-type vehicle endorsement

   (d) appraisal clause

5. All of the following are considered uninsured vehicles under the PAP EXCEPT:

   (a) a motor vehicle not covered by bodily injury liability insurance at the time of an accident.

   (b) a vehicle covered by bodily injury liability insurance at the time of an accident, but the insurer writing the coverage is insolvent.

   (c) a hit-and-run vehicle.

   (d) a vehicle covered by bodily injury liability up to the state-required minimum, but this amount is less than the injured person's bodily injury claim.

6. Mike borrowed Susan's car with her permission. While driving Susan's car, Mike negligently injured another driver. Both Mike and Susan have purchased PAPs. How will this loss be settled?

   (a) neither policy will respond as borrowed autos are excluded

   (b) Susan's coverage is primary, Mike's coverage is excess

   (c) Susan's and Mike's insurers will each pay their pro-rata share of the loss

   (d) Mike's coverage is primary, Susan's coverage is excess

7. Which statement(s) is(are) true with regard to collision coverage under the PAP?

   I. If you are at fault in the accident, your insurer will not pay for damage to your auto.

   II. If a negligent driver hits your car, you can collect from the negligent driver or from your own insurer.

   (a) I only

   (b) II only

   (c) both I and II

   (d) neither I nor II

8. Which of the following losses would be covered under Part D of the PAP?

   (a) Bill's car was stolen on Thursday morning. His cab fare to work Monday morning was $15.

   (b) Thieves broke into Jennifer's car and stole her portable CD player.

   (c) Geraldine's radar detector was stolen from her car.

   (d) Harold's right front tire blew out after only 800 miles of use.

9. All of the following are exclusions under the liability coverage of the PAP EXCEPT:
   (a) intentional losses.
   (b) use of a vehicle without reasonable belief permission would have been granted to use the vehicle
   (c) losses for which the insured is liable.
   (d) liability resulting from an accident that occurred while the vehicle was being used as a taxi.

10. Gina carelessly injured another motorist while driving her own car and must pay damages of $50,000 as a result of the accident. If Gina has two PAPs that will respond to the loss, how will the claim be settled?
    (a) neither policy will respond as duplication voids coverage
    (b) one policy will be primary and the other policy excess
    (c) contribution by equal shares will be used to settle the loss
    (d) each policy will respond on a pro-rata basis

11. A car damaged in an auto accident may lose market value or resale value. This reduction in value, for which some insureds have sought recovery, is called:
    (a) gap insurance.
    (b) diminution of value.
    (c) underinsured motorists coverage.
    (d) collision damage waiver.

■ True/False

Circle the T if the statement is true, the F if the statement is false. Explain to yourself why a statement is false.

T F 1. The PAP is a package policy.

T F 2. The most important coverages you can purchase under a PAP are physical damage coverages

T F 3. If you cross the center line and hit a car, bodily injuries suffered by the driver of the other car are covered under your medical payments coverage.

T F 4. If you are driving in a state that has a financial responsibility requirement with higher liability limits than the limits of your policy, the PAP automatically provides these higher limits.

T F 5. Underinsured motorists coverage duplicates the coverage provided by uninsured motorists coverage.

T F 6. Under the PAP, collision losses are settled based on replacement cost.

T F 7. Your PAP covers you while you are driving in Mexico.

T F 8. If you borrow a friend's car and are involved in an accident, any physical damage insurance on the borrowed car is primary and your physical damage coverage is excess.

T F 9. The miscellaneous-type vehicle endorsement can be added to the PAP to insure motorcycles, mopeds, and golf carts.

T F 10. Although the insurer may be required to pay up to the limit of liability under the PAP, the insurer will not cover legal defense costs.

T   F   11. Under supplementary payments, the insurer will reimburse up to $200 daily for loss of earnings and to cover other reasonable expenses.

T   F   12. Coverage for towing and labor costs can be added to the PAP by endorsement.

T   F   13. The purpose of the collision damage waiver is to relieve someone who rents an auto from financial responsibility if the auto is damaged or stolen.

Case Applications

Case 1

Kirk owns a 1975 Ford Torino that has been driven 165,000 miles. Kirk purchased a PAP. He carries the minimum liability insurance limits required by his state. He does not carry uninsured motorists coverage or medical payments coverage. He purchased collision and other-than-collision coverage, both with a $100 deductible. Critique Kirk's auto insurance coverages.

Case 2

Carolyn owns a 2005 Toyota Camry. She insured the car under a PAP and purchased the following coverages: bodily injury and property damage liability, medical payments coverage, collision and other-than-collision loss coverage, uninsured motorists, and towing and labor costs. Are the following losses covered under Carolyn's PAP? If the loss is covered, which PAP coverage would respond?

a)   While driving the Camry, Carolyn slid off an icy road and hit a tree. Her car was damaged and the passenger riding with her sustained a broken nose and a severe laceration on her forehead.

b)   Carolyn's car was hit by a car that ran a stop sign. The driver did not have insurance. Although Carolyn's car was not damaged, Carolyn suffered whiplash and required medical care as a result of the accident.

c)   Carolyn's car broke down while she was driving on a busy freeway. She called a tow truck and had the car towed to a local service station.

(d) While driving late at night, Carolyn fell asleep and her car crossed the center line. She hit an approaching car. The driver of the other car sustained $20,000 in bodily injuries and the passenger i the other car sustained $10,000 in bodily injuries. The other car was a total loss, and Carolyn's car sustained $2,500 in damage. Carolyn broke her arm and leg in the accident.

(e) Carolyn was involved in a carjacking. She was not injured, but her stolen car was never recovered.

■ Solutions to Chapter 22

Short Answer Questions

1. The four classes of vehicles considered to be covered autos under the PAP include: any vehicle listed in the declarations, newly acquired vehicles, trailers owned by the named insured, and temporary substitute autos.

2. The six parts of the PAP include:
    (1) Part A—Liability Coverage
    (2) Part B—Medical Payments Coverage
    (3) Part C—Uninsured Motorists Coverage
    (4) Part D—Coverage for Damage to Your Auto
    (5) Part E—Duties After an Accident or Loss
    (6) Part F—General Provisions

3. The following groups are insured under the liability section of the PAP: the named insured and family members, persons using the named insured's covered auto, any person or organization upon whose behalf an insured person uses a covered auto, and finally any person or organization legally responsible for the named insured's or a family member's use of any auto or trailer.

4. The exclusions are: intentional damage or injury, property owned or transported, property rented or under the insured's care, bodily injury to an employee, use of auto as a public or livery conveyance, vehicles used in the automobile business, business vehicles, use of a vehicle without a reasonable belief of permission, nuclear energy exclusion, vehicles with fewer than four wheels, vehicles furnished or made available for the named insured's regular use, a vehicle owned by, furnished, or made available for the regular use of any family member, and racing vehicles.

5. Just two groups are eligible for medical payments coverage under the PAP. The first group is the named insured and family members. The second group is other persons while they are occupying a covered auto.

6. A number of important points must be recognized with respect to the uninsured motorists coverage insuring agreement. This coverage applies only if the uninsured motorist is legally liable. The maximum amount paid for any single accident is the amount shown in the declarations. The claim is subject to arbitration if there is disagreement over the amount of damages or whether the insured is entitled to damages. Finally, many states include coverage for property damage caused by an uninsured motorist.

7. Four groups of vehicles are considered uninsured. First, motor vehicles and trailers that have no liability insurance or applicable bond at the time of an accident. Second, a vehicle covered by liability insurance, but less coverage than the amount required under the state's financial responsibility law is considered uninsured. Third, a hit-and-run vehicle is considered uninsured. Finally, a vehicle to which bodily injury liability coverage applies, but the insurer denies coverage or is insolvent is uninsured.

8. A collision loss is defined as the upset of your covered auto or its impact with another vehicle or object. Some examples include: hitting another car, running into a utility pole, and hitting the side of a parking garage. Other forms of physical damage are not covered under collision, but are covered by other-than-collision loss insurance, unless excluded. Some examples of other-than-collision losses include: auto fires, hail damage, flood, theft, hitting a bird or animal, and vandalism.

9. In addition to requirements dictated by common sense and required by law, the PAP has a number of added requirements. The insurer (or its agent) must be notified that a loss has occurred. You must cooperate with the insurer in the investigation and settlement of the claim. The insurer should be given copies of any legal papers or notices you receive in connection with the accident. You may be required to take a physical exam if you are claiming medical expenses. You must also authorize the insurer to obtain medical reports and records. Finally, you must submit proof of loss. If you are trying to collect under uninsured motorists, you must notify the police of the accident and the other driver must be found liable. If you are trying to collect for physical damage, you must protect the vehicle from further harm and assist the insurer by making the vehicle available for inspection and obtaining damage estimates.

10. Either the insurer or insured may cancel the PAP. The named insured need only give the insurer notice of when he or she would like the coverage cancelled. The insurer must give 10 days notice if cancellation is for nonpayment of premiums, and 20 days notice for other causes. Nonrenewal is an option for the insurer when the policy comes up for renewal. The insurer may be unwilling to extend coverage for another time period. The insurer must give 20 days notice before the end of the policy period that the coverage will not be renewed. If the insurer decides to renew the PAP, an automatic termination provision becomes effective. This means that if the insured does not accept the company's offer to renew, the policy terminates at the end of the current policy period.

11. The PAP excludes some other types of vehicles. The insured, however, may need coverage for these vehicles. Coverage can be obtained by adding a miscellaneous-type vehicle endorsement to the PAP. This endorsement extends coverage to motorcycles, mopeds, motorscooters, golf carts, motor homes, dune buggies, and similar vehicles.

Multiple Choice Questions

1. (c) Vehicles with fewer than four wheels are excluded from coverage. Motorcycles can be insured through a miscellaneous-type vehicle endorsement added to the PAP.

2. (a) Unfortunately for Bruce, he purchased inadequate liability insurance. The first two numbers in the split limits are for bodily injury liability—$25,000 per person, subject to a maximum of $50,000 per accident. The $7,500 bodily injury claim is covered as it is less than $25,000. Only $25,000 of the $32,000 bodily injury claim is covered. The third number in the split limits is for property damage liability. Bruce has only $10,000 of coverage, so only $10,000 of the $16,000 covered. The total paid by the insurer is:

$$\$7,500 + \$25,000 + \$10,000 = \$42,500$$

   Bruce will have to pay the remaining portion of the claim out of his own pocket.

3. (c) Both statements are true. Collision coverage applies to impact with other vehicles or objects, such as trees, poles, and buildings. Contact with birds and animals is covered under other-than-collision loss coverage.

4. (d) The appraisal clause in the PAP specifies how disputes between the insurer and the insured with respect to valuation will be resolved.

5. (d) A vehicle is not uninsured if it has coverage up to the state-required minimum liability limits. The vehicle described in choice (d) is underinsured with respect to the described claim, however.

6. (b) Regarding nonowned autos, the insurance on the car is primary, the insurance on the driver is excess. So Susan's coverage applies first, and then Mike's coverage applies.

7. (b) Only the second statement is true. Collision losses are paid regardless of fault. If your car is damaged by a negligent driver, you can collect from the negligent driver or collect from your own insurer. If you collect from own insurer, your insurer will attempt to recoup this payment from the other driver through subrogation.

8. (a) Part D provides transportation expenses as a supplementary payment. If a covered auto is stolen after a 48-hour period, the insurer pays up to $20 a day for transportation expenses.

9. (c) The reason liability insurance is purchased is to have coverage for losses for which you are legally responsible. Such claims are the reason for purchasing the coverage.

10. (d) In the case of "other insurance" on an owned auto, each insurer is required to pay its pro-rata share of the loss.

11. (b) The loss described is the diminution of value of the vehicle.

True/False

1. **T**

2. **F** Physical damage losses are capped at the value of the property damaged. The most you could lose if your $15,000 car is totally destroyed is $15,000. If you injure someone while operating your vehicle, however, the resulting liability claim may make $15,000 look like a pittance. Liability coverage (bodily injury and property damage) is the most important coverage.

3. **F** Medical payments coverage applies to the people in your car (named insured, family members, and your passengers). Bodily injuries suffered by the driver of the other car would be covered under your liability coverage.

4. **T**

5. **F** The coverages address different situations. You can collect under one or the other, but not both. Underinsured motorists coverage applies if the negligent driver satisfies the state-required minimum liability limit, but the amount of coverage in force is not enough to cover the liability claim. The underinsured motorists coverage would pay the difference.

6. **F** The amount paid for a physical damage loss to a covered auto is the lesser of the actual cash value of the damaged or stolen property or the amount necessary to repair or replace the property.

7. **F** The PAP applies only when you are in the United States, its territories or possessions, Puerto Rico, and Canada.

8. **T**

9. **T**

10. **F** In addition to paying up to the limit of liability, the insurer agrees to defend you and pay legal defense costs.

11. **T**

12. **T**

13. **T**

Case Applications

Case 1

Kirk is not spending his auto insurance premium dollars wisely. He needs additional liability insurance as state minimum limits are generally far too low. He also needs to add uninsured motorists coverage and medical payments coverage. Finally, Kirk should consider dropping the physical damage coverage. Recalling the physical damage settlement rules, Kirk's old car is a prime candidate to be "totaled" if there is a physical damage claim. Carrying both physical damage coverages with such a low deductible is not a wise use of premium dollars.

Case 2

Although Carolyn has had some bad luck driving, fortunately all of the claims are covered.

(a) The physical damage caused by hitting a tree is covered under the collision coverage of the PAP. The medical treatment required by the passenger would be covered under the medical payments coverage.

(b) As the other driver is legally liable and did not have liability insurance, Carolyn's uninsured motorists coverage would respond.

(c) As Carolyn added the endorsement for towing and labor costs, the towing charge is covered.

(d) The bodily injury claims and property damage to the other car are covered under Carolyn's liability coverage. Damage to Carolyn's car is covered under her collision coverage. Carolyn can also recover the cost of her medical care under the medical payments coverage. Collision losses and medical payments are paid regardless of fault.

(e) Theft of an insured auto is covered under the other-than-collision loss coverage of the PAP.

Chapter 23
Auto Insurance and Society

■ Overview

Compensating innocent motorists who have been injured in auto accidents is an important issue for society. Private insurers are not anxious to insure high-risk drivers. But it is in society's interest that all motorists are financially responsible. This chapter examines a number of issues relating to auto insurance and society. Four major topics are addressed. First, approaches that are used to compensate innocent automobile accident victims are discussed, including no-fault insurance as an alternative to the traditional tort-based system. Second, methods of providing automobile insurance to high-risk drivers are examined. Third, factors affecting the cost of automobile insurance are discussed. Finally, some suggestions for shopping for automobile insurance are offered.

■ Learning Objectives

After studying this chapter, you should be able to:

● Describe each of the following approaches for compensating auto accident victims: financial responsibility laws, compulsory insurance laws, unsatisfied judgment funds, uninsured motorists coverage, low-cost auto insurance, and "no pay, no play" laws.

● Explain the meaning of no-fault automobile insurance and the rationale for no-fault insurance laws.

● Describe each of the following methods for providing auto insurance to high-risk drivers: automobile insurance plans, joint underwriting associations (JUAs), and reinsurance facilities.

● Identify the major factors that determine the cost of automobile insurance to consumers.

● Explain the suggestions that consumers should follow when shopping for auto insurance.

● Define the following:

Add-on plan	Multicar discount
Assigned-risk plans	No-fault auto insurance
Auto insurance plan	"No pay, no play" laws
Choice no-fault plan	Optional deductibles
Compulsory insurance law	Optional no-fault benefits
Essential services expenses	Pure no-fault plan
Financial responsibility law	Reinsurance facility (or pool)
Good student discount	Safe driver plans
Insurance score	Shared (residual) market
Joint underwriting association (JUA)	Specialty insurers
Low-cost auto insurance	Survivors' loss benefits
Maryland Automobile Insurance Fund	Uninsured motorists coverage
Modified no-fault plan	Unsatisfied judgment fund
Monetary threshold	Verbal threshold

■ Outline

I.   Approaches for Compensating Auto Accident Victims

    A. Financial Responsibility Laws

    B. Compulsory Insurance Laws

    C. Unsatisfied Judgment Funds

    D. Uninsured Motorists Coverage

    E. Low-Cost Auto Insurance

    F. "No Pay, No Play" Laws

    G. No-fault Auto Insurance

II.   Auto Insurance for High-Risk Drivers

    A. Automobile Insurance Plan

    B. Joint Underwriting Association (JUA)

    C. Reinsurance Facility

    D. Maryland Automobile Insurance Fund

    E. Specialty Insurers

III. Cost of Automobile Insurance

    A. Territory

    B. Age, Gender, and Marital Status

    C. Use of the Auto

    D. Driver Education

    E. Good Student Discount

    F. Number and Types of Cars

    G. Individual Driving Record

    H. Insurance Score

IV.   Shopping for Auto Insurance

    A. Carry Adequate Liability Insurance

    B. Carry Higher Deductibles

    C. Drop Collision Insurance on Older Vehicles

    D. Shop Around for Auto Insurance

    E. Take Advantage of Discounts

    F. Improve Your Driving Record

    G. Maintain Good Credit

Short Answer Questions

1. What approaches are available for compensating automobile accident victims?

2. Under what circumstances are drivers typically required to demonstrate proof of financial responsibility under state financial responsibility laws?

3. What are the advantages and shortcomings of compulsory automobile insurance laws?

4. What are the advantages and disadvantages of uninsured motorists coverage as a method of compensating innocent automobile accident victims?

5. Differentiate between the four principal types of no-fault plans.

6. What are the arguments for no-fault laws and against no-fault laws?

. How can high-risk drivers who are unable to obtain insurance in the voluntary automobile insurance market obtain auto insurance?

. How does an automobile insurance plan differ from a joint underwriting association?

. What impact do territory, use of the vehicle, and age of the driver have upon automobile insurance premiums?

. What suggestions should you consider when shopping for automobile insurance?

■ Multiple Choice Questions

Circle the letter that corresponds to the BEST *answer.*

1. In a certain state, all high-risk automobile insurance business is placed in a common pool, and each auto insurer operating in the state pays its proportional share of pool losses and expenses based upo the proportion of automobile insurance coverage written in the state by the insurer. Such a plan is called a(n):
   (a) joint underwriting association.
   (b) reinsurance facility.
   (c) specialty automobile insurer.
   (d) auto insurance plan.

2. Which statement(s) is(are) true with regard to pure no-fault automobile insurance?
   I.   Under pure no-fault insurance, after an automobile accident involving bodily injury, each party collects from his or her own insurer regardless of fault.
   II. Most states that have adopted no-fault insurance use pure no-fault.
   (a) I only
   (b) II only
   (c) both I and II
   (d) neither I nor II

3. A number of states have established special funds for compensating innocent accident victims who have exhausted all other means of recovery. These funds are called:
   (a) joint underwriting associations.
   (b) unsatisfied judgment funds.
   (c) reinsurance facilities.
   (d) auto insurance plans.

4. All of the following are approaches for protecting innocent victims of automobile accidents EXCEPT:
   (a) uninsured motorist coverage.
   (b) no-fault automobile insurance.
   (c) financial responsibility laws.
   (d) higher deductibles on collision coverage.

5. Parker lives in a state that has a no-fault automobile insurance law. If Parker is injured in an accide he has the right to sue a negligent driver if his bodily injury claim exceeds a certain dollar threshol What type of no-fault plan is used in Parker's state?
   (a) tort liability
   (b) pure no-fault
   (c) modified no-fault
   (d) add-on no-fault

6. Which statement(s) is(are) true with regard to the cost of automobile insurance?

    I. Insurers are not permitted to consider the age of the driver when determining the premium for coverage.

    II. Urban drivers typically pay more for their coverage than do drivers in rural areas.

    (a) I only

    (b) II only

    (c) both I and II

    (d) neither I nor II

7. Acme Auto Insurance began operations in a new state last year. It wrote 4 percent of the automobile insurance premiums written in the state. Acme was just given a list of high-risk drivers that it is required to insure this year. The number of people on the list is 4 percent of all high-risk drivers in the state. What approach does this state use to provide coverage to high-risk drivers who are unable to obtain coverage in the voluntary market?

    (a) joint underwriting association

    (b) reinsurance facility

    (c) specialty automobile insurers

    (d) auto insurance plan

8. All of the following are arguments in favor of no-fault automobile insurance EXCEPT:

    (a) determination of fault is often difficult.

    (b) claim payments are often inequitable.

    (c) safe drivers may be penalized.

    (d) a large proportion of premium dollars are used to pay legal costs.

9. In a number of states, insurers must accept all applicants for automobile insurance. If an applicant is considered high-risk, the insurer has the option of placing the applicant in a state pool. Although the applicant is placed in the state pool, the original insurer services the policy. Losses incurred by the state pool are shared by the auto insurers in the state. This type of arrangement is called a(n):

    (a) reinsurance facility.

    (b) automobile insurance plan.

    (c) joint underwriting association.

    (d) specialty automobile insurer.

10. Which statement(s) is(are) true with respect to uninsured motorists coverage?

    I. It provides payments to insureds who have bodily injury caused by an uninsured motorist, a hit-and-run driver, or a driver whose insurer is insolvent.

    II. Benefits under uninsured motorists coverage are paid without regard to fault.

    (a) I only

    (b) II only

    (c) both I and II

    (d) neither I nor II

■ True/False

Circle the T if the statement is true, the F if the statement is false. Explain to yourself why a statement is false.

T   F   1. Adequate physical damage coverage for your auto is the most important consideration when purchasing auto insurance.

T   F   2. Some insurance companies specialize in insuring motorists with poor driving records.

T   F   3. No-fault insurance typically provides benefits for essential services expenses.

T   F   4. If you double the amount of liability insurance you carry under your auto insurance policy, your premium will double.

T   F   5. Compulsory insurance is the only foolproof method of assuring that innocent victims of auto accidents will receive compensation.

T   F   6. Carrying limits of automobile liability coverage equal to the state financial responsibility limits assures adequate protection.

T   F   7. Under an add-on no-fault plan, the injured person retains the right to sue the negligent driver.

T   F   8. An insured who owns two vehicles will pay twice as much for auto insurance as will an insured who owns one vehicle, other factors being equal.

T   F   9. Under state financial responsibility laws, a motorist is not required to prove financial responsibility until after he or she has been involved in an accident or until after a conviction for certain auto-related offenses.

T   F   10. High-risk drivers are assigned to specific companies through joint underwriting associations.

T   F   11. Under a "no pay, no play" law, uninsured drivers are not permitted to sue for noneconomic damages, such as pain and suffering.

T   F   12. Low-cost insurance plans provide minimum amounts of liability insurance at reduced rates to motorists who cannot afford regular insurance or who have limited financial assets to protect.

■ Case Applications

Case 1

Granite Insurance Company is a newly formed auto insurer. Rod Williams, president of Granite, hired Janet Barnes, a math professor at State University, to be in charge of ratemaking. Using what she considered relevant rating factors, Janet calculated net premiums. Then she added an allowance to the net premiums to cover expenses. When she explained the premium calculation to Rod Williams, Rod said, "Of course you still need to allow for losses in the residual market. One of the states where we operate has an auto insurance plan and another has a joint underwriting association." Not wanting to appear uninformed, Janet said, "Yes, of course." Janet has no idea what Rod meant, and she has asked you for an explanation. What would you tell Janet?

Case 2

Betty is an underwriter at Last Resort Insurance Company, an insurer specializing in insuring high-risk drivers. Last Resort has a reputation in the industry as a "high premium" insurer. Last year, Last Resort experienced some financial difficulties. In an unprecedented move, the two largest automobile insurance companies operating in the state each gave Last Resort one million dollars to strengthen Last Resort's financial position.

a)   How does Betty's job as an underwriter with Last Resort differ from a similar position with an auto insurer that does not specialize in insuring high-risk drivers?

(b)   Why would the two largest auto insurers operating in the state each give Last Resort one million dollars?

■ Solutions to Chapter 23

Short Answer Questions

1.   There are a number of approaches available for compensating automobile accident victims. These approaches include: financial responsibility laws, compulsory insurance laws, unsatisfied judgment funds, uninsured motorists coverage, low-cost auto insurance, "no pay, no play" laws, and no-fault automobile insurance.

2.   Proof of financial responsibility is typically required under the following circumstances: after an accident involving bodily injury or property damage exceeding a specified amount, failure to pay a final judgment resulting from an automobile accident, and conviction for certain offenses, such as driving while intoxicated or reckless driving.

3. On the positive side, compulsory insurance laws are considered superior to financial responsibility laws because they provide a stronger guarantee of protection to the public. Advocates argue there are fewer uninsured vehicles in states with compulsory insurance laws.

   However, in general there is no correlation between compulsory insurance laws and the number of uninsured vehicles on the highway. According to a respected industry group, compulsory auto insurance does not reduce the number of uninsured drivers. Finally, although states have computer reporting systems to track uninsured drivers, the reporting systems have not effectively met their major objective of identifying and tracking uninsured drivers.

4. The advantages of uninsured motorists coverage include: some level of protection against uninsured drivers and settlement is faster and more efficient if you collect under uninsured motorists coverage than if you collect from the other party through a tort liability claim. Uninsured motorist coverage also has some defects as a method of compensating automobile accident victims. These disadvantages include: inadequate limits, the insured person must establish that the uninsured motorist is legally liable, and in some states, property damage is not covered under uninsured motorist coverage.

5. One type of no-fault is pure no-fault. Under a pure no-fault plan, the injured person cannot sue the other driver regardless of the seriousness of the claim and no payments are made for pain and suffering. The only source of recovery is your own insurer. No states have enacted a pure no-fault statute.

   A second type of no-fault plan is modified no-fault. Under a modified no-fault plan, an injured person is permitted to sue the other driver if his or her bodily injury claim exceeds a dollar or a verbal threshold. Otherwise, the accident victim collects from his or her insurer only.

   The third type of no-fault, an add-on plan, pays benefits to an accident victim without regard to fault. However, the injured person still has the right to sue the negligent driver who caused the accident. These plans are called "add-on" because in addition to collecting from an insured's own insurer, the accident victim also has the right to sue the negligent driver who caused the accident.

   Some states have adopted a fourth alternative called choice no-fault. Under a choice no-fault plan, a motorist can choose to purchase no-fault insurance and pay lower premiums, or retain the right to sue under the tort liability system and pay higher premiums.

6. Those who favor no-fault insurance laws cite several problems with the tort liability system. The alleged problems with the tort liability system include: difficulty in determining fault, inequality in claim payments, high transaction costs and attorney fees, fraudulent and excessive claims, and delays in payment.

   Supporters of the tort-based system argue that no-fault laws are not needed. They argue that the defects in the tort-based system are exaggerated, claims of efficiency and premium savings under no-fault are exaggerated, court delays are not universal, safe drivers may be penalized under no-fault, no-fault does not allow for payment for pain and suffering, and the tort liability system needs only to be reformed not eliminated.

7. High-risk drivers can obtain coverage from a number of sources. These sources include: automobile insurance plans, joint underwriting associations, reinsurance facilities, state insurance funds, and insurers that specialize in insuring high-risk drivers.

8. While the intent of automobile insurance plans and joint underwriting associations is the same, making coverage available to high-risk drivers, the plans differ in how this goal is accomplished. Under an automobile insurance plan, each auto insurer that operates in the state is assigned a proportion of high-risk drivers based on the total volume of coverage written in the state. Thus, if an insurer writes 5 percent of the auto insurance coverage in a state, the insurer will be required to insure 5 percent of the high-risk drivers. Under this approach, specific high-risk drivers are assigned to specific insurers.

Under a joint underwriting association (JUA), all high-risk automobile business is placed in a common pool, and each company pays its pro-rata share of pool losses and expenses. So if an insurer writes 10 percent of the auto insurance coverage in a state, the insurer will be responsible for 10 percent of JUA underwriting losses. The JUA influences the design of the policy used and the premiums charged. Under this approach, specific high-risk drivers are not assigned to individual insurers.

9. The base rate for auto liability insurance is determined largely by the territory where the auto is principally used and garaged. An urban driver normally pays a higher rate than a rural driver pays because of the higher number of automobile accidents in congested urban areas. Use of the vehicle is another important rating factor. Insurers classify autos based on how the car is used (e.g., for pleasure, to and from work, business use, and farm use). Age of the driver is another rating factor. Young drivers are involved in a disproportionately high number of accidents, therefore they must pay more for their coverage.

10. The following suggestions are offered when shopping for automobile insurance: have adequate liability insurance, carry a higher deductible, consider dropping collision coverage on older vehicles, shop around for auto insurance, take advantage of discounts, improve your driving record, and maintain good credit.

Multiple Choice Questions

1. (a) What is described is a joint underwriting association (JUA). An important characteristic of JUAs is that high-risk motorists are not specifically assigned to individual insurers. Instead, the high-risk drivers are pooled and each insurer bears its proportional share of any underwriting loss.

2. (a) Only the first statement is true. Under a no-fault plan, you collect from your own insurer, regardless of fault. No states however, have adopted a pure no-fault law.

3. (b) These funds designed to compensate innocent accident victims are called unsatisfied judgment funds.

4. (d) Higher collision deductibles have nothing to do with protecting innocent victims of automobile accidents. Collision coverage protects the owner of a vehicle from a physical damage loss to the owner's vehicle. Damage to someone else's auto as a result of your negligence would be paid through your property damage liability coverage.

5. (c) Parker lives in a state that uses modified no-fault. Under this form of no-fault, the injured person cannot sue the negligent driver unless injuries satisfy a monetary or verbal threshold.

6. (b) Age is an important rating factor. Younger drivers are charged more for coverage because they are involved in a disproportionate number of accidents. Urban drivers typically pay more for auto insurance because of the higher number of accidents in congested urban areas.

7. (d) The state uses an automobile insurance plan. Under this residual market device, specific applicants are assigned to specific insurers on a proportional basis. If an insurer writes 4 percent of the auto coverage in a state, it is assigned 4 percent of the high-risk applicants.

8. (c) "Safe drivers may be penalized" is an argument against no-fault. As you collect from your own insurer under a no-fault plan, there is a fear that "safe" drivers who are injured by "unsafe" drivers may be forced to pay more for their coverage, even though they are innocent.

9. (a) A state reinsurance facility is described. Applicants who the insurer does not wish to insure are placed in the pool even though the insurer services these policyowners.

10. (a) Only the first statement is true. The first statement describes the situations in which uninsured motorists coverage will respond to claims. The second statement is incorrect because the other driver must be legally responsible for the claim before uninsured motorists coverage will respond.

True/False

1. **F** Physical damage losses are limited to the value of the vehicle. Liability losses can be far more severe than property losses. Adequate liability insurance should be your greatest concern.

2. **T**

3. **T**

4. **F** Doubling the liability coverage does not mean that the premium will double. As the limit of liability increases, the probability that each additional dollar will be paidout as part of a claim settlement decreases. Looked at another way, the "new" coverage will not be needed until the "old" coverage is exhausted for any claim. Hence the additional liability coverage has a lower cost per thousand.

5. **F** Compulsory insurance is not a foolproof assurance that innocent accident victims will be compensated. For example, an individual could purchase coverage in order to license and register the vehicle, and then cancel the coverage.

6. **F** The state financial responsibility limits are very, very low. Insurance only at these levels makes you vulnerable to large liability claims.

7. **T**

8. **F** Multicar discounts are available if the insured owns two or more autos. The discount is based on the assumption that two cars owned by the same person will not be driven as frequently as one car.

9. **T**

10. **F** Under automobile insurance plans, high-risk drivers are assigned to specific companies. Under joint underwriting associations, insurers bear a proportionate share of the underwriting experience of the group, rather than insuring individual drivers.

11. **T**

12. **T**

Case Applications

Case 1

A residual is something that is "left over." In automobile insurance, private insurers select all of the "good" risks and what is "left over" are high-risk drivers that no company wants to insure. As it is believed to be in the public interest for such drivers to have insurance, a number of techniques for making coverage available to these drivers have been developed. Two such techniques are automobile insurance plans and joint underwriting associations. Through these techniques, insurers are required to take a proportionate share of "bad" risks and often this business is unprofitable. Rod simply wants Janet to consider the fact that the company will be forced to insure some bad risks that may be unprofitable.

Case 2

a) Underwriters at companies that do not specialize in insuring high-risk drivers face a broader range of applicants. Some of the applicants are above average, some are below average, but most are average risks. The underwriter must select and classify the applicants based upon various underwriting factors.

Underwriters at companies that specialize in high-risk drivers do not have "above-average" (superior) risks to offset substandard risks. Given that Last Resort is known for high premiums, if an application has been forwarded to the company, chances are that the applicant has been turned down for coverage by other insurers that charge lower premiums. For Betty, the rating categories likely are different— instead of above average, average, and below average; the categories may be below average, slightly below average, and significantly below average. Premiums must be higher given the additional risk that is underwritten by insurers that specialize in covering high-risk drivers.

b) The generosity of the two largest insurance companies operating in the state is not hard to understand. These companies, as well as other insurers operating in the state, "skim the cream" (take the best risks) from the market. What remains are the high-risk drivers that few companies wish to insure. However, it is important to society that these drivers have liability insurance. The two large companies may view the contribution to the solvency of Last Resort as protection against state regulatory action that may cost them even more. If Last Resort is insuring the "bad risks," then perhaps an auto insurance plan, joint underwriting association, or some other residual market mechanism is not needed. The insurers may view these alternatives as more costly than the continued operation of an insurer specializing in insuring high-risk drivers.

Chapter 24
Other Property and Liability Insurance Coverages

Overview

This chapter examines a wide range of personal property and liability insurance coverages. It opens with a discussion of coverage for dwellings that don't qualify for coverage under the homeowners program and/or situations where less coverage than that provided by a homeowners policy is desired. Next, coverage for mobilehomes and special coverage for personal property are examined. As homeowners and dwelling forms usually exclude boats exceeding certain length and horsepower limits, coverage is needed for recreational boats. This coverage can be provided through the boatowners package form and yacht insurance.

In addition to private insurers, the federal government is involved in providing property coverages. Federal flood insurance and FAIR plans are discussed in this chapter. The chapter concludes with a discussion of title insurance and personal umbrella policies. Title insurance protects the insured from defects in clear title to property. The personal umbrella policy is designed to provide protection against catastrophic liability claims and to fill gaps in underlying liability coverages.

Learning Objectives

After studying this chapter, you should be able to:

- Describe the following ISO dwelling forms: Dwelling Property 1 (basic form), Dwelling Property 2 (broad form), and Dwelling Property 3 (special form).
- Explain how a mobilehome can be insured.
- Identify the types of property that can be insured under a personal articles floater.
- Explain how recreational boats can be insured.
- Explain the basic provisions of the national flood insurance program.
- Describe the basic characteristics of title insurance.
- Explain the major characteristics of a personal umbrella policy.
- Define the following:

Boatowners package policy	National Flood Insurance Program (NFIP)
Dwelling Property 1 (basic form)	Personal articles floater (PAF)
Dwelling Property 2 (broad form)	Personal injury
Dwelling Property 3 (special form)	Personal umbrella policy
FAIR plans	Retained limit
Flood	Self-insured retention
Inland marine floater	Title insurance
Mobilehome insurance	Yacht insurance

■ Outline

I.   ISO Dwelling Program

   A.   Dwelling Property 1 (Basic Form)

   B.   Dwelling Property 2 (Broad Form)

   C.   Dwelling Property 3 (Special Form)

   D.   Endorsements to the Dwelling Program

II.   Mobilehome Insurance

   A.   Eligibility

   B.   Coverages

III. Inland Marine Floaters

   A.   Basic Characteristics of Inland Marine Floaters

   B.   Personal Articles Floater

   C.   Scheduled Personal Property Endorsement

IV.   Watercraft Insurance

   A.   Boatowners Package Policy

   B.   Yacht Insurance

V.   Government Property Insurance Programs

   A.   National Flood Insurance Program

   B.   FAIR Plans

VI.   Title Insurance

VII. Personal Umbrella Policy

   A.   Basic Characteristics

   B.   ISO Personal Umbrella Policy

■ Short Answer Questions

   1.   Why would someone insure his or her home through an ISO dwelling form rather than through an ISO homeowners insurance policy?

2. What are the basic characteristics of the three ISO dwelling forms?

3. What coverages are provided under mobilehome insurance?

4. What are the basic characteristics of inland marine floaters?

5. What are the classes of personal property that can be insured under the personal articles floater?

6. What coverages are provided through the boatowners package policy?

7. Why is federal government involvement needed in the market for flood insurance?

8. Why were FAIR plans created? What coverages are typically available through FAIR plans?

9. What protection is provided by title insurance? How do title insurance policies differ from other insurance contracts?

10. What are the basic characteristics of a personal umbrella policy?

■ Multiple Choice Questions

Circle the letter that corresponds to the BEST *answer.*

1. All of the following are characteristics of a personal umbrella policy EXCEPT:
   (a) the umbrella policy provides excess liability insurance over basic underlying contracts.
   (b) coverage is broad and covers certain losses not covered under the underlying contracts.
   (c) a self-insured retention must be met for certain losses covered by the umbrella policy but not covered by underlying contracts.
   (d) the premium is expensive given the coverage provided.

2. Which of the following statements is(are) true with regard to flood insurance?
   I. Flooding caused by unusually heavy rainfall is excluded.
   II. Although private insurers service insureds, if an insurer's losses exceed premiums and investment income, the federal government is responsible for the underwriting loss.
   (a) I only
   (b) II only
   (c) both I and II
   (d) neither I nor II

3. Mandy owns expensive furs, jewelry, and antique furniture. Her husband, Brian, owns a valuable coin collection and a gun collection. As the coverage provided under their homeowners coverage is limited with respect to this property, Brian and Mandy added a special endorsement to their policy to provide the necessary coverage. This endorsement is called a(n):
   (a) scheduled personal property endorsement.
   (b) umbrella liability endorsement.
   (c) protection and indemnity insurance endorsement.
   (d) extended coverage endorsement.

4. While piloting his yacht, Ted lost control of the vessel and smashed into a dock and another yacht at the marina. Which coverage under yacht insurance would cover the resulting claims?
   (a) property damage
   (b) medical payments coverage
   (c) liability coverage
   (d) uninsured boater coverage

5. All of the following statements about inland marine floaters are true EXCEPT:
   (a) the coverage can be tailored to meet the specific type of personal property insured.
   (b) inland marine floaters provide named-perils physical damage coverage for non-oceangoing vessels.
   (c) most inland marine floaters cover insured property anywhere in the world.
   (d) desired amounts of insurance can be selected.

6. Amy purchased property insurance coverage on her home. The form she purchased provided actual cash value, named-perils coverage on the dwelling. Personal property was covered on a named-perils basis and the policy did not provide personal liability coverage. What type of policy did Amy purchase?

    (a) mobilehome insurance
    (b) Dwelling Property 1
    (c) Homeowners 3 policy
    (d) Dwelling Property 3

7. Which statement is true concerning the boatowners package policy?

    I.   It provides limited, named-perils physical damage coverage.
    II. It combines property, liability, and medical payments coverage in one contract.

    (a) I only
    (b) II only
    (c) both I and II
    (d) neither I nor II

8. Which of the following insurance programs is designed to make property insurance available to urban property owners who are unable to obtain affordable property coverage in the private market?

    (a) FAIR Plans
    (b) ISO Homeowners Program
    (c) ISO Dwelling Program
    (d) federal flood insurance

9. All of the following are common personal umbrella liability policy exclusions EXCEPT:

    (a) obligations under workers compensation.
    (b) intentional acts.
    (c) performance of professional service.
    (d) personal injury.

10. Which statement(s) is(are) true with regard to title insurance?

    I.   The policy covers defects in title that have occurred prior to the effective date of the coverage.
    II. The policy term runs indefinitely in the future.

    (a) I only
    (b) II only
    (c) both I and II
    (d) neither I nor II

■ True/False

Circle the T if the statement is true, the F if the statement is false. Explain to yourself why a statement is false.

T   F   1. Some homes ineligible for coverage under a homeowners policy can be insured under a dwelling form.

T   F   2. The risk of property damage from flooding is easy for private insurance companies to insure.

T   F   3. Even though the policy term of title insurance is indefinite, the premium is paid only when the policy is issued.

T   F   4.   An umbrella policy insures property from damage caused by weather-related risks.

T   F   5.   Mobilehome insurance excludes coverage for personal property.

T   F   6.   Under the Dwelling Property 2 form, losses to the dwelling are settled based on replacement cost.

T   F   7.   The ISO Dwelling forms include coverage for personal liability and theft.

T   F   8.   Inland marine floaters cover property only when it is at a fixed location.

T   F   9.   Insurance for mobilehomes may be written through a mobilehome policy or provided throug a homeowners policy that has been properly endorsed.

T   F   10. When written as a separate contract, the Personal Articles Floater (PAF) provides "open perils" (all-risks) coverage on the property insured.

■ Case Applications

Case 1

Sal and Vicky's home is not eligible for coverage under a homeowners policy. Their agent explained the ISO dwelling forms. Sal and Vicky would like to have "all-risk" coverage on their home, personal liabilit insurance, and additional coverage for some valuable personal property that has limited coverage under th dwelling forms. How can these coverages be provided through an ISO dwelling form?

Case 2

Dr. Reggie Barnes, MD, is a surgeon. He owns an expensive home and two expensive autos. He purchase a homeowners policy and an auto insurance policy. To provide additional liability protection, he purchase a personal umbrella insurance policy. A number of liability claims have been filed against Dr. Barnes. Ignoring the underlying coverages (auto liability and homeowners liability), would the umbrella policy respond to these claims?

(a)   Dr. Barnes serves on the Board of Directors of a drug company. When an outside company tried to acquire the company, the Board blocked the takeover. Irate shareholders, who would have earned substantial profits if the takeover had been successful, filed suit against Dr. Barnes.

b)   A doberman owned by Dr. Barnes attacked a guest. The guest was horribly disfigured and filed a lawsuit against Dr. Barnes.

c)   Dr. Barnes is alleged to have slandered a lawyer at a medical malpractice panel discussion. The lawyer filed a lawsuit against Dr. Barnes.

d)   Dr. Barnes botched a simple operation. The patient has filed a medical malpractice claim against Dr. Barnes.

Solutions to Chapter 24

Short Answer Questions

1.   Some dwellings are not eligible for coverage under the homeowners policy. Other individuals do not need a homeowners policy or cannot afford the broad coverage provided under the homeowners policy. The dwelling forms are designed to meet the needs and desires of such homeowners.

2.   The Dwelling Property 1 (basic) form is similar to homeowners insurance. Losses to the dwelling are settled on an actual cash value basis, unless there is a state requirement to the contrary. In addition to the dwelling, this form provides coverage for other structures, personal property, fair rental value, and additional living expenses. The basic form provides coverage for a limited number of perils. Some additional perils may be added by endorsement.

The Dwelling Property 2 (broad) form expands the coverage provided under the basic form. Losses to the dwelling and other structures are settled on a replacement cost basis. Additional perils are covered under this contract.

The Dwelling Property 3 (special) form provides "open perils" coverage on the dwelling and other structures. Personal property is covered for the same perils as the broad form.

The dwelling forms do not provide liability insurance or theft coverage as part of the standard contract. These coverages can be added to the contract through endorsements.

3. Mobilehome coverage is similar to coverage under a homeowners policy. Coverage A insures the mobilehome against physical damage. Coverage B insures other structures (e.g., a tool shed, garage or stable). Coverage C insures personal property and Coverage D is loss of use coverage. The Sectic II coverages under the homeowners policy, personal liability and medical payments to others, are al: provided under a mobilehome policy.

4. Inland marine floaters have a number of common characteristics. They are: the ability to tailor coverage to meet specific types of personal property, the desired amount of coverage can be selecte: broader and more comprehensive coverage can be obtained, worldwide coverage is provided, and inland marine policies usually do not impose a deductible.

5. The classes of personal property that can be insured under the personal articles floater include: jewelry, furs, cameras, musical instruments, silverware, golfer's equipment, fine arts, and stamp an: coin collections.

6. The boatowners package policy provides a number of coverages. All-risk physical damage coverag: is provided on the boat. The insured is also covered for bodily injury and property damage liability arising out of negligent ownership and operation of the boat. Medical expense coverage, similar to that found in auto insurance policies, is provided; and some boatowners package policies provide uninsured boaters coverage.

7. Government involvement is needed because the risk of flood is difficult to insure privately. The exposure units susceptible to flood are not independent and there is potential for a catastrophic loss occur. As only those people who live in flood zones are likely to seek flood coverage, the premium for the coverage would be too high for most insureds to purchase the coverage without federal government involvement.

8. Many property owners in riot-prone areas are unable to obtain property insurance at affordable premiums. The basic purpose of FAIR plans is to make property insurance available to urban property owners who are unable to obtain coverage in regular insurance markets. The coverage typically provided through FAIR plans includes: fire and extended-coverage insurance, vandalism, malicious mischief, and, in a few states, crime insurance and sprinkler leakage coverage.

9. Title insurance protects the property owner or lender against unknown defects in title to the propert: A defective title can result from an invalid Will, an incorrect description of the property, defective probate of a Will, undisclosed liens, easements, and other defects. A title may also be forged.

Distinguishing characteristics of title insurance include: protection against title defects that occurre: prior to the effective date of coverage, the policy is written by an insurer assuming that no losses wi occur, the premium is paid only when the policy is issued, the policy term is indefinite, and if a loss occurs, the insured is indemnified up to the policy limit.

10. Personal umbrella policies have several common characteristics. These policies provide high-limit, excess liability insurance over basic underlying contracts. The coverage is broad and covers some claims not covered by the underlying contracts. A self-insured retention (SIR) must be met for certai losses covered under the umbrella policy but not covered under any underlying policies. Finally, the umbrella policy is available at a reasonable cost.

Multiple Choice Questions

1. (d) Given the high limit of liability and the broad coverage provided by the umbrella policy, the premium is quite reasonable.

2. (b) Only the second statement is true. Floods caused by unusually heavy rainfall are covered. Should the losses to the private insurers servicing the coverage exceed premiums and investment income, the federal government bears the loss, not the insurers.

3. (a) A scheduled personal property endorsement was added to their policy to provide the additional coverage for their valuable personal property.

4. (c) These claims would be covered under the liability coverage of the policy. Damage to his own boat would be covered under the property damage insurance.

5. (b) Inland marine floaters are not used to provide coverage on vessels. Inland marine floaters are used to insure valuable personal property that is frequently moved from one location to another.

6. (b) Amy purchased the Dwelling Property 1 form. This form provides named-perils, actual cash value coverage on the dwelling. The dwelling forms do not provide personal liability coverage.

7. (b) Only the second statement is true. The physical damage coverage provided under the boatowners package policy is "open perils" (all-risks) coverage rather than named perils coverage. As a package policy, the contract does provide coverage for property, liability, and medical payments coverage through one policy.

8. (a) FAIR plans were established to make property insurance available to urban property owners who are unable to obtain coverage in the regular market.

9. (d) Although homeowners policies generally exclude personal injury, usually it is covered under personal umbrella policies. The other choices are all common umbrella policy exclusions.

10. (c) Both statements are true. If there is some defect in the title that occurred prior to the effective date of coverage, the insured is protected. The coverage is not written for a specific time period and covers all title defects that occurred before the effective date of the contract.

True/False

1. **T**

2. **F** Flood coverage is difficult for private insurance companies to write as losses can be catastrophic, only those who face the risk are likely to purchase the coverage, and premiums may not be affordable. As a result of these difficulties, the federal government is involved in providing flood coverage.

3. **T**

4. **F** The personal umbrella policy provides protection against catastrophic liability claims.

5. **F** Coverage C of mobilehome insurance provides coverage for personal property of the insured.

6. **T**

7. **F** Both of these loss exposures are excluded from coverage under the dwelling forms. They can be added, however, through endorsements.

8. **F** Inland marine floaters cover property anywhere in the world. These policies are especially valuabl█ for travelers who take valuable personal property with them on trips.

9. **T**

10. **T**

Case Applications

Case 1

By using the appropriate dwelling form, and attaching the necessary endorsements, the desired coverage can be obtained. As Sal and Vicky want "all-risk" coverage on their home, the agent should recommend the Dwelling Property 3 form. The liability insurance they desire can be provided by attaching a personal liability supplement endorsement to the policy. Finally, to provide the desired coverage for their valuable personal property, a scheduled personal property endorsement can be added to the contract.

Case 2

(a) Liability as a Director or Officer of a for-profit enterprise is excluded under the personal umbrella policy. The coverage is available through a type of liability insurance called Director's and Officer's Liability Insurance.

(b) This claim would be covered under the umbrella policy. In this case the homeowners policy would respond first, with the umbrella policy providing excess coverage if needed.

(c) Slander is a form of personal injury, excluded under the homeowners policy. This coverage is provided, however, by most personal umbrella policies.

(d) Liability as a professional, in this case as a surgeon, is excluded by the personal umbrella policy. Dr. Barnes should have purchased physicians liability coverage (medical malpractice insurance) to respond to such claims.

Chapter 25
Commercial Property Insurance

▌ Overview

Business enterprises make a large investment in property—plant, equipment, vehicles, inventory, furniture, and other property. This property may remain at a fixed location or may be moved between several locations. The business also may take possession of a customer's property temporarily. Obviously the business suffers a loss if its property is damaged or destroyed. In addition to direct physical damage to property, businesses can also incur indirect (consequential) losses if physical damage renders property unusable. This loss is a combination of continuing expenses and lost profits. This chapter discusses a wide range of commercial property insurance coverages. Coverages examined include: the commercial package policy (CPP), business income insurance, inland and ocean marine insurance, the businessowners policy (BOP), and a variety of other property coverage forms. Commercial property insurance is an important part of a business entity's risk management program.

Learning Objectives

After studying this chapter, you should be able to:

Explain the basic provisions of the building and personal property coverage form, including: covered property, additional coverages, optional coverages, and extensions of coverage.

Identify the causes of loss that are covered under the following forms: causes of loss basic form, causes of loss broad form, and causes of loss special form.

Explain how a business income loss is determined under the business income (and extra expense) coverage form.

Explain what is covered by each of the following ocean marine policies: hull insurance, cargo insurance, protection and indemnity (P&I) insurance, and freight insurance.

Identify the types of property that can be covered by an inland marine insurance policy.

Describe the major provisions in a businessowners policy (BOP) including: coverages provided, additional coverages, and optional coverages.

Define the following:

Annual transit policy

Bailee

Builders risk coverage form

Building and personal property coverage form

Business floater

Business income (and extra expense) coverage form

Business income insurance

Businessowners policy (BOP)

Cargo insurance

Causes-of-loss forms (basic, broad, special)

Collision liability clause (running down clause)

Commercial package policy (CPP)

Condominium association coverage form

Condominium commercial unit-owners coverage form

Difference in conditions (DIC) insurance

Equipment breakdown protection coverage form	Nationwide marine definition
Extra expense coverage form	Ocean marine insurance
Freight insurance	Package policy
General average	Particular average
Hull insurance	Perils of the sea
Implied warranties	Protection and indemnity (P&I) insurance
Inland marine insurance	Reporting form
Means of transportation and communication	Trip transit policy

■ Outline

I.   ISO Commercial Property Program

    A.   Common Policy Declarations

    B.   Common Policy Conditions

    C.   Coverage Parts

II.   Building and Personal Property Coverage Form

    A.   Covered Property

    B.   Other Provisions

III. Causes-of-Loss Forms

    A.   Causes-of-Loss Basic Form

    B.   Causes-of-Loss Broad Form

    C.   Causes-of-Loss Special Form

IV.   Reporting Forms

V.   Business Income Insurance

    A.   Business Income (and Extra Expense) Coverage Form

    B.   Extra Expense Coverage Form

    C.   Business Income from Dependent Properties

VI.   Other Commercial Property Coverages

    A.   Builders Risk Insurance

    B.   Condominium Insurance

    C.   Equipment Breakdown Insurance

    D.   Difference in Conditions (DIC) Insurance

VII. Transportation Insurance

    A. Ocean Marine Insurance

    B. Basic Concepts in Ocean Marine Insurance

    C. Inland Marine Insurance

    D. Nationwide Marine Definition

    E. Major Classes of Inland Marine Insurance

    F. Filed Inland Marine Forms

    G. Nonfiled Inland Marine Forms

VIII. Businessowners Policy (BOP)

    A. Eligible Business Firms

    B. BOP Coverages

■ Short Answer Questions

1. What common conditions apply to the commercial package policy?

2. What are the components of a complete commercial package policy (CPP)?

3. What additional coverages are provided under the building and personal property coverage form of the CPP?

4. Explain the deductible, coinsurance, and optional coverages provisions of the commercial package policy.

5. How do the three causes-of-loss forms used in the commercial package policy differ?

6. In what situations are reporting forms used?

7. Does business income insurance cover direct losses or indirect losses? What types of losses (e.g., property damage, expenses, liability, lost earnings, medical expenses, etc.) is this insurance designed to cover?

8. What is builders risk insurance?

9. What protection is provided through a difference in conditions (DIC) insurance policy?

10. What protection can be provided through the purchase of ocean marine and inland marine insurance

11. What are the major classes of ocean marine and inland marine insurance?

12. For whom was the businessowners policy (BOP) designed? What coverages are provided by the businessowners policy (BOP)?

Multiple Choice Questions

Circle the letter that corresponds to the BEST answer.

1. One customer is responsible for over 90 percent of a company's sales. The risk manager of the company is concerned that if this customer goes out of business temporarily, the company will lose income. To protect against this risk, what endorsement should be added to the company's business income policy?
    (a) leasehold interest insurance
    (b) business income from dependent properties
    (c) extra expense insurance
    (d) differences in conditions (DIC) insurance

2. One class of ocean marine insurance provides ship owners comprehensive liability insurance for property damage and liability to third parties. This type of coverage is called:
    (a) hull insurance.
    (b) cargo insurance.
    (c) protection and indemnity insurance.
    (d) freight insurance.

3. Which statement(s) is(are) true with respect to the commercial package policy (CPP)?
    I.   The CPP is rigid and not easily adapted to various coverage situations.
    II. The packaged coverages cost less than purchasing the same coverages separately.

    (a) I only
    (b) II only
    (c) both I and II
    (d) neither I nor II

4. Decorations by Dora specializes in holiday decorations. The business is seasonal. Dora builds up inventory in preparation for holiday demand, and after holidays, the inventory level is low. Because inventory fluctuates, Dora is required to periodically inform the insurer of the inventory value. What form does Dora's insurer require?
    (a) a reporting form
    (b) an agreed amount endorsement
    (c) a replacement cost endorsement
    (d) a waiver of inventory clause

5. A physician, dentist, or business firm may own individual office space in a building legally organized as a condominium. To insure the business personal property of the owner and personal property of others, the owner would purchase:
    (a) condominium commercial unit-owners coverage.
    (b) Homeowners 6 insurance.
    (c) condominium association coverage.
    (d) businessowners policy (BPO).

6. Professional Dry Cleaners (PDC) desires insurance to cover damage to customers' property while the property is in PDC's possession, if PDC is at fault. PDC should purchase:
   (a) leasehold interest coverage.
   (b) difference in conditions (DIC) coverage.
   (c) extra expense insurance.
   (d) bailee's customer insurance.

7. All of the following property can be covered under the building and personal property coverage form EXCEPT:
   (a) business personal property of the insured at the insured location.
   (b) personal property of others in the care, custody, or control of the insured.
   (c) business personal property of the insured off the premises at an exhibition.
   (d) the insured's building.

8. Which statement(s) is (are) true with respect to the businessowners policy (BOP)?
   I.   The BOP covers the building, business personal property, loss of business income, extra expenses, and business liability.
   II. The BOP is designed primarily for large corporations.
   (a) I only
   (b) II only
   (c) both I and II
   (d) neither I nor II

9. Inter-Ocean Transit purchased cargo insurance, hull insurance, and protection and indemnity insurance on one of its ships, the *Southern Cross*. While navigating through fog just off Long Island, the *Southern Cross* negligently hit another cargo ship, severely damaging the other ship and its cargo. Inter-Ocean Transit would be covered for this property damage liability under:
   (a) cargo insurance.
   (b) hull coverage of hull insurance.
   (c) running down clause of hull insurance.
   (d) protection and indemnity insurance.

10. Taylor Enterprises purchased an "all-risk" policy that covers other perils not insured by basic property insurance contracts. Taylor Enterprises purchased:
   (a) difference in conditions (DIC) insurance.
   (b) extra expense insurance.
   (c) a commercial package policy.
   (d) a business floater policy.

■ True/False

Circle the T if the statement is true, the F if the statement is false. Explain to yourself why a statement is false.

T F 1. If the insured underreports the property value under a reporting form, recovery is limited to the proportion that the last value reported bears to the correct value that should have been reported.

T F 2. Continuing expenses are not covered under business income insurance.

' F   3. Insurers marketing equipment breakdown insurance offer loss prevention services to their policyowners.

' F   4. The causes-of-loss broad form provides broader coverage than the causes-of-loss special form.

' F   5. Business Income (and Extra Expense) Coverage provides limited coverage if business is interrupted as a result of a computer hacker breaking into a company's computer system.

' F   6. Business income insurance is written with a coinsurance requirement.

' F   7. If the insured cancels the commercial package policy, the premium refund may be less than pro rata.

' F   8. The extra expense coverage form is a separate form that covers the extra expenses incurred to continue operations during a period of restoration.

' F   9. The condominium association coverage form is purchased to provide coverage on the personal property of the unit owners.

' F   10. In ocean marine insurance, a general average loss falls entirely upon one insurable interest.

' F   11. The nationwide marine definition defines the property that marine insurers can insure.

Case Applications

Case 1

Power Pack Battery Company manufactures a variety of batteries for consumer, industrial, and defense industry use. The company purchased an ISO commercial package policy (CPP) to cover property exposures. In addition to common declarations and conditions, Power Pack selected the commercial property coverage, crime coverage, and equipment breakdown insurance. The company elected the causes-of-loss broad form. A number of losses have occurred. Are these losses covered?

a)   An explosion in the assembly building caused extensive damage to the building.

b)   In the explosion described above, a caustic acid was released. The acid contaminated a thirty square-yard area.

c)   A sprinkler accidentally discharged in the finished goods building. The finished stock of batteries was ruined because of the resulting corrosion.

(d)   One of Power Pack's customers left a machine with the company so that Power Pack engineers coul custom-design a battery for the machine. While the machine was in Power Pack's possession, a fire destroyed the machine.

Case 2

Kerry Ann is owner of Fast Foto Finishing (FFF), a retail camera, film, and photo-developing business. She purchased an ISO businessowners policy (BOP) with a standard property coverage form. A number of losses have occurred. Are these losses covered under Kerry Ann's BOP?

(a)   Vandals broke into the store while it was closed and damaged business personal property.

(b)   Kerry Ann lost business income and incurred continuing expenses after a fire damaged the store.

(c)   A large outdoor sign, shaped like a camera, was destroyed in a windstorm.

(d)   A part-time sales clerk absconded with the daily receipts.

■ Solutions to Chapter 25

Short Answer Questions

1. The common conditions include: the cancellation rights for each party, a provision stating that the only permissible changes are endorsements, the insurer has the right to audit the insured's books at any time during the policy period and up to three years after coverage expires, the insurer has the right to make inspections and surveys that relate to insurability and premiums charged, the first named insured in the declarations is responsible for premium payments, and the insured's rights and duties under the policy cannot be transferred (assigned) to another party without the consent of the insurer.

2. The necessary components of a complete commercial package policy (CPP) include: common policy declarations, common policy conditions, and two or more coverage parts. The two or more coverage parts are selected from these coverages: commercial property coverage, commercial general liability coverage, commercial crime coverage, equipment breakdown coverage, inland marine coverage, commercial auto coverage, and farm coverage.

3. Debris removal is an additional coverage. If property is moved to another location for safekeeping after a covered loss occurs, the property is covered on an all-risk basis for up to thirty days after the property was first moved. A maximum of $1,000 is available for fire department service charges. The policy will provide up to $10,000 for the cleanup and removal of pollutants if the release or discharge is caused by a covered peril. The policy covers increased cost of construction because of ordinance or law. Finally, the policy covers the cost to replace or restore data lost because of an insured peril.

4. A standard deductible of $250 applies to each occurrence. If a coinsurance percentage is stated in the declarations, the insured must satisfy the coinsurance requirement. Three optional coverage provisions are available. An agreed value option suspends the coinsurance clause and covers losses in the same proportion that the limit of insurance bears to the agreed value shown in the declarations. Inflation guard coverage automatically increases the amount of insurance by an annual percentage stated in the declarations. Finally, replacement cost coverage can be substituted in place of actual cash value coverage.

5. The basic form provides coverage for specified perils, including: fire, lightning, explosion, windstorm or hail, smoke, aircraft or vehicles, riot or civil commotion, vandalism, sprinkler leakage, sinkhole collapse, and volcanic action.
    The broad form expands the basic form perils to include coverage for falling objects, weight of snow, ice, or sleet, and water damage. The broad form also covers certain collapses.
    The special form provides coverage against "risks of direct physical loss," meaning that all physical damage losses are covered unless specifically excluded or limited in the form.

6. Reporting forms are used in situations where there are fluctuations in inventory. The reporting form requires the insured to periodically report the value of the insured property. As long as the report is accurate, the amount of insurance on the inventory is automatically adjusted based on the inventory reported.

7. Business income insurance covers indirect (or consequential) losses that occur as a result of direct physical damage to covered property. Business income insurance is designed to cover the loss of business income, expenses that continue during the shutdown period, and extra expenses incurred because of direct physical loss to insured property.

8. Builders risk insurance is coverage for a building under construction. The form can be used to cover the insurable interest of a general contractor, a subcontractor, or the building owner.

9. Difference in conditions (DIC) insurance is an all-risk property insurance policy that covers perils not insured through basic property insurance contracts. The coverage excludes perils insured by other property contracts, however most other property perils are covered. DIC coverage fills coverage gaps and can be used to insure unusual and catastrophic exposures. Firms with international operations often use the DIC policy to insure overseas properties.

10. Ocean marine insurance provides protection for goods transported over water. All types of oceangoing vessels and their cargos can be insured by ocean marine contracts. The legal liability of ship owners and cargo owners can also be insured.

Inland marine insurance provides protection for goods shipped on land. This coverage includes insurance on imports, exports, domestic shipments, and means of transportation such as bridges and tunnels. Inland marine insurance can also be used to insure fine art, jewelry, furs, and other property

11. The major classes of ocean marine insurance include: hull insurance, cargo insurance, protection and indemnity (P&I) insurance, and freight insurance.

    The major classes of inland marine insurance include: domestic goods in transit, property held by bailees, mobile equipment and property, property of certain dealers, and means of transportation and communication coverage.

12. The businessowners policy (BOP) is a package policy specifically designed for small- to medium-sized retail stores, office buildings, apartment buildings, and similar businesses.

    The businessowners policy covers the building, business personal property, loss of business income, extra expenses, and business liability exposures. Optional coverages are available for outdoor signs, money and securities, employee dishonesty, and mechanical breakdown.

Multiple Choice Questions

1. (b) The appropriate coverage for this situation is business income from dependent properties coverage. This type of coverage provides protection if a key supplier or a key customer incurs property damage that interrupts operations.

2. (c) Protection and indemnity (P&I) insurance provides this liability coverage to ship owners.

3. (b) Only the second statement is true. The CPP is flexible and can be tailored to cover most commercial property and liability exposures in a single policy. The purchaser receives a discount by combining coverages purchased in a single policy.

4. (a) Dora's coverage is subject to a reporting form. Because her inventory fluctuates, Dora is required to periodically report the value of the inventory to her insurer.

5. (a) Condominium commercial unit-owners coverage will provide the necessary insurance.

6. (d) Professional Dry Cleaners enters into an arrangement called a bailment when PDC accepts laundry from customers. Bailee's customers insurance will provide the desired coverage.

7. (c) Personal property of the insured off the premises at a fair or exhibition is not covered.

8. (a) Only the first statement is true. The BOP provides all of the coverages listed in the first statement. The BOP is primarily designed for small- to medium-sized business entities, not for large corporations.

9. (c) The property damage liability would be covered under the running down clause of the hull insurance.

10. (a) Difference in conditions (DIC) insurance covers other perils not insured by basic property insurance contracts.

True/False

1. **T**

2. **F** Business income insurance covers continuing expenses, as well as lost business income and extra expenses.

3. **T**

4. **F** The special form is broader, providing coverage for "risks of direct physical loss," covering all losses except those excluded. The broad form provides named-perils coverage.

5. **T**

6. **T**

7. **T**

8. **T**

9. **F** This coverage is for the buildings and equipment to maintain or service the buildings. The form may also cover fixtures, improvements, alterations, and appliances. However, personal property of the unit owners is specifically excluded. This property can be insured by the unit owner through the Homeowners 6 policy.

10. **F** A general average loss is incurred for the common good and is shared by all parties to the venture. A particular average loss falls upon a single interest.

11. **T**

Case Applications

Case 1

(a)   As explosion is a covered peril under the broad form, this loss is covered.

(b)   One of the "additional coverages" under the CPP is pollutant cleanup and removal. As the discharge of the acid was caused by a covered cause of loss, up to $10,000 is available for the cleanup of the caustic battery acid.

(c)   Sprinkler leakage is a covered peril under the broad form. The damage to the completed stock as a result of sprinkler leakage would be covered.

(d)   Personal property of others in the care, custody, or control of the insured is covered under the "Personal Property of Others" coverage.

Case 2

(a)   Vandalism is not excluded under the current form of the businessowners policy. Therefore, this claim would be covered.

(b)   Business income coverage is provided as an additional coverage. The lost income and continuing expenses incurred as a result of this covered peril, fire, are covered.

(c)   Coverage for the outdoor sign is an "optional coverage" under the BOP. If Kerry Ann chose to include this coverage, then the loss would be covered.

(d)   Employee dishonesty is also an optional coverage under the BOP. If Kerry Ann chose to purchase this coverage, the loss is covered. If she did not choose to purchase this coverage, the loss is not covered.

Chapter 26
Commercial Liability Insurance

■ Overview

Property risks have a common characteristic—the amount of the loss is capped by the value of the property lost and any indirect loss. Unlike commercial property risks, liability exposures are not limited in amount. In this chapter we turn our attention to business liability risks and their treatment. Business enterprises and professionals face a wide variety of liability exposures developing out of premises and operations, products and completed operations, contractual liability, contingent liability, errors and omissions, and other exposures. A number of commercial liability insurance coverages have been developed to address these risks, including commercial general liability insurance, workers compensation and employers liability insurance, business auto coverage, commercial umbrella policies, professional liability insurance, and other liability coverages. A thorough understanding of commercial liability loss exposures and insurance coverages is required for a successful risk management program.

■ Learning Objectives

After studying this chapter, you should be able to:

Identify the major liability loss exposures of business firms.

Describe the basic coverages provided by the commercial general liability (CGL) policy.

Explain the coverage provided by a workers compensation and employers liability policy.

Describe the important provisions of a commercial umbrella policy.

Identify the basic coverages provided by a businessowners policy (BOP).

Describe the basic characteristics of a professional liability policy for physicians.

Define the following:

Advertising injury	Employers liability insurance
Aircraft insurance	Employment-related practices liability
Basic extended reporting period	coverage
Bodily injury or property damage	Errors and omissions insurance
Business auto coverage form	Fire legal liability
Business liability coverage form	Garage coverage form
Claims-made policy	General aggregate limit
Commercial general liability (CGL) policy	Liquor liability law (dramshop law)
Commercial umbrella policy	Long-tail claims
Completed operations	Medical payments
Contingent liability	Occurrence
Contractual liability	Occurrence policy
Directors and officers (D&O) liability policy	Other-states insurance
Each occurrence or per-occurrence limit	Personal injury

Physicians, surgeons, and dentists professional liability coverage form

Products-completed operations aggregate limit

Products-completed operations hazard

Products liability

Property damage to impaired property

Property damage to the insured's product

Property damage to the insured's work

Retained limit

Self-insured retention (SIR)

Ultimate net loss

Voluntary compensation endorsement

Workers compensation and employers liability insurance

■ Outline

I.   General Liability Loss Exposures

A.   Premises and Operations

B.   Products Liability

C.   Completed Operations

D.   Contractual Liability

E.   Contingent Liability

F.   Other Liability Loss Exposures

II.   Commercial General Liability (CGL) Policy

A.   Overview of the CGL Occurrence Policy
   1.   Section I—Coverages
      (a)   Coverage A—Bodily Injury and Property Damage Liability
      (b)   Coverage B—Personal and Advertising Injury Liability
      (c)   Coverage C—Medical Payments
      (d)   Supplementary Payments: Coverages A and B
   2.   Section II—Who is an Insured?
   3.   Section III—Limits of Insurance
   4.   Section IV—Commercial General Liability Conditions
   5.   Section V—Definitions

B.   Overview of the CGL Claims-Made Policy
   1.   Meaning of "Claims-Made"
   2.   Rationale for Claims-Made Policies
   3.   Retroactive Date
   4.   Extended Reporting Period

III.   Employment-Related Practices Liability Insurance

A.   Insuring Agreement

B.   Co-payment

C.   Legal Defense

D.   Exclusions

V.   Workers Compensation Insurance

    A.   Part One: Workers Compensation Insurance

    B.   Part Two: Employers Liability Insurance

    C.   Part Three: Other-States Insurance

.   Commercial Auto Insurance

    A.   Business Auto Coverage Form
        1.   Liability Insurance Coverage
        2.   Physical Damage Coverage

    B.   Garage Coverage Form

I.   Aircraft Insurance

    A.   Aviation Insurers

    B.   Aviation Insurance for Private Business and Pleasure Aircraft

II.   Commercial Umbrella Policy

    A.   Coverages

    B.   Required Underlying Coverages

    C.   Exclusions

III. Businessowners Policy

    A.   Business Liability

    B.   Medical Expenses

    C.   Legal Defense

    D.   Exclusions

X.   Professional Liability Insurance

    A.   Physicians, Surgeons, and Dentists Professional Liability Insurance

    B.   Errors and Omissions Insurance

    C.   Directors and Officers Liability Insurance

■ Short Answer Questions

1. What are the major general liability loss exposures that businesses face?

2. How does products liability differ from completed operations liability?

3. Coverage A of the commercial general liability (CGL) policy provides coverage for bodily injuries and property damage. What important exclusions apply to Coverage A?

4. What six limits of liability apply under the commercial general liability (CGL) policy?

5. How does claims-made coverage differ from occurrence-based coverage?

6. What three coverages are provided under workers compensation and employer liability insurance?

7. What two important coverages are provided under the business auto coverage form?

8. What are the basic characteristics of a commercial umbrella policy?

9. What are the major characteristics of physicians, surgeons, and dentists professional liability insurance?

10. What is errors and omissions insurance? Who needs to purchase this type of liability coverage?

■ Multiple Choice Questions

Circle the letter that corresponds to the BEST *answer.*

1. In some business operations, it is common to hire independent contractors to perform some activities. A business organization can be held liable in certain situations for injuries and property damage caused by these contractors. This type of liability is called:
   (a) contractual liability.
   (b) contingent liability.
   (c) completed operations liability.
   (d) premises and operations liability.

2. Park Rite is a business that builds and operates underground parking garages in major metropolitan areas. To provide protection against damage to or theft of a vehicle parked for a fee in a Park Rite facility, the company should purchase:
   (a) garagekeepers coverage.
   (b) completed operations insurance.
   (c) business auto insurance.
   (d) commercial general liability insurance.

3. Which statement(s) is(are) true with respect to the commercial umbrella policy?
   I. Coverage is provided for claims exceeding the coverage limit in underlying policies.
   II. Personal injury is typically excluded from coverage under commercial umbrella policies.
   (a) I only
   (b) II only
   (c) both I and II
   (d) neither I nor II

4. All of the following losses would be covered under a standard aircraft insurance policy EXCEPT:
   (a) the plane was destroyed while on the ground as a result of a hangar fire.
   (b) the plane crashed short of the runway because of fog, and a passenger required medical attention for injuries sustained.
   (c) a passenger was killed when the owner/operator made a navigational error and the plane crashed.
   (d) property in the owner/operator's custody was destroyed when the plane crashed.

5. Brenda has worked for a bank for eight years. Several times she's been passed over for promotions that were given to less qualified coworkers. When she complained, she was demoted and given menial tasks that newly hired workers were typically assigned. Brenda sued the bank and was successful in proving injury to her career by failure to promote and retaliation. Which insurance coverage would pay the damages Brenda was awarded?
   (a) workers compensation and employer liability insurance
   (b) directors and officers liability insurance
   (c) employment-related practices liability insurance
   (d) commercial general liability insurance

6. Which statement(s) is(are) true with respect to the commercial general liability insurance form?
    I.   Advertising injury liability is not covered under the policy.
    II. In addition to liability protection, the insurer provides for the cost of a legal defense.

    (a) I only
    (b) II only
    (c) both I and II
    (d) neither I nor II

7. All of the following are common exclusions under workers compensation and employer liability insurance EXCEPT:
    (a) intentional acts.
    (b) injuries that are not employment-related.
    (c) punitive damages.
    (d) occupational disease.

8. A wide range of professionals (e.g., accountants, architects, and lawyers) need liability insurance to provide protection in case a negligent act, mistake, or failure to perform harms a client. What type of insurance is designed to meet the needs of these professionals?
    (a) difference in conditions insurance
    (b) errors and omissions insurance
    (c) commercial general liability insurance
    (d) directors and officers liability insurance

9. All of the following statements about the businessowners policy (BOP) are true EXCEPT:
    (a) The BOP provides liability and medical payments coverage.
    (b) Liability arising out of workers compensation, pollution, and professional services is excluded.
    (c) Legal defense costs are counted against the policy limits.
    (d) The BOP has two aggregate limits on the total amount of covered claims that can be paid during the policy period.

10. Which statement(s) is(are) true with respect to claims-made coverage?
    I.   Premiums, losses, and loss reserves can be estimated with greater accuracy under claims-made coverage than under occurrence coverage.
    II   To be covered under a claims-made form, occurrences must occur after the retroactive date and must be reported during the present policy term.

    (a) I only
    (b) II only
    (c) both I and II
    (d) neither I nor II

■ True/False

Circle the T if the statement is true, the F if the statement is false. Explain to yourself why a statement is false.

T   F   1. The "long tail" refers to the fact that years after a liability policy is first written, claims may be reported.

T   F   2. Personal injury is not covered under the commercial general liability policy.

T   F   3. Physicians, surgeons, and dentists professional liability insurance forms always require the medical professional's consent before the insurer can settle a claim.

T   F   4. The commercial umbrella policy shares losses on a pro-rata basis with any applicable underlying coverage.

T   F   5. The legal liability of another party can be assumed by an oral or written contract.

T   F   6. Employers liability insurance is not needed if the employer has coverage for workers compensation.

T   F   7. Damage to property in the care, custody, or control of the insured is a common liability insurance exclusion.

T   F   8. A loss covered under an occurrence general liability policy may not be covered under a claims-made general liability policy.

T   F   9. Workers compensation insurance excludes coverage for occupational disease.

T   F   10. Commercial general liability insurance covers the cost of a product recall.

T   F   11. Aircraft insurance provides property damage liability coverage.

T   F   12. Garage owners purchase business auto insurance to provide liability coverage for damage to customers' autos while in the garage owner's care.

■ Case Applications

Case 1

Kimball Manufacturing makes windows. All windows are manufactured on the premises and are shipped to wholesalers, retailers, and consumers using company vehicles. To protect against liability claims, the company bought commercial general liability insurance (with products liability and completed operation coverage), workers compensation and employer liability insurance, and business auto coverage. Are the following claims covered, and if so, under which policy?

(a) A Kimball Manufacturing delivery vehicle failed to yield the right of way and hit a school bus. A lawsuit has been filed against Kimball Manufacturing.

(b) An employee sustained a severe laceration when a window shattered.

c) Kimball won the window contract for a new arena. The windows were custom-built and installed by Kimball workers. The first time the arena hosted an event, a window fell out of its frame and injured four people. A lawsuit has been filed against Kimball Manufacturing.

d) A former employee who had been fired because of repeated absenteeism and tardiness returned to Kimball Manufacturing to pick up his last paycheck. While walking down a stairway, a wooden step broke. The former employee fell and sustained a concussion, a broken arm, and a broken pelvis. He has filed a lawsuit against Kimball Manufacturing.

Case 2

Right on Target Gun Shop is a sole proprietorship located in a rural area. The store is owned and operated by Carl Gibson. The store sells a wide range of firearms, including rifles, shotguns, and handguns. Carl Gibson purchased a businessowners policy (BOP) to cover property and liability exposures. A number of coverage questions have arisen with regard to the liability coverage. Are each of the following claims covered under the policy?

a) When Carl was showing a customer a rifle, another customer called Carl's name. As he turned to see who called his name, he hit the customer with the barrel of the gun. The customer received a severe facial laceration and is suing Right on Target.

b) Carl is required by state law to provide workers compensation coverage on his employees. An employee injured his back while stacking boxes of ammunition. The employee would like to sue Carl as a result of his injuries.

c) A lawsuit was just filed against Right on Target by a candidate running for public office. The candidate favors gun control legislation. She alleges that a Right on Target radio advertisement slandered her.

■ Solutions to Chapter 26

Short Answer Questions

1. The major general liability loss exposures that businesses face include: premises and operations, products liability, completed operations, contractual liability, and contingent liability. Some other general liability loss exposures include: pollution, fire legal liability, liquor liability, directors and officers liability, personal injury liability, damage to property in the insured's care/custody/control, and employment-related practices liability.

2. Products liability refers to the legal liability of manufacturers, wholesalers, and retailers to persons who are injured by defective products or property damage from defective products. Completed operations refers to liability arising out of faulty work performed away from the premises after the work or operations are completed.

3. The major exclusions are: expected or intended injury, contractual liability, liquor liability (if the insured is in an alcohol-related business), workers compensation, employers liability, pollution, aircraft/watercraft/autos exclusion, mobile equipment, war, property in the care/custody/control of th insured, property damage to the insured's product, property damage to the insured's work, property damage to impaired property, the recall of products, and personal and advertising injury.

4. The first limit is a general aggregate limit the insurer will pay for medical expenses and damages under Coverages A, B, and C; excluding claims under products liability and completed operations. The second limit caps the amount the insurer will pay under Coverage A for the "products-complete operations hazard." The third limit is the maximum amount that the insurer will pay under Coverage B for personal injury and advertising injury. Fourth, there is a per-occurrence limit on the amount th insurer will pay for the sum of damages covered under Coverage A and Coverage C for the same occurrence. Fifth, the amount the insurer will pay under Coverage A for property damage to a rented premises caused by fire is limited. Finally, there is a maximum limit placed on the amount the insure will pay per-person for medical expenses because of bodily injury.

5. Occurrence-based coverage provides protection against occurrences that take place during the policy period, regardless of when the claim is reported. This form of coverage may create problems for insurers because they are required to pay claims on policies that have already expired. This delay makes it difficult for insurers to calculate premiums and loss reserves. To alleviate these problems, claims-made coverage was introduced. Claims-made coverage provides protection for claims that ar first reported during the policy period, provided the event occurred after a retroactive date stated in the policy. Such coverage is easier to price and more accurate loss reserves can be established.

6. There are three separate coverages in the workers compensation and employer liability insurance policy. These coverages include: Workers Compensation Insurance, Employers Liability Insurance, and Other-States Insurance.

7. The two important coverages provided by the business auto coverage form are liability coverage and physical damage insurance. The liability coverage provides protection for liability arising out of a bodily injury or property damage claim arising out of the ownership, maintenance, or use of a covered auto. The physical damage coverage protects the insured against damage claim because collision and other-than-collision losses to the covered auto.

8. Although there are some variations in commercial umbrella liability policies, they do include a number of common characteristics. First, commercial umbrella policies provide high limits of liability and broad coverage in excess of underlying coverages. Second, the insured is required to carry minimum underlying limits before an insurer will write a commercial umbrella policy. Third, the umbrella policy covers some claims not covered by the underlying policies, after the insured pays a self-insured retention. Fourth, the umbrella policy provides coverage for losses attributable to bodily injury and property damage liability, personal injury, and advertising liability. Finally, there are some important exclusions typically found in umbrella policies.

9. The major characteristics of physicians, surgeons, and dentists professional liability coverage include: broad coverage, liability protection not restricted to accidental acts, the insured's liability for the negligent acts of an employee is covered, there is a maximum limit per medical incident and an aggregate limit for each coverage, other liability insurance coverages are necessary because medical malpractice coverage is not a substitute for them, the form may allow the insurer to settle a claim without the insured physician's or surgeon's consent, and an extended reporting period can be added.

10. Errors and omissions insurance provides protection against losses incurred as a result of some negligent act, error, or omission by the insured. A wide range of professionals need the protection provided by errors and omissions insurance. Some examples include lawyers, accountants, employee benefit managers, insurance agents and brokers, and architects.

Multiple Choice Questions

1. (b) This form of liability is called contingent liability.

2. (a) Garagekeepers coverage will provide protection against damage to or theft of vehicles parked in a Park Rite facility.

3. (a) Commercial umbrella policies provide coverage for claims exceeding underlying coverage limits. Coverage for personal injury is provided under most commercial umbrella policies.

4. (d) Aviation insurance excludes property in the care, custody, and control of the insured, with the exception of the personal property of passengers (up to a specified limit).

5. (c) Employment-related practices liability insurance provides coverage for employment discrimination, wrongful termination, failure to promote, harassment, retaliation, and other employment-related wrongful acts.

6. (b) Only the second statement is true. Commercial general liability insurance does provide coverage for advertising injury liability. The insurer writing the coverage also provides for the cost of a legal defense.

7. (d) Occupational illness is covered under workers compensation and employers liability insurance.

8. (b) Errors and omissions insurance protects professionals from claims arising from negligence, failure to perform, and mistakes.

9. (c) Coverage for legal defense costs is in addition to the policy limits, not counted against policy limits. The other statements are true.

10. (c) Both statements are true. Claims-made coverage reduces long-tail claims, thus premiums, losses, and loss reserves are more easily estimated. The injury need not occur during the policy period for coverage to apply. For coverage to apply, the injury must occur after the retroactive date and must be reported during the present policy term.

True/False

1. **T**

2. **F** Coverage B of the commercial general liability policy provides coverage for personal and advertising injury liability.

3. **F** Many current medical malpractice forms permit the insurer to settle a claim without the medical professional's consent.

4. **F** The underlying coverage pays first. If the underlying coverage limit is exhausted, then the umbrell policy will respond on an excess basis.

5. **T**

6. **F** Employers liability insurance is needed for a variety of reasons. For example, an injury or disease that occurs on the job may not be considered work-related. Employer liability insurance also respone in a variety of other situations.

7. **T**

8. **T**

9. **F** Occupational disease is covered under workers compensation insurance.

10. **F** Product recall expenses are specifically excluded from coverage under the commercial general liability insurance form. This coverage can be added through an endorsement.

11. **T**

12. **F** Garage owners purchase garagekeepers insurance to provide this liability coverage.

Case Applications

Case 1

(a) This claim would be covered under the business auto coverage, provided the appropriate coverage had been purchased and the delivery vehicle is an insured vehicle. The commercial general liability form excludes liability arising from vehicles.

(b) As the injury developed out of and in the course of employment, workers compensation coverage would respond to the claim.

(c) Based on the facts presented, it appears that either the window was defective, or the installation of th window was faulty. This loss would be covered under the general liability policy as either a product liability claim or as a completed operations claim.

(d) As this claim involves a former employee, workers compensation insurance does not apply and the former employee has the right to sue Kimball Manufacturing. The company's general liability coverage will respond to this premises liability claim.

Case 2

a) The businessowners policy (BOP) provides coverage for bodily injury liability claims, so this claim would be covered.

b) The BOP excludes workers compensation claims, so there is no coverage for this claim under the BOP. Carl may be self-insuring the workers compensation exposure or may have purchased workers compensation insurance, which would respond.

c) This claim would be covered under the BOP. The BOP provides coverage for advertising liability and personal injury.

Chapter 27
Crime Insurance and Surety Bonds

Overview

In addition to the property and liability risks faced by businesses, losses can also occur as a result of crime. Losses attributable to crime take many forms, including burglary, employee theft, arson, shoplifting, embezzlement, robbery, and other types of crime. In response to the need for coverage of such losses, the Insurance Services Office (ISO) has developed a number of crime insurance forms that are discussed in this chapter. This chapter also examines surety bonds. These bonds provide monetary compensation if a bonded party fails to perform a promised obligation. A variety of surety bonds, each designed for a special purpose, are discussed.

Learning Objectives

After studying this chapter you should be able to:

Define theft, robbery, burglary, and safe burglary.

Identify the insuring agreements in the commercial crime coverage form (loss sustained form).

Explain the difference between the discovery form and the loss sustained form.

Identify the basic insuring agreements in a financial institution bond for a commercial bank.

Show how surety bonds differ from insurance.

Identify the major types of surety bonds and give an example where each can be used.

Define the following:

Attachment bond	Judicial bond
Bail bond	License and permit bond
Burglary	Loss-sustained form
Cancellation as to any employee	Loss sustained during prior insurance
Commercial crime coverage (loss sustained form)	Obligee
Contract bond	Other property
Court bond	Outside the premises
Discover form	Performance bond
Federal surety bond	Principal
Fidelity coverage	Public official bond
Fiduciary bond	Retroactive date endorsement
Financial institution bond	Robbery
Inside the premises—theft of money and securities	Safe burglary
	Surety bonds
Inside the premises—robbery or burglary of other property	Surety (obligor)
	Theft

■ Outline

I.   ISO Commercial Crime Insurance Program

II.   Commercial Crime Coverage Form (Loss Sustained Form)

    A.   Basic Definitions

    B.   Insuring Agreements

    C.   Exclusions

    D.   Policy Conditions

III. Financial Institutions Bonds

    A.   Fidelity Coverage

    B.   On Premises Coverage

    C.   In-Transit Coverage

    D.   Forgery or Alteration Coverage

    E.   Securities Coverage

    F.   Counterfeit Money

    G.   Fraudulent Mortgages

IV.   Surety Bonds

    A.   Parties to a Surety Bond

    B.   Comparison of Surety Bonds and Insurance

    C.   Types of Surety Bonds

■ Short Answer Questions

1.   Name the five basic ISO crime coverage forms and policies.

2. Name the two versions under which the ISO crime coverage form can be written.

3. For the purposes of insurance, how are burglary, robbery, and theft defined?

4. What exclusions apply to the ISO commercial crime coverage form?

5. What seven insuring agreements are available under a financial institution bond?

6. Many financial institution losses are attributable to employee dishonesty. Which of the seven coverages under a financial institution bond is designed to cover these losses?

7. Who are the three parties to a surety bond, and what is the role of each of the parties?

8. What are the major differences between surety bonds and insurance?

9. What are the major types of surety bonds?